UNDERGROUND
EMPIRE

UNDERGROUND EMPIRE

How America Weaponized the World Economy

HENRY FARRELL AND

ABRAHAM NEWMAN

HENRY HOLT AND COMPANY

NEW YORK

Henry Holt and Company
Publishers since 1866
120 Broadway
New York, New York 10271
www.henryholt.com

Henry Holt® and ⓗ® are registered trademarks of Macmillan Publishing Group, LLC.

Library of Congress Cataloging-in-Publication Data is available.

ISBN: 9781250840554

Our books may be purchased in bulk for promotional, educational, or business use. Please contact your local bookseller or the Macmillan Corporate and Premium Sales Department at (800) 221-7945, extension 5442, or by e-mail at MacmillanSpecialMarkets@macmillan.com.

First Edition 2023

Designed by Gabriel Guma

Printed in the United States of America

1   2   3   4   5   6   7   8   9   10

To Nicole and Craig

CONTENTS

INTRODUCTION

All Roads Lead to Rome

I t's easy to descend into the underground empire. There are entrances everywhere. Some of them are even signposted. In the Washington, DC, area, where both of us live, the multilane artery of Route I-66 connects the Virginia suburbs to the capital city of the United States. Smaller roads diverge from it toward the Pentagon and the CIA's headquarters in Langley. Route I-66 passes through the Beltway, which loops around the city toward Fort Meade, where the spies and hackers of the National Security Agency (NSA) and U.S. Cyber Command go to work. The road terminates in Foggy Bottom, the home of the U.S. Department of State, a few blocks away from the U.S. Department of the Treasury and the White House.

These buildings are the surface manifestations of American empire. Some were designed for public display. The White House and Department of the Treasury have Palladian facades constructed according to principles descending from the Roman architect Vitruvius, who began as an engineer in Julius Caesar's army. Others are built from reinforced steel and concrete for more utilitarian purposes, barricaded behind fences, cameras, and armed guards.

All are connected to the underworld. Every empire's architecture of rule and display would fall into ruin were it not joined to a filigree of tunnels and pipes, conveying resources and information like the mycelium that spreads out from a mushroom through the surrounding soil. The threads of empire operate in both directions, spreading influence and power outward as they gather resources to the center.

The rulers of the ancient world built their capitols from stones like porphyry and marble. Their living empires were made out of more everyday stuff; the trade routes, grain ships, and aqueducts that tied towns, cities, and countryside in a densely connected web of economic activity. Imperial Rome built a network of roads that allowed merchants to convey their wares as well as legions to march quickly across provinces. When a traveler entered the empire from the hinterlands, they departed a world of villages and winding cattle tracks for one of trading cities, joined by long, straight thoroughfares that carried both commerce and coercion.

Many centuries after the empire had fallen, a medieval proverb maintained that all roads lead to Rome. The infrastructure that Rome built still casts a shadow on the modern economy. History is lazy. Once something has been built, it is easier to build on top of it. Highways in France and Italy follow routes that were decreed by an imperial censor thousands of years ago.

In modern times, much of the real business of empire has moved underground. American imperium still uses military power to keep surface trade routes open, deploying the U.S. Navy to patrol global sea-lanes. But American power also travels along buried fiber-optic cables, insinuating itself into networks like the Internet and the complex financial infrastructures used by banks to send money around the world. Beneath the open markets that facilitate global trade and manufacturing lies a less tangible network of intellectual property and technological expertise. Again, this provides American leaders with unparalleled levers of control.

These world-spanning systems were not created as part of a deliberate plot for political domination. They were mostly built by private companies, pursuing efficiency and profit. But that was also true of older empires, whose legionaries often followed in the footsteps of their merchants.

Modern empire has turned the subterranean machineries that enable global markets and information flows—fiber-optic cables, server farms, financial payment systems, and the manufacturing systems that produce complex products such as semiconductors—into tools of coercion. On a casual glance, these systems seem simultaneously dull and arcane—the complicated wiring and plumbing arrangements of the global economy. But the plumbing is political. Just as all roads once led to Rome, the world's fiber-optic networks, financial systems, and semiconductor supply chains converge on the United States, allowing it to project its might.

Indeed, if you want to understand how these systems work, it's helpful to imagine them as roads. Every morning, commuters leave the quiet residential streets they live on, turning onto busier ones, which in turn connect to arterial highways. So, too, people enter the underground empire every morning. They turn on their mobile phones, log on to their work computers, perhaps send some money to a family member. Without thinking about it, they are sending their information across buried wires that might connect to global information arteries such as the so-called Internet backbone of high-speed cables, a highway with millions of lanes, on which local and international traffic mix indiscriminately. On this virtual road, American cars with local license plates—"End Taxation without Representation," or "Virginia Is for Lovers"—might weave between trucks with logos in Chinese script, Persian, French, and Russian, each heading to their own local destinations. People in other countries, too, are checking their email, buying products from Amazon or its local competitors, and paying their bills.

All these different people in their different countries use the same highway. It is as if Route I-66, instead of just connecting Washington, DC, to its surrounding hinterland, also wound invisibly through other cities such as Beijing, Ankara, Paris, and Vladivostok, connecting everywhere to everywhere. The big catch is that travelers from these various parts of the world might be diverted through the DC suburbs, even if they are taking a short local trip between different neighborhoods in Dublin or in Kirkuk. As Irish or Kurdish drivers take their obligatory detour, they pass the headquarters of the National Security Agency (NSA), which might photograph their vehicle, just in case someone in the U.S. government later wants to know who they are and where they were going. A driver with Iranian plates might unexpectedly be pulled over to the side of the road by Treasury agents with dark suits and neat haircuts. Traffic on the virtual highway can spill back over into the logistics of the physical world. As the federal government sieves online traffic for information, it might discover an email that leads to the sequestration of a container of advanced semiconductors departing Seoul for Shanghai.

A quarter century ago, Vice President Al Gore described the new world of global networks as an "Information Superhighway." As he half-admitted at the time, it was a corny metaphor. Gore used it because he wanted people to think of these networks as a necessary infrastructure that the United States should invest in. He didn't want intrusive regulation, but he believed there had to be rules of the road, to eliminate bottlenecks and open these networks to everyone. Technical experts never liked Gore's language. When they thought about global networks, they thought they were like the Internet, a network of networks that seemed like a wild free-for-all with no traffic cops, allowing people to go wherever they wanted.

Now, the Internet has been tamed. We're back in a world of information highways, which feed into bottlenecks that the United States has turned into choke points, allowing it to surveil and control everyday commerce and interaction across the globe. And the highways carry the traffic of the global economy, supporting financial services and production systems. Unsurprisingly, other governments don't like this. Some of them want to build new routes to circumvent the bottlenecks. Others hope to capture or create choke points of their own. Their clashing imperatives give rise to new conflicts, which catch multinational corporations and individuals in the cross fire.

In 1989, we saw the triumph of one world order over another, as the political and economic confrontation of the Cold War gave way to world-spanning networks. The Internet, global finance, and supply chains proliferated as business took advantage of new economic freedoms. Then, after the 9/11 attacks, when the U.S. government was at its most vulnerable, it stumbled onto the political power hidden amid the plumbing of this new global economy.

At first, it sought to use this discovery to target the "bad guys." Focused on the immediate threat of terrorists and rogue states, the agencies and bureaucracies involved didn't anticipate how the powers they were wielding would transform America's relationship with allies such as Europe, competitors like China, and the global business community. Nor did officials understand how tempting it would be to use network capabilities not just to subdue villains but to subjugate friends that had largely accepted interdependence as a source of market efficiencies. To protect America, Washington has slowly but surely turned thriving economic networks into tools of domination. The United States sleepwalked its way into a new struggle for empire, breaking bad without ever quite realizing it.

As you read this book, you will discover how this underground empire came into being. How did a world of open networks become a subterranean imperium, which allowed the United States to spread its influence across the borders of other countries, gathering information, interdicting goods, and cutting entire countries out of the global economy? More important, you'll find out what is happening now and what's likely to happen in the future. How are other powerful countries such as China, or jurisdictions like the European Union, protecting themselves or retaliating? What will happen if others try to build and extend their own subterranean realms? If you are a company trapped in the middle, what options do you have to protect yourself?

For the first time, people—U.S. administration officials, foreign leaders, and CEOs—are beginning to think through what has happened and what is next. We will tell you how the coming disputes between nascent empires can best be managed and how the tools of empire can be turned to different purposes, closing down tax havens, or helping build the structures to fight climate change. What we will not do, because we cannot, is map plausible escape routes from the underground empire. It's easy to descend into it but not so easy to get out.

Why was a world of open global networks so well suited to American empire? Some think that the answer is simple: empire and global networks were different phases of a vast and complex plot, which has slowly unfolded over decades. Vladimir Putin, for example, has claimed that the Internet is a "CIA project," designed to empower America by undermining Russia and other autocratic states. He seems to believe the Cold War never finished: it just evolved from power games in the shadow of nuclear confrontation to semi-clandestine information war, conducted via networks that were purposely built to be weaponized against America's adversaries.

Those who built this new world thought just the opposite, claiming that it had put an end to old-style geopolitical maneuvering between states. In a 1999 article, Thomas Friedman, an evangelist of the new age, declared that an old world divided by a Wall had given way to a new one bound together by a Web. Back then, the World Wide Web seemed new and exciting. It provided an easy synecdoche for the broader post–Cold War transformation of the world economy. Information networks such as the Internet conveyed torrents of information across borders, building new global markets as businesses found customers and suppliers in other countries. Financial networks expanded, allowing money to move rapidly across the world in search of fleeting opportunities for arbitrage or longer-term investments. Global trade was no longer the exchange of raw commodities and finished products. The global trading system was transformed into an intricate decentralized factory floor, where complex products could be designed in one country and assembled in another from components and subcomponents produced around the planet. The world was now flat.

In theory, information would flow freely in this new global order, resisting even the most determined autocrats. Bill Clinton told China that trying to control information was like nailing Jell-O to the wall; it would just wobble its way around the impediment and escape. Governments would no longer control financial flows. Instead, financial flows would control governments, as politicians cowered in the face of changes to sovereign credit ratings. Clinton's adviser James Carville famously joked that he wanted to be reincarnated as the bond market so that he could "intimidate everybody." Friedman claimed that no one would want to go to war in a world of globalized supply chains, since by attacking your neighbor, you would just be attacking your own economy. From his perspective, the new world was an emporium, not an imperium, a thriving marketplace where the very notion of empire was irrelevant and antiquated.

The truth is more interesting and complicated than either Putin's world of conspiracies or Friedman's two-dimensional flatland. If the Cold War hadn't ended, the great era of global network building would never have begun. A world that was divided into mutually distrustful power blocs would never have allowed networks to entangle their economies together. Furthermore, it wasn't the United States government that built the networks. Following the collective wisdom of the day, officials believed that their job was to get out of the way of private enterprise, which was overwhelmingly U.S.-based or U.S.-focused.

As in previous historical moments, the network builders were businesses and business consortiums, pursuing profit and efficiency rather than conquest. Those who had political aspirations more often wanted to undermine empire than maintain it, hoping that they were building a networked world in which people and private organizations would be able to make their own connections, regardless of whether their governments wanted to.

Yet these networks—which were supposed to undermine the old world of power politics—never quite escaped the shadow of America's Cold War empire. Historically minded economists and social scientists often talk about path dependence, the way in which decisions taken long ago (where to locate cities; what to say in a constitution) constrain our actions today. The new networks of the global world economy were path dependent in a quite literal sense. Like medieval road builders, their architects often found it easier to lay down new routes on the foundations of old ones. As they built, others built on top of what they had constructed, and others still again, in a process of continual accretion. This meant that the paths that they built followed the older arteries of power, connecting to the heart of the old post–World War II empire, the physical territory of the United States of America.

The supposed world without empire seemed remarkably familiar. Without any need for a grand plan, the map reflected and reinforced the Cold War victory of the United States. The networks that connected the world together didn't just follow the contours of past economic and political power relations. They froze a moment in time, the brief period when the United States was at the apex of its power and at the center of everything, so that it lasted for decades.

Take the undersea and underground cables that tied the world's communications system together. According to an NSA estimate, by 2002 less than 1 percent of global Internet bandwidth passed between two regions of the world without passing through the United States. The global messaging system that allowed banks to talk with each other was based in Belgium—but its board was dominated by U.S. banks, and it was hostage to its data center in Northern Virginia. International banks carried out international transactions in U.S. dollars, exposing them to the "dollar clearing system," a set of complex financial arrangements controlled by U.S. regulators. And even as the production of complex semiconductors moved from the United States to Asia, American companies kept key aspects of semiconductor design and intellectual property at home.

The pipes and plumbing of globalization didn't just carry power to the center. They also made it more vulnerable to attacks, as the United States found out on September 11, 2001. Decentralized communications systems made it much easier for terrorists to communicate, while an open global financial system allowed them to send money and resources across borders without anyone knowing or taking responsibility for stopping them.

But so long as the United States had the will to change things, the means were close at hand. Key global networks were centered on the United States, allowing U.S. authorities in the NSA, the Department of the Treasury, and elsewhere to turn the broader network to their own purposes. The global economy relied on a preconstructed system of tunnels and conduits that the United States could move into and adapt, nearly as easily as if they had been custom-designed by a military engineer for that purpose. By seizing control of key intersections, the U.S. government could secretly listen to what adversaries were saying to each other or freeze them out of the global financial system.

At the beginning, the U.S. government did this opportunistically and sporadically. U.S. officials saw themselves as responding to an immediate, urgent threat rather than self-consciously building the foundations of a new kind of power. When the United States deployed this power, it targeted terrorist organizations like Al-Qaeda and belligerent states with few friends, like North Korea. Some of what the United States did was controversial, but the disagreements mostly centered on the sweeping interpretations of presidential power behind the imposition of new surveillance techniques and collateral damage to the civil rights of U.S. citizens.

Yet governments, too, can follow paths without anticipating where they lead. As departments and agencies developed new tools, they kept on finding new uses for them. Whenever a new use was discovered, it created a possible precedent for others. When bureaucrats got a taste of power, they liked it.

America's control of global communication networks allowed it to tap into the communications of allies as well as adversaries. Before the Internet, surveillance was difficult and expensive, meaning that it was usually reserved for "high-value targets": terrorists, senior foreign officials, and other people whose communications were strategically valuable. After September 11, U.S. surveillance agencies had free rein and massive resources, which they used to turn global telecommunications networks into a distributed surveillance system. They literally built a system that allowed them to record every single phone call in an entire country and store the data for up to a month, so that they could later "rewind" individual conversations that they suspected might be interesting. In this new world, the problem wasn't gathering information. It was storing the massive amounts of data that were collected and sifting them for valuable nuggets. When the U.S. government started taking full advantage of America's position in global networks, its surveillance state was transformed.

So, too, was America's system of financial coercion. Within a couple of weeks of the September 11 attack, the U.S. Department of the Treasury had started to aggressively investigate its options for gathering data from the world, so that it could detect future attacks. It quickly identified the SWIFT (Society for Worldwide Interbank Financial Telecommunication) messaging system—which plays a core role in global financial transfers—as a crucial source of information, and demanded access to SWIFT's information under pain of criminal subpoenas. Treasury also began to develop a new kind of sanction, which used its control of "dollar clearing" to force international banks to implement U.S. policy outside its borders. Control of SWIFT and dollar clearing were combined to cut Iran out of the world's financial system, forcing it to the negotiating table to discuss its nuclear weapons program. The U.S. officials who planned these steps often thought of them as once-off emergency measures. Instead, they became the precedent for a more general transformation of U.S. financial power.

Slowly, and without ever really thinking through what it was doing, the United States transformed the subterranean networks that tied the world's economy together into an underground empire, where it could listen in on the world's conversations and isolate its enemies from the world economy. Once-radical proposals became commonplace tools of policy. The United States was no longer just the world's remaining superpower. It was a state with superpowers. Like a spider at the heart of a global web, it could detect the subtle percussions of what enemies and friends were saying to each other from thousands of miles away. And when it thought it necessary, it could tightly wrap an adversary's economy in smothering strands that were stronger than steel.

But with great power comes great responsibility. And by the end of Barack Obama's second term as president, officials had begun to worry about what they had wrought. The Snowden revelations, which detailed secret U.S. surveillance efforts put in place after the attacks of September 11, 2001, had not only left the American intelligence community backfooted but threatened the political arrangements underlying the Internet. When the revelations led the European Union to cancel its data transfer deal with the United States, Eric Schmidt, the chair of Google's parent company, warned that the Internet itself was at risk. Jack Lew, Obama's Treasury secretary, gave a much reported speech warning that if the United States overused its powers, "financial transactions may begin to move outside of the United States entirely—which could threaten the central role of the U.S. financial system globally."

———————

Once, the underground empire was cloaked by its dullness. The visible trappings of empire—lost legions, battles, assassinated heirs— make for enthralling stories, but few people outside Colson Whitehead novels get excited about the infrastructure beneath. The result was that few people had any comprehensive understanding of the struggles below. Occasional tremors shook the surface. Most important, Edward Snowden's willingness to leak intelligence files revealed the massive subterranean machineries that the NSA and its sister agencies had built to monitor the world. International banks complained about the massive costs that the United States was willing to impose on them, but to little avail. The United States began taking quiet action against Chinese companies such as the telecommunications giant Huawei, which it saw as an extension of the state. But these seemed disconnected rather than parts of any whole.

The picture started to come together during the Trump administration, which believed that the United States, far from overusing its powers, wasn't nearly aggressive enough. Trump did not build the underground empire, but he made it more visible and far more controversial. This certainly wasn't because Trump himself connected the dots. When he discovered new tools of coercion, he was as delighted as a toddler with new toys, but he didn't have sufficient attention span to really understand how to make other countries bend beneath the yoke. While he wanted tribute, Trump was often willing to settle for attention. Regardless, the United States extended its underground empire in increasingly belligerent ways. And as its victims started paying attention, they began to piece together a different understanding of U.S. power. Trump's administration used the power of the U.S. financial system, for example, to target not just terrorists but human rights officials. Over time, it lurched haphazardly but irreversibly toward developing tools to target not just rogue states like North Korea but core assets of other great powers, like China.

And as the United States began to confront China, the imperial struggle became overt. The subterranean conflict moved aboveground as the old power and the new challenger battled for dominion. The United States targeted Huawei because it feared that it was building the roads that would allow China to create its own empire. Huawei—a company with a murky relationship with China's government—was building the world's next-generation Internet infrastructure.

As a cynical European official put it, America was angry with China for trying to do what America had already done, by turning the global communications system into an empire of surveillance. To stop this from happening, America turned to the tools that it had and developed new ones. U.S. newspapers covered its actions as a business section story. In China, the U.S. campaign looked like a national crisis, making the dangers of the underground empire visible and visceral.

America's new belligerence frightened traditional allies as well. Their companies had long been subjected to "secondary sanctions"— economic tools that can force foreign businesses to comply with U.S. demands, even if they aren't located in the United States. When the United States started threatening its allies for sticking to a deal that the United States itself had negotiated, these allies began to see the U.S.-dominated financial system as a yoke that they had to pass under. They started thinking about building their own "strategic autonomy," fearing, in French president Macron's words, that the "day that cooperation becomes dependence, you have become somebody's vassal and you disappear."

It was easier for China and Europe to understand the threat than to know what to do about it. It was hard for China to build its own technology. When Russia invaded Ukraine, Europe discovered how much it needed America. Businesses and individuals, too, faced impossible dilemmas. As the United States began to confront China, they were stranded in the no-man's-land between warring empires, one trying to retain its grasp on global networks and the other struggling to displace it. Once, when multinational corporations thought about political risk, they feared kleptocratic dictators. Now they worried that America might press them into service or China might retaliate.

Skirmishes between these two powers and lesser ones may blow up, posing existential threats to the businesses caught in economic conflicts between states. As they respond to the threat, and states respond in turn, the global economy may be transformed from an open system into a frozen conflict between armed and hostile camps. We already know how much damage can be done when accidental catastrophes strike. In 2011, an earthquake led to months of disruption in the semiconductor industry, which relied on a few key suppliers in Japan, and when the wave of coronavirus rolled over the globe in 2020, it revealed similar vulnerabilities. We may be on the verge of a greater catastrophe still, brought about not by chance but by battles that tear apart the silken webs that weave the world economy together.

A verting breakdown will require the United States to work toward a different vision of security. It will have to acknowledge the responsibility that comes with power, allowing others to secure themselves from America's network imperialism. At the same time, it must lead the way in working out rules of the road, for a world where adversaries are inextricably tied together by global networks. In the Cold War, the United States was willing to talk to the USSR to figure out what each side was able to accept and to avoid destabilizing misadventures with nuclear weapons. Historical precedent shows it can do this, and *must* do this—it is American fingers that are closest to the power switches. Building resilience and mitigating vulnerabilities will lead to a better future than crude nationalism and reshoring. No one likes or trusts a bully, but people are willing to accept power if it's used benevolently.

International superpower that it is, the United States might even support a vision of commonwealth rather than empire, in which it and other actors secure collective benefits rather than contending over narrow interests. It is easy to see how the United States could use its sanctions against carbon producers or countries like Brazil that keep allowing rain forests to be cut down. The United States has already used its powers in the past to go after other issues, such as tax havens in Switzerland. Why not egregious polluters?

Such a commonwealth would have its problems. It would be most active where U.S. self-interest and global self-interest overlapped. It would have to strike deals, which means that certain problems would be carved out and left unaddressed. For example, it's hard to see China signing on to proposals that use networked coercion to spread democracy. Finally, this regime would be most effective in pushing other countries to make necessary choices that they already know they have to make instead of raising new ones.

Nevertheless, this would represent a far better path than the one that the United States is going down. The United States was able to retain its empire so long because it was hidden in the shadows. Now that it has been exposed to the light, it will crumble, or worse. The old conflicts will become more bitter and intractable, and the new fights are just getting going. If this system ever made the United States safe, it won't for much longer. Instead, it is precipitating a spiral that may undermine the United States, and surely will if the United States continues to believe that it can enforce its demands with impunity. When you have built the economic equivalent of a nuclear arsenal, you shouldn't be surprised when others think about striking first or striking back.

1

WALTER WRISTON'S WORLD

In his time, Walter Wriston was one of the most powerful people on the planet, the chairman of the financial giant Citibank and its parent corporation, Citicorp. He was also a man with a vision. His book, *The Twilight of Sovereignty*, is nearly forgotten today, but it predicted how the information revolution would transform global politics. The sovereign power of states, which had grown since the waning of the Middle Ages, was now in decline. New technologies and market freedoms were about to "decentralize power," rendering "once vital strategic 'choke points'" irrelevant, and "shifting the tectonic plates of national sovereignty." Global flows of information, money, and trade were not only flooding across national borders but washing them away, creating a true global marketplace in which agile individuals and businesses could evade government regulation.

When novel ideas succeed, they decay into stale clichés. Wriston's arguments became the common wisdom of the business bestsellers stacked on tables in every airport bookstore. But he had begun speaking and writing about the irresistible challenge that global information technology and markets posed to government power in the 1970s, long before others were really paying attention. Back then, financial flows were largely restricted by national borders, and the Internet was an obscure government-funded experiment. Even when he published his book in 1992, it wasn't clear that technology would transform everything. The Berlin Wall had fallen only three years before, and the Cold War still hadn't yet relinquished its skeletal grasp on the world's politics and markets.

Wriston inherited his zeal for economic liberty and deep distrust of the state from his father. Henry Wriston, a university president and president of the prestigious Council on Foreign Relations, was personally invited by the famous economist Friedrich von Hayek to help found the Mont Pèlerin Society, a highly influential group of libertarian and conservative thinkers who tended the flame of free market thinking after World War II. Like his father, Walter was a globalist who was deeply influenced by Hayek's vision of a world in which market freedoms were the basis of individual liberty.

But Walter Wriston wasn't an academic or a think-tank president. As Roy Smith, who worked for Citibank's rival, Goldman Sachs, described it later, Wriston was "the most influential banker" of his time, the man who had turned Citibank into the "one bank that all others copy shamelessly." When Wriston said in 1992 that he had written his book "from the perspective of a participant in the evolving global financial marketplace," he was engaging in polite and perhaps ironic understatement. The histories of globalization pay close attention to the politicians and high officials who cleared the way for open markets, and the thinkers who argued for them, but they regularly ignore the business leaders who actually built them. Wriston was the Zelig of globalization. Look closely at the burgeoning of international finance, of information networks, of the logistical innovations that transformed trade. You'll find him everywhere.

In his personal relations, Wriston was a little awkward and stiff, exemplifying the virtues and scruples of his Methodist upbringing. His business philosophy, in contrast, displayed a distinct piratical flair. He disdained borders and national rules in favor of the high seas of global markets, where Citibank and its rivals could outsail the grasping monarchs who ruled the land, creating their own freebooter's republic on the waves.

Already as a trainee officer at National City Bank (now Citibank), Wriston had risked causing apoplexy in his superiors by lending $42 million to Malcom [*sic*] McLean, a trucking entrepreneur with a new and controversial idea about how to transport goods cheaply by water as well as land. McLean used the money to launch the containerization revolution, which dramatically lowered the costs of transporting goods around the world. Wriston's financial innovations helped create the modern Eurodollar market—a vast offshore realm of financial transactions in U.S. dollars happening outside of U.S. borders. His efforts to build a private global payments system under Citibank's control in the early 1970s prompted other banks to build their own collective system, so as to avoid being drawn inside Citibank's gently smiling jaws.

Wriston's willingness to put his ideas into action changed the world. As he explained in 1979, the "current banking network, with its Euromarkets and its automated payments system" seemed dull and technical, but it had immense political consequences. He believed that if money could move rapidly from country to country, it could no longer be mastered by states. Instead it might master them, replacing the whimsical tyranny of political rulers with the austere rigor of market discipline. Equally, the free movement of information across global telecommunications networks would prevent governments from halting the spread of ideas that they did not like. As Wriston explained later, telecommunications networks could transform high technology manufacturing, allowing multitudes of different producers in different countries to coordinate together on building a common product.

Wriston was right that these changes would have immense political consequences, but he misunderstood what these consequences would be. He once told a friend that "centralization . . . is a fascist state," and believed till his death that he and his peers were building a freer world with limited government. The irony was that he and other business leaders were centralizers by their nature: they sought to dominate markets, so that other businesses would have to use their systems and pay tribute to them. They built world-spanning networks that centered on a few key choke points. Eurodollar markets and global payment systems redirected the world's financial flows through U.S. banks and U.S.-dominated institutions. Global information flowed through networks centered on U.S. territory and subject to U.S. surveillance. And as global manufacturing came to rely on information and financial networks, it, too, became concentrated in ways that made it vulnerable to U.S. authority. The tragedy of globalization was that men and women like Wriston built a world that seemed to escape the control of government but in fact was wide open to government power and its own undoing.

———————

Wriston eventually came to believe that "international banking is a system designed by fate to exist in a certain state of economic tension, with all governments, including the most democratic." But at the beginning of his career, international banking barely existed. The banking industry that Wriston and others confronted in the 1960s was sluggish, timid, and lazy. Banks were trapped inside national borders by complex and clashing rules put in place after the financial crash of the Great Depression. These regulations meant that most banks faced little international competition and had scant incentive to invest in new ways of doing things. It was nearly impossible to be a true international bank.

The 1960s banking industry was a Victorian survival into the modern era, a clattering steampunk engine of rusting pistons and gutta-percha-covered cables, with a few incongruously modern parts bolted on. Eric Sepkes, who helped build the European payments system, later recalled how Citibank's London operation relied on a system of pneumatic tubes to communicate between its payments and authorizing offices. Staff had to handwrite payment instructions on a form, which they then stuffed into a canister and inserted into a partial vacuum conduit that ferried it to its destination (the City of London had built miles of pneumatic tube networks in the nineteenth century). One day, when the payments people didn't hear back from authorization, they discovered that the tube had become blocked. Citibank had to call in a chimney sweep to fix the problem, re-enabling payments processing for the entire continent of Europe.

Global banking was a system of mysterious tubes on a much larger scale, with various portals that took money in, did expensive and incomprehensible things to it, and spat it out somewhere else. No one fully understood the machinery, least of all the people who were supposedly in charge. The gentlemanly activities of merchant banking, where men with excellent pedigrees built on their social connections to win deals, remained rigidly distinct from the mundane tasks of payments processing, which were performed by female clerks surrounded by vast piles of paper. It took a very long time to send money across borders. At one point, Citibank's Argentinian branch had to convert its profits into cases of Scotch whisky, to prevent them from being inflated away before they could be sent to New York.

Wriston helped rebuild this clanking machine into an engine of transformation, welding disjointed national markets into a true world economy. His strategy was built around two insights. The first was that global markets could—if they were allowed—circumvent the labyrinthine systems of rules constructed by national regulators and eventually replace them. The second was that banking was a "branch of the information business." Market prices provided one crucial source of information, summarizing as they did the decisions of millions of individuals over what to buy and sell. Technology provided another, allowing banks to discover the information they had buried within their own bureaucracies and to better exchange information with each other and their customers. With proper technology, the dull-seeming backroom activities of banking such as payments processing could become a source of profit and power.

When Wriston began to remake Citibank, money had already begun to seep through the seams in the ductwork. Businesses outside the United States desperately wanted U.S. dollars, which were needed, for example, to buy and sell oil, while businesses in the United States wanted to earn higher returns. U.S. regulators had capped interest rates for ordinary consumers and stopped interest payments altogether on corporate deposits. Bankers had already begun to figure out crafty means to connect demand to supply.

Wriston and his colleagues built the institutional infrastructures that allowed this to happen at scale. They created financial instruments like the certificate of deposit, which provided a legal pipeline to smoothly convey the dollars owned by American businesses to the international banks that needed them for their customers. Citibank's competitors, like J. P. Morgan and Warburg, adapted these instruments and came up with their own ideas. What was once a small and disconnected trade in Eurodollars, based primarily in London, became a vast marketplace for buying, selling, and lending in dollars outside the United States.

As the political economist Eric Helleiner describes it, the Euro-dollar market became a legal gray zone where vast amounts of U.S. dollars circulated beyond U.S. borders. As the market grew, the U.S. dollar became established as the universal basis of international trade. If you were a Japanese company selling goods to a business in Italy, it was hard to convert the Italian lira that you were paid in directly into Japanese yen. The economic relationship between Japan and Italy wasn't big enough to support a liquid market where the two currencies could be exchanged directly. The Eurodollar market provided an easy detour, where you could turn lira into dollars and then dollars into yen. And as the supply of Eurodollars grew, it increasingly made sense for companies to simply buy and sell in dollars, which they could then convert into their home currencies.

The result was that the dollar became a global currency, without anyone really planning it. More dollars circulated outside the United States than within it. U.S. officials at the Federal Reserve and elsewhere paid surprisingly little official attention to what was happening. This made the market attractive, for example, to the Soviet Union, which needed dollars for international trade but worried that they might be seized by the U.S. government if they were deposited directly in American banks. By using Eurodollars, which were bought and sold in London and Italy, they thought they could avoid this risk.

These markets all depended on an infrastructure of clever financial engineering. Banks weren't trading physical stacks of hundred-dollar bills. Looked at closely, Eurodollars were an accounting fiction, imaginary dollars traded between real banks. They couldn't be used for anything other than buying other currencies. But every single Eurodollar had to be backed by a real dollar, sitting in a U.S bank operating under U.S. law and responsible to U.S. regulators. As Wriston explained, "All the dollars in the world—except [physical] currency—are deposits in a bank in America, because that is the only place anyone can spend a dollar."

This meant that transactions using Eurodollars had to be cleared through a U.S. bank's internal processes (moving money from one customer's account to another's) or through a clearing institution run by U.S. banks, such as CHIPS, the Clearing House Interbank Payments System. Foreign banks had to maintain clearing accounts in U.S. financial institutions if they were to trade dollars and participate in global finance. The Eurodollar market might indeed have been a pirate kingdom, but it was one where the buccaneers had to regularly provision themselves in the monarch's ports. The more that foreign banks came to depend on access to U.S. dollars, the more vulnerable they were to U.S. regulators, whenever those regulators finally woke up.

Gradually, the "dollar clearing system" run by U.S. banks like Citibank and J. P. Morgan and clearing institutions like CHIPS became the beating heart of the world's financial system, circulating dollars around the world in a regular systole and diastole. The Eurodollar market, far from creating a decentered new realm of finance, had made the global financial system more fragile and more vulnerable to American jurisdiction.

This became clear in 1974, when Chase froze the dollar clearing account of a small German bank, Herstatt, which had run into financial difficulties. Flaws in the system meant that other banks' transactions with Herstatt couldn't be cleared, which meant that other banks' transactions with those banks failed to clear, and so on, in an ever-growing cascade. Citibank pulled the plug on its automatic money transfer system to stop payments to banks that might no longer be creditworthy. The global financial system went into heart failure; Citibank's decision "virtually brought the [world's] payment system to a halt." Wriston spent the next couple of days corralling elite bankers to put the system together again. He succeeded, but as he noted later, the episode showed how twenty to thirty private banks had become the "de facto payments mechanism of the world." In his dry and understated description, this made central banks nervous, "and it also makes us nervous."

———————————

Over the 1970s, the other key element of global banking—automated settlement messaging—became centralized, too. Again, Wriston's Citibank played a crucial role in the story.

Financial transactions between banks in different countries have always been difficult. In the eighteenth and nineteenth centuries, banks relied on close relationships with their "correspondent" banks in other countries. They would issue physical letters of credit, signed instructions telling a correspondent bank to provide money to the bearer on the promise that the bank would be paid. However, such letters could be forged and were difficult to verify in a world where sea voyages could take weeks or months (much of the plot of *Golden Hill*, Francis Spufford's novel of pre-Revolutionary New York, turns on the difficulties of establishing whether an individual carrying a large letter of credit is who he says he is). The telegraph of the nineteenth century and the telex machines of the twentieth century made communication faster, but they were still awkward and cumbersome. In the 1960s, telex payments required the operators for both banks to perform logarithmic calculations using shared code books to ensure that security had not been breached.

As Citibank became the most internationalized bank in the world—it had branches in over ninety countries—Wriston recognized an opportunity to standardize the ways in which banks talked to each other across borders. Every important international bank had to do business with Citibank. That meant that if Citibank decided on a new technological standard for payments messages, there was a good chance that it would stick and spread. And if it did spread, Citibank would become "the nexus of the world's payments system," giving it a permanent advantage over its competitors. Every time that money went from one country to another, it would have to go through Citibank's system, providing it with a potential stranglehold on the market.

Wriston and his eventual successor, John Reed, were both obsessed with technology and had set up their own skunk works, Transaction Technologies, Inc., to build specialized hardware and software. Transaction Technologies was tasked with building MARTI (Machine-Readable Telegraphic Input), a kind of secure post office system just for banks. After MARTI was launched, Citibank's senior operations officer Richard Matteis reportedly demanded that all its correspondent banks use MARTI to communicate with it or have their telexes returned. As banker Renato Polo described it decades later, Citibank more or less said, "We advise you to use MARTI from now on. If you don't use it, we will not execute your instructions."

The problem was that Citibank was too big to be trusted. Citibank might want to control a messaging system that every other bank depended on, but those other banks had excellent reason to be wary. They had no desire to depend on a technology that was outside their control and that Citibank could change at will to squeeze them. As Polo went on to explain, "[E]ither you make yourself captive to one correspondent, which no one in his right mind would ever do, or you say no." Many indeed said no, leading to utter chaos as Citibank's backroom operations struggled to deal with a blizzard of failed transfers and the temporary near collapse of Citibank's network of correspondent banks.

Citibank's MARTI wasn't the only possible system for payments messages. A Dutch banker, Johannes (Jan) Kraa, had persuaded a group of European banks to found the Society for Worldwide Interbank Financial Telecommunication (SWIFT) in 1973 to create an alternative system for secure communications between banks. SWIFT was based in Belgium, to sidestep the rivalry between the two financial centers of London and New York. However, it had a hard time getting European banks to agree to participate. Each wanted its own country's standards to prevail, making it hard for SWIFT to reach consensus or attract enough banks to make the system workable. By 1974, it looked increasingly likely that SWIFT would fail. Then the MARTI debacle persuaded European banks that if they didn't come up with a shared standard, someone else, like Citibank, would come up with a standard for them.

Citibank's campaign to force MARTI on its correspondents led to a "decisive landslide" in SWIFT adoption. By the end of 1975, SWIFT had 270 member banks located across fifteen countries. Although Wriston blamed MARTI's failure on the difficulties of getting banks to agree with each other, Matteis later admitted that "people's resistance to MARTI made SWIFT a success."

Soon, SWIFT membership was a necessary condition for participating in the global financial system. And the more that SWIFT grew, the more essential it became to the world's financial system, including America's. Eleven years after its founding, Robert Moore of Chemical Bank became the first American chairman of SWIFT's board, while Citibank's Yawar Shah became chairman in 2006. Today, SWIFT's messaging system carries over ten billion messages annually, facilitating 1.25 quadrillion dollars in transactions. Like the dollar clearing system, it plays a central role in global finance. As the writers of SWIFT's official history acknowledged, SWIFT has become an "'obligatory passage point' . . . if you want to participate in financial services you must join because there is no real alternative."

SWIFT's central importance created its own problems. Willie Sutton is supposed to have said that he robbed banks because "that's where the money is." Now, the money flows through complex technical networks such as SWIFT, and criminal minds have taken notice. North Korean hackers exploited weaknesses in SWIFT's system to transfer $81 million out of the Bank of Bangladesh's accounts at the New York Federal Reserve Bank in 2016. If they hadn't made a typo, they might have gotten away with a billion.

The cops noticed, too: SWIFT came under political pressure from the United States, which wanted it to do more to prevent and detect crime. For a long time, SWIFT's officials managed to fend off these requests, arguing that SWIFT was a purely technical organization, dedicated to managing the world's financial plumbing.

Even though SWIFT was based in Belgium, it was run by a consortium of international banks. It had succeeded in replacing a Dickensian tangle of pneumatic tubes with a system for sending money that actually worked. SWIFT had defeated an alternative system that would have been controlled by a single American bank if Walter Wriston had had his way. But some of the banks were American, and all of them needed access to the dollar clearing system to carry out their work. Most people didn't pay attention to SWIFT, which seemed to be a boring but useful organization dedicated to maintaining a boring but useful part of the world's financial plumbing. But SWIFT's ability to fend off politics depended on U.S. willingness to tolerate its apparent independence. If the U.S. government ever really used its muscle, SWIFT would have to cave.

In 1996, Walter Wriston enthused that "there is no way on God's green Earth government can exercise censorship on the Net in any meaningful way." But *The Twilight of Sovereignty*, which he wrote just a few years earlier, had nothing to say about the Internet. Its index jumped straight from "International Monetary Fund" to "Investment spending." Back when the Internet was one specialized network among many, the most important change seemed to be the physical transformation of the world's telecommunication network, which the Internet and its competitor networks rode upon. A few years later, when technological evangelists celebrated the liberatory potential of the Internet, they paid little attention to the wires and cables that carried it.

Wriston had intimate and painful experience of the world before it had been transformed. The first transatlantic cable capable of carrying voice transmissions had been laid in 1956. It allowed a grand total of thirty-six phone calls to happen at once. There were so few phone circuits available between Brazil and New York that Citibank's local branch hired "squads of Brazilian youths" as dialers, who kept calling and calling for days until they got an open line. When they succeeded, Citibank's employees stayed on the phone, reading books and newspapers to keep the line open until it was needed.

Things began to change in the 1970s and 1980s. Electronic switches—specialized computers—began to replace mechanical arrays in which human operators had connected one caller to another by plugging their cables together. These switches could handle many conversations at once. Digital fiber-optic technology allowed human voices to be turned into information, and information into rapid pulses of light, so that a thin strand of flexible glass could carry a myriad of individual conversations. The first transatlantic fiber-optic cable, which was laid in 1988, could carry forty thousand simultaneous phone calls. As other fiber-optic cables were laid, flows of money, information, and ideas became "utterly dependent on the new world communications network" and the "path to prosperity" it offered. Wriston believed that this new, apparently decentralized system of communication required governments to "surrender control over the flow of information."

As the Internet swallowed up other networks over the 1990s, it seemed to reinforce Wriston's arguments about decentralization. After all, the Internet was designed from the ground up to avoid central control. As a popular dictum described it, the Internet "interprets censorship as damage and routes around it." But something funny started happening with the physical networks that the Internet relied upon. The more that they spread around the world, notionally escaping their American origins, the more centralized they became, so that their key flows were channeled through switches and exchange points on American soil.

This new empire of information had its heart next door to the capital of the old empire of regulation and coercion that Wriston wanted to escape. If you leave Washington, DC, and travel westward along I-66 by car for forty minutes or so, you will pass through the unincorporated community of Tysons Corner into Loudoun County. Once this was farmland; now it is a wilderness of office parks and industrial facilities. Ten minutes after passing the turnoff for Dulles Airport, with its swooping concrete wings, you reach Ashburn, Virginia, which was the single most important crossroads of the nascent Internet that Wriston celebrated, and which plays a crucial role in the new universe of cloud computing.

Ashburn doesn't look as though it was ever an Internet boomtown. Instead of Palo Alto's ostentatiously low-key bungalows and boutique restaurants catering to the newly ultrarich, it has retirement communities, chain restaurants, and affordable town houses. Even so, fortunes were made and lost here in the boom years of the dot-com frenzy, as property speculators bought cheap land to create facilities for Internet start-ups. In the early 2000s, Ashburn was the "bullseye of America's Internet" and a crucial hub in the world's communication infrastructure. Today, the major cloud computing centers of Amazon Web Services, Microsoft, and Google cluster around Ashburn, jostling for room with colocation centers and other dull-seeming but crucial aspects of the Internet's plumbing.

Places like Ashburn wouldn't exist if the people who invented the Internet had been right. The Internet wasn't ever supposed to have any hubs or bull's-eyes. Instead, it was supposed to be a "distributed network"—one in which every node on the network is linked to several other nodes, without any real center. Such networks are much more robust against breakdown and control than centralized networks like the hub-and-spoke routing systems used by such airlines as United. Dulles Airport, for example, is one of United Airlines' key hubs, along with Denver, Chicago O'Hare, and Houston. This handful of nodes is central in the network. When these hubs are hit by storms, United passengers, even those outside the hubs, suddenly discover that they can't make their connections. Distributed networks, in contrast, are supposed to avoid hubs and single failure points, so that it is always possible to find an alternative route when one node goes down. Paul Baran, who came up with the idea of a distributed network, was trying to figure out how to make nuclear "command and control networks" less vulnerable to disruption in a war with the Soviet Union. A distributed network could allow the U.S. military to communicate, even if its central facilities had been taken out by nuclear strikes.

But the people who invented the Internet didn't control it, especially after it left the control of the government in the 1990s. Some entrepreneurs realized that if they could capture an Internet choke point—a crossroads in the network—they could make a lot of money. Internet "exchanges" were one kind of crossroad. They seemed technical and unimpressive to the casual observer: rooms full of cables, all connecting to the switches that figure out which information has to be sent where. But these exchanges play a crucial role in the physical infrastructure of the Internet, bridging the different networks run by big telecommunications providers, so that digitized phone calls, email messages, and video can find the best path from sender to receiver. Like airport hubs, they are the places where connections are made.

When they fail, large parts of the Internet slow to a crawl or become completely inaccessible.

It wasn't an accident that the biggest choke point of all was in Northern Virginia. If Silicon Valley was where personal computers started getting built in the 1970s and 1980s, Northern Virginia was where they got connected. Instead of Stanford University (the center of Silicon Valley's innovation economy), Northern Virginia had ARPA (now DARPA), the Pentagon agency that had invented the Internet's predecessor and employed Robert Kahn and Vint Cerf, who developed the basic "protocols" (rules and technical expectations) that allow the Internet to work. MCI WorldCom, which was based in Ashburn, built the national fiber-optic network that the government-controlled Internet ran on.

A new microeconomy started to flourish around these centers, catering to the federal government and other big customers, giving rise to AOL and other near-forgotten technological giants of the 1980s. One crucial strand of fiber-optic cable extended out from Washington, DC, into Northern Virginia along a long spike following an old railway route. Small technology firms swarmed around it like bees sipping nectar from a foxglove.

When the Internet (which had originally been a network for academics and research) went commercial, local entrepreneurs were ready to get rich. Rick Adams, a self-described computer "mutant," had founded UUNET, one of the first commercial Internet Service Providers, connecting homes and firms to the Internet, in his house. He started talking strategy with the man who sold him access to fiber-optic networks, Scott Yeager, of Metropolitan Fiber Systems (MFS), over forty-eight-ounce porterhouses in Morton's steakhouse.

The National Science Foundation, which ran the noncommercial Internet, was about to announce which big companies were going to run the Internet's physical infrastructure. But Adams and Yeager understood how the Internet worked and saw how they could preempt the National Science Foundation's decision. Because the Internet was distributed, no one was really in charge of it—autonomous "router" computers continuously figured out the most efficient ways to send information. If UUNET could persuade enough other ISPs to connect to it, and if MFS could provide enough bandwidth to serve them all, they could organize a quiet coup. The rest of the Internet would discover that the most efficient way to send data was through UUNET and its partners, so that "UUNET would become the default route for the entire Commercial Internet," and the competition would be over long before the government announced the winner.

This was how Adams and Yeager came to build MAE-East (Metropolitan Area Ethernet, East; later Metropolitan Area Exchange, East), in a room at the bottom of a Northern Virginia parking-lot garage. MAE-East provided an exchange where different Internet Service Providers like MCI and Sprint could physically connect their networks together. Exactly as Adams had hoped, MAE-East became a central exchange for the early commercial Internet. By 1994, Yeager's biographer claimed that it carried over 90 percent of all Internet traffic.

MAE-East became a fountain of monopoly power. Adams was in charge—businesses had to have Adams's approval to get access to MAE-East. Very soon, MCI, Sprint, and America Online were members of MAE-East, while smaller companies were turned away. UUNET went public at a price of $14 a share in 1995 at the beginning of the dot-com boom, hitting $93.25 a share a few months later, and went on an acquisition spree. When Al Gore complained about "bottlenecks," he was worried that big telecommunications companies like Verizon and Sprint might use their control to turn the Internet into their own private monopoly, choking off competition from new entrants in the industry like UUNET. Now, Adams and his peers were building their own old-boys club.

This created opportunities for entrepreneurs like the late Al Avery and Jay Adelson. Equinix, the company that they founded, eventually became a giant in its own right. In December 2020, it enjoyed its seventy-second consecutive quarter of growth, pulling in approximately $6 billion in annual revenue. But Avery and Adelson's original idea was to provide an alternative to bottlenecks like MAE-East. Avery, who worked for Digital Equipment Corporation, had hired Adelson to help set up the Palo Alto Internet Exchange (PAIX) in a basement near Stanford University. As Adelson described it to us, Avery's work on PAIX inspired them to build a "neutral exchange," which would "isolate the business model from conflicts of interest."

Even if Avery and Adelson's business model was very different from Rick Adams's, they needed to move next door. They built near MAE-East's location in Tysons Corner, because it was the "most dense [interconnection point] in the world." But they also needed cheap land and digging permission to bury the fiber-optic cables that connected all the servers together. Avery and Adelson went to the jurisdiction next door, Loudoun County. County officials didn't have a strong understanding of the underlying technologies—they promoted their central location with posters showing a hand grasping a bunch of old-school analog phone cords together. But they were plenty capable of recognizing an opportunity when they saw it.

Instead of a centralized switchboard between the major telecommunications networks run by a club of insiders, Equinix created an exchange that any paying customer could join, combined with the equivalent of a long-stay hotel, where customers could park their own servers. If Spotify and Google need to communicate with each other quickly, they do not need to move data from Stockholm to San Jose. Instead, they can each locate servers in the same facilities and hook them up via fiber-optic cables. A neutral exchange would allow their servers to talk to the world, while "colocation" of servers in the same place would allow them to have rapid conversations with each other.

Today, Equinix is the largest colocation provider on the planet by market share and Ashburn is its largest facility. Adelson, reflecting on the company's position a few years after he stepped down in the wake of the September 11, 2001, attacks, worried that they might just have replaced one centralized monopoly with another. "Equinix is now a dominating force and this means it can be dangerous. When we started we were trying to disrupt monopolies but how ironic that now its success means it will be the only force."

UUNET eventually disappeared, and MAE-East became redundant, but Ashburn didn't need them anymore. More server farms attracted more high-speed fiber, which in turn attracted more server farms, in a self-reinforcing loop.

That was why Amazon went to Northern Virginia when it wanted to pioneer a new business model—cloud computing. In the early 2000s, most people thought of Amazon either as a consumer-focused company or as a marketplace. But Amazon's then CEO, Jeff Bezos, recognized early on that Amazon's information infrastructure could be turned into a profit center by renting it out to other businesses. The result, Amazon Web Services (AWS), not only became Amazon's great "engine of profitability" but spurred a new explosion of e-commerce. Hungry young start-ups didn't have to spend precious capital to buy their own servers anymore. Instead, they could just lease as much "compute" (basic computing power) from Amazon as they needed to serve the customers they had right now. Established businesses like Airbnb, Baidu, Lyft, and Netflix could lease compute, too, focusing on their core missions rather than maintaining the online infrastructure. When other companies realized how much money Amazon was making from AWS, they rushed to build their own "cloud computing" services.

Nebulous terms such as "cloud computing" make it easy to forget that all the information processing had to happen in buildings full of servers, connected to the Internet via fast fiber-optic cables. Amazon was even more secretive about where the buildings were than it was about the enormous profits they generated. By poring through municipal property records, Ingrid Burrington discovered in 2016 that the first AWS facilities were housed in colocation facilities in Ashburn and its neighboring towns.

Cloud computing services are notoriously sticky. As a recent biographer of Jeff Bezos describes it, "Once [companies] moved their data onto Amazon's servers, [they] had little reason to endure the inconvenience of transferring it back out." But the places where cloud computing actually happens—physical colocation facilities and data centers—are even stickier. As Adelson told us:

> If I put my half-a-million-dollar [communications switch] right next to my peers' infrastructure, and I invest all this money, and then I trench $15 million's worth of services into a fiber into that location, and then I physically run those cross connections to a thousand other people in that room, how am I ever going to move from there? I don't know if it's technically *feasible* to move from there.

That stickiness is why today's global Internet is highly centralized in places like Ashburn, making it vulnerable to attacks and accidents. In November 2020, websites across the globe from Adobe.com to the *Washington Post* crashed, thanks to a mistake made by technicians in Northern Virginia. People working in an Amazon Web Services facility had attempted to add some new servers. Instead, they crashed the network. A few months later, Ashburn became a bull's-eye in a very literal sense, when a right-wing extremist plotted to "kill off about 70 percent of the Internet." Seth Pendley, twenty-eight, of Wichita Falls, Texas, had started planning his attack after coming to Washington, DC, with a sawed-off rifle on January 6, 2021. He fell for an FBI sting operation, when he began talking on the encrypted Signal messaging system about his plan to "fuck up the Amazon servers." Pendley had hand-drawn maps of facilities in Ashburn and was arrested after trying to purchase C-4 plastic explosives from an undercover FBI agent.

Ashburn's information complex has over seventy nondescript low-slung warehouses, sprawling across 18 million square feet (with another 5.7 million square feet under construction), occupying more space than eight Empire State Buildings flipped on their sides. The data centers that power large swathes of the Internet consume an estimated 4.5 giga-watts of electricity a year, as much as nine coal-fired power plants would produce. Local officials still try to claim that up to 70 percent of daily global Internet traffic flows through Loudoun County. This is surely an exaggeration, but one with a light dusting of truth. In 2021, Northern Virginia still had the largest concentration of data centers in the world, with nearly twice the capacity of its closest competitor, London. This no doubt helped lure Jeff Bezos to open Amazon's second corporate head-quarters in Virginia.

Nobody intended that the networks and servers that support the Internet should become centralized. It happened because the builders of the economic networks that would weave the new world together typically began by building on what was already there. And those who came after them often found it easier to build on top of their efforts, laying new roads on top of old ones and joining them together where old crossroads already existed. It was clear from early on that the found-ing myth of the Internet—that it is a centerless network, inherently resistant to damage and control—is untrue. As a hacker told the writer Neal Stephenson back in 1996, "Virtually all communications between countries take place through a very small number of bottlenecks." But back then, no one wanted to think about the implications. The result is that today an obscure town in Northern Virginia has become a kind of vast parabolic mirror, concentrating the Internet into a tiny point that is easy to observe and perhaps to exploit.

G lobal finance and information networks transformed the physical economy, too. Before global networks, nearly all trade involved raw commodities, like oil, or finished products, such as radios. If you owned a company that built complicated things, like cars or computers, you wanted to have subcontractors who built components for you close by. If they were abroad, you couldn't talk to them quickly if a problem developed in the production process, while paying them was messy and tedious. That was one reason why production happened in clusters like Silicon Valley (which was a semiconductor hub before it started churning out software and services) or the car manufacturing complex centered around Detroit.

When globalization really got going in the 1990s, the infrastructure for cheap global transport could be combined with easy money and cheap communication to transform the global economy. Wriston argued that this marked a "fundamental change in the world's work." Human intelligence, as crystallized in intellectual capital, was "the dominant factor of production," and it was free to travel across borders, whether governments liked it or not. Adam Smith's wealth of nations had become the wealth of the world. Traditional trade was gradually subsumed by a new transnational system of production, in which design might happen in one country, production of different parts in many others, and assembly of the parts into a final product somewhere else again. In *The Twilight of Sovereignty*, Wriston used the example of an IBM computer, assembled in Florida from parts from Malaysia,

France, South Korea, Japan, and Singapore to illustrate how the world economy had changed in ways that trade statistics and politicians' speeches didn't capture.

Nowhere was this change more obvious than in Silicon Valley. The historian Margaret O'Mara has documented how Silicon Valley was an outgrowth of U.S. military spending. The missile and space programs' insatiable demand for complex electronics spawned big laboratories and contractors, which in turn spawned start-ups like Shockley Semiconductor. It was the first manufacturer of semiconductors, perhaps the single technology that did the most to make the modern economy. The original Silicon Valley was a cluster of manufacturing companies that alternatively competed and collaborated, offering easy opportunities for skilled engineers to find good jobs or, when their boss was as impossible as William Shockley, to go out and start their own businesses. As military spending dried up, Silicon Valley companies found new customers in the private sector and spawned a thriving subculture of homebrew computer clubs and self-taught hackers.

The culture survives in a modified form today, but the manufacturing has mostly moved on. For example, Apple Computer Company famously had its beginnings in a Silicon Valley garage. But as it grew larger, it had to find other places to build the computers that had made it famous. In addition to facilities in Fremont, California, and the East Bay of San Francisco, it had plants in Singapore and Ireland, where it could take advantage of cheap labor and assemble its computers closer to Asian and European customers. As O'Mara explained to us, chipmakers started outsourcing early. National Semiconductor set up its first Singapore plant in 1968.

However, Apple did everything it could to keep its manufacturing in-house. Apple's CEO, Steve Jobs, was notoriously focused on quality control and for a long time wanted Apple to design everything itself and source components from a single supplier. This allowed Apple to maintain high quality, but at the cost of much lower flexibility than competitors like Dell, which outsourced as much of the production process as it could. Fast logistics and information technology allowed mass-market manufacturers to move from a system where they had to make their products in advance, guessing at what demand would be, to one where they only started making a product after they had received an order.

By 1998, Jobs recognized that Apple needed to change course. He hired Tim Cook, a specialist in supply chain management, who had helped Compaq shift to "on demand manufacturing." Cook, who later became Jobs's successor, understood that logistics and information management were as important to business success as brand building, just as Wriston had understood the value of banks' back offices and Bezos of Amazon's computing infrastructure. Cook famously believed that inventory was "evil" and spent the next several years rebuilding Apple's supply chain, developing intense relationships with subcontractors like LG and Foxconn, a Taiwan-headquartered company that employs an estimated 1.3 million workers in mainland China alone. These relationships provided a degree of flexibility that would have been impossible in a world without fast communications—Apple could make last-minute design changes and have them implemented nearly immediately by its Chinese subcontractors.

However, Apple kept the key stages of product design, where much of the value was added, at home in Cupertino. The famous statement printed on the back of its iPhones, "Designed by Apple in California. Assembled in China," described a business model copied by many other companies. American design ingenuity combined well with Asian manufacturing capacity and expertise, especially as global trade rules shifted to make importing and exporting easier. The "China shock" saw low-tech American manufacturing jobs in industries such as textiles, and high-technology industries such as computer manufacture shift overseas. When President Barack Obama asked Steve

Jobs whether iPhones could be made in the United States rather than abroad, Jobs bluntly told him that it wasn't going to happen. International supply chains provided a degree of flexibility that America itself couldn't come close to matching.

What was true of iPhones was even more true of the semiconductors that Silicon Valley had pioneered. As semiconductors became more sophisticated, it became exponentially more expensive to manufacture them. Today, a 5-nanometer "fab" or "foundry" (a factory making integrated circuits), which is close to the leading edge of technology but not quite on it, can cost $12 billion to build. Since a fab has a lifetime of around five years, that means that it costs more than $75 a second to own one—even before you start making anything in it.

The semiconductor giant Intel, which had been founded by two of Shockley's former employees, Robert Noyce and Gordon Moore, could afford to stick to an integrated model, where the same company designed the chip and manufactured it in its own fabs. But other companies, including Intel's longtime competitor Advanced Micro Devices (AMD), moved away from the old model.

Creating and manufacturing a semiconductor requires deep, continued, and extensive communication throughout design and manufacturing. Easy, rapid, cheap communications meant that it could be done by different companies in completely different parts of the world. In the mid-1980s, companies began to realize that it was possible to design semiconductors without building them. Before then, manufacturing semiconductors was a process of trial and error. You designed the chip, built a prototype, figured out why the prototype didn't work, and kept on redesigning and building until you got a working version. But then, specialized companies started to put together professional design software that could run countless simulations of the chip under different conditions, to iron out errors before they reached the manufacturing stage. This, in turn, made it far easier for companies to start specializing in design without having to build their own expensive fabs. When they needed to build their final product, they could go to a company that had excess capacity in their fab and get them to build it.

The person credited with figuring this out was Gordon Campbell, a well-known entrepreneur. As Morris Chang, the founder of the Taiwan Semiconductor Manufacturing Company (TSMC), recounted decades later, Campbell came to him, looking for a $50 million investment in a new company. However, Campbell never followed up on his request. When Chang tracked him down, Campbell said that he'd discovered that he only needed $5 million to create a company that just focused on design and not the capital-intensive stage of manufacturing. Chang was intrigued. He had hoped to become the CEO of Texas Instruments but had been passed over and left for General Instruments, a smaller company, which had turned out to have its own disappointments.

Chang recognized that if some companies started specializing in pure design, there was a market opportunity to create a "pure play" foundry, which would specialize in manufacturing chips that other companies had designed. With $100 million in support from the Taiwanese government, he went to Taiwan to set up TSMC. Rather than just providing a commodity service, TSMC would specialize in building deep, ongoing relationships with its customers.

Already in the mid-1990s, one company might provide the software to design the chip, another might do the design work based on intellectual property provided by a third company, while a fourth ran the fab where billions of transistors are laid down on silicon wafers to create the final product. By 2020, the combination of specialized design and pure play foundry companies had completely transformed the semiconductor industry.

Firms like Qualcomm ensured that the United States continued to dominate the design of complex semiconductors, while pure play foundries like TSMC manufactured the complex semiconductors that Qualcomm and its competitors designed, continually improving their fabs to build smaller, more powerful, and less power hungry chips. Specialized companies based in the United States like Cadence Design Systems and Synopsys provided the automated tools that were necessary to design chips with billions of semiconductors. Companies like ARM—which was originally a joint venture between Apple, VLSI Technology, and the United Kingdom's Acorn Computers—licensed their intellectual property for particular processes on chips, creating, for example, the RISC (Reduced Instruction Set Computer) architecture that both cell phones and Apple's new M1 chips rely on.

The industry had truly gone global. *Beyond Borders*, a 2016 report by the Semiconductor Industry Association, depicted semiconductor manufacturing as a beautiful and extraordinarily complex global ecology, in which no one country dominated and cross-border cooperation provided far better innovation and growth than any national system ever could. The association's consultants proclaimed that "one U.S. semiconductor company had over sixteen thousand suppliers worldwide" and that a "globally interdependent industry that pools the best each participant has to offer provides the best path to the future." One could hardly have asked for a better illustration of Walter Wriston's vision of a world where business collaboration and the spread of ideas had rendered borders irrelevant.

The problem was that this picture was terribly misleading. In fact, semiconductor manufacture had gone global in ways that posed enormous potential risks. TSMC wasn't simply the biggest foundry. It was the sole source of advanced logic chip production. TSMC was a single point of failure for the U.S. economy, but it was outside U.S. borders. Indeed, it was located on an island just one hundred miles from the United States' emerging competitor and adversary, China. Without TSMC's chips, whole sectors of the U.S. economy might grind to a halt.

Equally, however, the United States could potentially use the semiconductor supply chain to threaten other countries. The most sophisticated design companies, such as Qualcomm, were based on U.S. soil. Without their plans, other countries' products wouldn't work. The software that was needed to design new complex semiconductors was the exclusive property of U.S. companies. U.S. intellectual property wound through the entire semiconductor production chain, like a fisherman's longline with barbed and baited hooks. Ideas had spread beyond borders, but instead of undermining government control, they potentially enabled it. Though few people paid attention during the boom years, the United States reserved the right to control technologies where more than a certain percentage of the intellectual property was American.

In peaceful times, manufacturers and governments focused on the benefits of globalization, ignoring the geopolitical risks. They were taking an enormous gamble. As the supply chain became more specialized, they became more brittle. If the risks ever became salient and visible, the entire global system for manufacturing semiconductors might become a war zone.

W riston had hoped to build a world where business, not government, was in charge. He and his peers helped markets spill over the confines of national borders into each other, a confluence that grew into a world ocean of information, money, and production. But even if business leaders like Wriston did not aspire to become sovereigns, they wanted to build their own business empires. Firms hoped to make monopoly profits by dominating their market and centralizing economic control.

As these businesses went global, a few glimpsed what might happen. Wriston had enthused about the power of Eurodollars and electronic money flows to transform the world. In 1998, the Canadian political economist Eric Helleiner wrote a skeptical riposte to his vision. It wasn't just that Eurodollar markets existed on the sufferance of governments and would have withered if the United States had not let them flourish. It was that global finance was "increasingly concentrated" in great financial centers like New York and London where electronic money had to pass through various "central 'choke points.'" As Helleiner speculated, this might actually increase the power of governments like the United States rather than undermining it. The question was when these governments would take up their power, and what they would do when they did.

2

THE STORMBREW MAP

One of the thousands of highly classified files that Edward Snowden took from the National Security Agency (NSA) was a secret map. At first glance, it seems unremarkable. Colored lines connect the Americas, Europe, and Africa, heading to the margins en route to Asia and Australia. The map has a title, "STORMBREW at a Glance," and a bristling thicket of intelligence community acronyms, denoting who is allowed to read it and who is not. Behind the map's contours and code words lie a long history and a graphical key to the underground empire.

Maps don't just depict physical locations. They reduce them into comprehensibility, turning a complex physical geography into a subset of essential features—power, territory, authority, reach. Every map of the countries of the world condenses the long, bloody history that created those countries' borders. But maps don't just represent physical space. They can remake it according to the priorities of the mapmakers, laying down sovereign claims over where one country's laws start and others end.

That is why maps have long been a tool of empire. In 1493, Pope Alexander VI issued a papal bull that sundered the world in half. The pope decreed that a line be drawn across the globe, stretching from the North Pole to the South, one hundred leagues west and south of the Azores and Cape Verde Islands. Alexander declared that all territories past that line belonged to the kings of Spain and Portugal, to do with as they willed. This legal map defined the New World as a kind of terra nullius, a nobody's land, whose native peoples had no rights to rule or govern themselves and no redress beyond whatever the rulers of the Iberian Peninsula chose to bestow on them.

Other rulers drew up their own maps in competition. The wizard John Dee was Queen Elizabeth I's court astrologer and is believed to have coined the term "British Empire." He believed that angels spoke to his scryer through a mirror, disclosing the hidden secrets of the world. Dee also drew up exquisite maps, which he combined with laborious legal arguments to defend Queen Elizabeth's "iust Arthurien clayme and title Imperiall" over the countries of the New World, asserting that they were rediscovered lands that had once been ruled from Camelot.

On its face, the NSA map appears no more than a technical depiction of a technical project for acquiring information. STORM-BREW was one of the NSA's many surveillance programs put in place after the attacks of September 11, 2001, capturing information from international cable traffic that crossed the United States. Created by the Truman administration in the 1950s, the NSA is perhaps the least well understood member of the U.S. intelligence community. Formally responsible for "signal" intelligence, it is tasked with sifting the billions of daily global clicks, emails, and phone calls for useful strategic information.

STORMBREW At a Glance

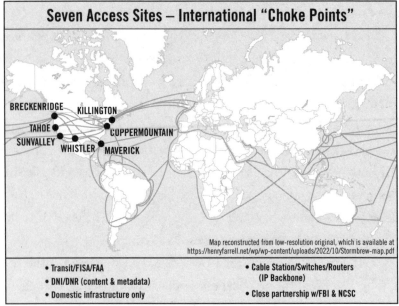

Seven Access Sites – International "Choke Points"

BRECKENRIDGE KILLINGTON

TAHOE   COPPERMOUNTAIN

SUNVALLEY   WHISTLER   MAVERICK

Map reconstructed from low-resolution original, which is available at
https://henryfarrell.net/wp/wp-content/uploads/2022/10/Stormbrew-map.pdf

- Transit/FISA/FAA
- DNI/DNR (content & metadata)
- Domestic infrastructure only

- Cable Station/Switches/Routers (IP Backbone)
- Close partnership w/FBI & NCSC

TOP SECRET // COMINT // NOFORN //20291130

The map depicts "Seven Access Sites—International 'Choke Points,'" inside the United States, with the code names Breckenridge, Tahoe, Sunvalley, Whistler, Maverick, Copper Mountain, and Killington (someone in the NSA liked to ski). Each of these "Choke Points" is located at a cable landing site or a switch in the Internet backbone. Like Dee, the U.S. government desperately wanted to uncover the world's hidden secrets. However, the NSA didn't have to converse with angels. Instead, as it explained in the materials accompanying the map, it just had to ask its STORMBREW "corporate partner" (which has been identified as Verizon/MCI) to sieve the data flowing through the Internet backbone for nuggets of precious and actionable information.

Programs like STORMBREW provided the NSA with upstream access to the torrents of information flowing through telecommunications networks. Other programs, such as PRISM, enabled it to demand downstream data, which was more narrowly targeted and better organized, from companies like Microsoft and Google. Nor was the NSA the only U.S. agency discovering new worlds. Shortly after September 11, 2001, the U.S. Treasury Department started to map the apparent chaos of the world's financial system, using its new knowledge to spy on enemies and eventually cut them out of the global economy.

These and other agencies of the U.S. government found out how to reduce the blooming, buzzing confusion of a globalized world, where it seemed as though everyone was shouting at each other at once, into simple, orderly maps. It turned out that everything converged on a handful of connections and bottlenecks, most of which were conveniently accessible to U.S. authorities (or at a pinch, allies such as the United Kingdom). An astonishingly complex reality could be reduced into something that was both graspable and tractable—lines on a page.

The maps didn't just explain how to get from one point to another. They defined the territory of U.S. surveillance and control. The NSA could parse the world's conversations by turning network hubs into clandestine listening posts, while the U.S. Department of the Treasury secretly tapped into the messages that banks used to send money across national boundaries. Over time, it discovered choke points, allowing it to cut off businesses and even whole countries from access to the key global networks that wove the world's economy together.

The United States started by isolating despised adversaries such as terrorist groups and pariah states like North Korea. It developed new legal tools to push Iran to abandon its nuclear program. After Trump came to power, the United States threatened to turn its tools against allies, too, punishing human rights officials who had the temerity to press for U.S. military accountability. Like the pope's map half a millennium before, the STORMBREW map and its equivalents didn't just simplify the world. They helped turn the terra nullius of the globalized economy into a territory that the United States could dominate.

Lieutenant General Michael Hayden of the U.S. Air Force surely wasn't thinking about world dominion as he prepared to give testimony to the House Permanent Select Committee on Intelligence in April 2000. He had more immediate worries.

Hayden had become director of the NSA the previous year. His professional life was bedeviled by a line that U.S. lawmakers had drawn across the world, dividing people in the United States—who had constitutional and legal protections from U.S. government surveillance—from those elsewhere, who had none.

Foreigners were still fair game, but past historical abuses (the NSA had wiretapped critics of the Vietnam War, including the Rev. Martin Luther King Jr.) had led the U.S. government to sharply restrict the NSA's ability to conduct surveillance within U.S. territory and against U.S. persons. As Hayden described it in his congressional testimony a year and a half before the attacks of September 11, 2001, if Osama bin Laden walked "across the bridge from Niagara Falls, Ontario, to Niagara Falls, New York, as he gets to the New York side, he is an American person. And my agency must respect his rights against unreasonable search and seizure."

Back in 2000, Hayden wanted to defend his embattled agency against accusations that it was spying on Americans as well as foreigners. Complaints from European Union politicians about U.S. surveillance had bled over into suggestions from U.S. civil liberties groups that the NSA was targeting the homeland. The 1998 movie *Enemy of the State*, starring Will Smith, showed the NSA murdering a congressman who threatened to block anti-terrorism surveillance legislation. Hayden watched the movie in a theater in Yongsan Army Garrison in South Korea, immediately after he learned that he was getting the job of NSA director. He shrank into his seat.

The NSA's problems didn't end in Hollywood. In the past, it had been easy for the NSA to spy because analog phone systems, using copper wire and satellites, were leaky. The NSA had relied on programs like ECHELON, built with its British partner, the Government Communications Headquarters (GCHQ), to tap into global satellite communications. But as communications went digital, they were far harder to eavesdrop on and much easier to encrypt. Fiber-optic cables, which use light rather than electric current to transmit information, don't leak. Most international communication had shifted to submarine cables that might lie nearly as far beneath the ocean's surface as the peak of Everest soars above it. European governments expected that the NSA would have a far harder time tapping into their conversations. The NSA's efforts to block the export of sophisticated encryption in the 1990s had apparently failed dismally.

American politicians agreed that the NSA had lost its technological edge. In its early years, the NSA had pushed out the boundaries of computer science, designing and testing highly advanced supercomputers while developing cutting-edge encryption and decryption systems. It held thousands of patents on everything from tamper-proof envelopes to new and improved car seats for children. But as the NSA grew, its technical acumen had disappeared into a chaos of complex procedures and internecine bureaucratic wars. After starting the job, Hayden received an urgent phone call from the NSA's head of technology. The NSA's internal network had collapsed thanks to an error installing new equipment, bringing "the *whole* system" down. The crash lasted for days, during which no one could access or analyze the NSA's data. Earlier, when Hayden tried to send out an all-hands update to the NSA's workforce, he was told, "We can't actually do that" (the agency had sixty-eight different email systems at its Fort Meade base).

In 2000, when Hayden testified about bin Laden, the NSA had an uncertain future. The House Permanent Select Committee on Intelligence had already warned that the NSA was failing to keep up with emerging commercial technologies and was "in serious trouble." Politicians had cut 30 percent from its budget. They were skeptical about spending taxpayers' money on a technologically moribund agency that had fractured into warring bureaucratic fiefdoms and was dedicated to a Cold War task that now seemed far less relevant and far harder to carry out.

A little over a year after Hayden's testimony, everything had changed, due to the attacks on September 11, 2001. In 2000, Hayden had used the example of Osama bin Laden walking across a bridge to demonstrate the depth of the NSA's commitment to U.S. law. Even America's most hated enemy would have strong legal rights, so long as he was standing on American soil.

When Hayden returned to this imaginary example in 2002 and 2006, he drew a quite different lesson. Bin Laden had struck a grievous and direct blow against the United States, without himself entering into U.S. territory. Instead of reassuring politicians that the NSA obeyed the law, Hayden wanted to push the law's envelope. What had once been a "stark hypothetical" was now "about life and death." The hijackers had turned globalization to their advantage, employing unencrypted email to communicate with each other and with the attack's planners in Hamburg. Al-Qaeda funded the hijackers through ordinary wire transfers, as well as credit cards and physical transfers of cash.

While America's laws "did" and "should" draw a sharp line between the United States and the rest of the world, Hayden argued that "[o]ur enemy in the global war on terrorism" didn't make such nice distinctions, and "the global telecommunications system [didn't] either." War had come to the U.S. homeland, and Hayden argued that U.S. law and practice needed to change. Communication between enemy combatants should not enjoy civil liberties protections. As Hayden saw it, terrorists' efforts to communicate and coordinate attacks coexisted with "innocent and even constitutionally protected messages on a unitary, integrated global communications network."

Hayden had no principled objection to a line dividing the world into U.S. persons (who had Fourth Amendment rights against search and seizure) and non-U.S. persons (who had none). He and his Bush administration colleagues simply wanted to redraw the line to provide the NSA with the greatest possible freedom to protect U.S. interests as it understood them. On one side lay a country of rights protected by laws and the U.S. Constitution. On the other, according to Hayden, lay the strife-tattered world described by the political theorist Thomas Hobbes, a perpetual "Mogadishu" in which there was no rule of law.

Even if bin Laden never physically crossed a bridge into the United States, his associates could wander digitally backward and forward across the line dividing the lawless world of war from the peaceable land of civil liberty protections, using email services located in the United States to evade the attention of the NSA's scryers. Hayden concluded that protecting U.S. security required existing rules to be aggressively reinterpreted, to ensure that the NSA's targets were on the unprotected side of the line, where they so obviously belonged.

Sometimes this was easy. As Charlie Savage documents in his book, *Power Wars*, the Europeans were wrong about the difficulties of tapping undersea fiber-optic cables. It wasn't hard at all if you could get into the cable's landing site on land. U.S. telecommunications companies had this access, at the switches where they connected to the broader telecommunications network. As far back as the 1980s, the U.S. government had secretly formulated a legal doctrine—"transit authority"— allowing it to tap into communications between foreigners that passed across U.S. territory so long as they didn't involve Americans.

Sometimes it would push up to the limit of the law and past it, on the basis of dubious and classified legal interpretations. Writers, including Savage, have explained the complex secret history of how

U.S. surveillance law changed after September 11, 2001. Bush admin-istration lawyers like John Yoo provided a modern equivalent of Dee's "iust Arthurien clayme," arguing in clandestine memos that George W. Bush could do more or less whatever he believed was necessary to protect national security. This sometimes enabled outright illegality, as with the infamous "Stellar Wind" program, which allowed the war-rantless surveillance of the communications of U.S. citizens.

By redrawing a line on a map, the NSA could change the world. Hayden liked to compare the new age to the "last great age of globaliza-tion," when European empire builders had discovered and conquered the world. Back then Europeans had gotten "land, wealth, tobacco, and syphilis," while the colonized world had gotten "exploitation of entire populations, global piracy, and the global slave trade." The new empire was less visible and less savage. But like the old ones, it relied on the notion of terra nullius, a vast territory inhabited by people who weren't protected by the law. Hayden himself was surprised at the ease of the "remarkable transition" from a world where "radio waves seren-dipitously hit our antennas to what became a digital form of breaking and entering." But he was very happy to bank it. The NSA's job was to protect Americans. If "you were not protected by the US Constitution and your communications contained information that would help keep America free and safe, . . . it was game on." When Republican sena-tor Arlen Specter asked how the United States should protect the pri-vacy of foreigners, Hayden responded with silent contempt; the Fourth Amendment, after all, was not an international treaty.

After September 11, secret rulings enabled agencies like the NSA to sweep up the information of foreigners, even if it was commingled with that of U.S. citizens, so long as they took minimal legal precau-tions. The line between the United States and the rest of the world had been moved. But all the legal doctrines that Bush's lawyers could come up with would have been useless if the territory hadn't changed, too. The NSA's power to surveil rested not just on the law but on the map.

The networks that the world used to talk and conduct business had their physical center of gravity on U.S. territory.

———————

I n summer 2002, Mark Klein, a skilled technician working for AT&T in San Francisco, got an email saying that an NSA employee would be visiting to vet one of Klein's coworkers. A few months after the visit, Klein heard that a "secret room" was being built on the sixth floor of AT&T's facility at 611 Folsom Street, behind a door marked 641A.

The secret room lay beneath AT&T's "Internet room" on the seventh floor. Like MAE-East, AT&T's San Francisco Internet room was one of the central exchange points of the Internet. Long-distance fiber-optic cables entered the building on the eighth floor and were fed down into the long rows of routers that the room contained. These routers connected one part of the Internet backbone to other major telecommunications carriers and exchange points, including MAE-East's Californian sister, MAE-West, and the PAIX exchange in Palo Alto, which Avery and Adelson had helped to build before they founded Equinix.

Klein was a left-winger and union member and had protested the Vietnam War in the 1970s. He had his suspicions about the secret room, but at first he wasn't quite sure what was going on. Perhaps it was being built to tap into domestic telephone calls (which were routed through a room that was right next door to 641A). But when Klein asked his coworker, Bob, who managed the Internet room, he was told that the secret room tapped into the Internet. Bob took early retirement soon afterward, leaving Klein to maintain the Internet room in his place. Klein could start piecing together what was happening behind the door of 641A, reading misplaced manuals, poking around to see which cables connected where, and making deductions on the basis of his own technical know-how.

Klein had accidentally discovered how the NSA had solved the problem of tapping into fiber-optic cables. The cables terminated in Folsom Street, allowing the NSA to use a prism to split the beams of light carrying information along fiber-optic cables into two separate and identical signals. One conveyed people's emails, Web requests, and data to their expected destinations, while the other was diverted to room 641A. There, it was parsed and analyzed by a Narus STA 6400 machine, built by an Israeli company with deep intelligence community connections.

There was a lot of data to interrogate. Years later, another former AT&T employee, Philip Long, told reporters that he had been instructed to reroute "every internet backbone circuit [he] had in northern California" through the Folsom Street building. As he described it, "We were getting orders to move backbones. . . . We thought it was government stuff and that they were being intrusive. We thought we were routing our circuits so that they could grab all the data."

The NSA's corporate partners controlled other central points in the Internet. One of the documents that Klein discovered described the system in room 641A as "Study Group 3." He guessed that this anodyne term implied that there were at least two other facilities elsewhere. Talking to a colleague based in Atlanta, Klein "froze" in his seat when he heard that "splitters had been installed in cities along the West Coast." They had been put in on the East Coast, too. Just as the STORMBREW map relied on key switches owned by Verizon/MCI, the NSA's FAIRVIEW program tapped into AT&T's network at eight locations, including Folsom Street, with AT&T's full cooperation and permission. What Klein was witnessing was not a massive new surveillance program aimed at U.S. citizens. It was the expansion of an existing program, which used NSA's existing relationships with telecommunications companies to dramatically expand its grasp on information flows outside the United States.

Secret NSA documents describe the "extreme willingness" of

AT&T to help with the "NSA's SIGINT (signals intelligence) and Cyber missions," and the "amazing knowledge" of AT&T's workforce. The NSA was prepared to pay for access: in 2011, its secret budget included $394 million for its "Corporate Partner Access Project," most of which was paid to telecommunications firms that gave it access to information. But big companies like AT&T and Verizon had other reasons to want to keep the U.S. government happy. The telecommunications industry is heavily regulated, and the U.S. government could use the authority of the Federal Communications Commission to force telecommunications companies to accept wide-ranging security agreements under which they would cooperate with surveillance demands.

For example, Global Crossing, a firm that specialized in telecommunications infrastructure, had a fiber-optic network connecting twenty-seven countries on four continents. It was required to have a "'Network Operations Center' on U.S. soil that could be visited by government officials with 30 minutes of warning." When Global Crossing went bankrupt, U.S. government lawyers objected to a Hong Kong–based company buying a majority stake in the remnants of the company. They demanded that the Singapore company that eventually took over create a special subsidiary to manage the undersea cable network. The subsidiary's management and board of directors would be dominated by U.S. citizens with security clearances, all of whom had to be preapproved by the FBI and U.S. Departments of Defense, Justice, and Homeland Security. Companies that didn't play ball with such demands risked being frozen out of the market by U.S. regulators.

These telecommunications companies controlled the central points in the Internet, the crossroads where traffic briefly converged before it sped off again in millions of different directions. This wasn't just U.S.-bound traffic. As a secret NSA presentation noted, "a target's phone call, email or chat will take the cheapest path, not the physically most direct path." And that often led through what the NSA described as the "World's Telecommunications Backbone," the system of cables and routers that conveyed information across U.S. soil. Fiber-optic cables move data at the speed of light. An email from Rio de Janeiro to Fortaleza in the north of Brazil might travel more quickly along fiber-optic cables via Miami than if it crawled along the copper wires of Brazil's national network. Internet routers tried to send information via the fastest route, and that gave the United States access. If the email passed through U.S. systems, and mentioned a name or phone number or email address that had been flagged by the NSA, it could be captured for later analysis. The centrality of the United States was in part the result of policy. According to a former NSA employee, the U.S. government "quietly encourage[d] the telecommunications industry to increase the amount of international traffic that is routed through American-based switches" to make it easier to spy on the world.

The U.S. government had a harder time getting U.S.-based e-commerce and platform companies, like Google, Facebook, Microsoft, and Yahoo!, to play ball. They weren't regulated as heavily as telecommunications companies were. However, the effort was worth it, especially as these companies started to build a different kind of Internet backbone. Once, businesses had maintained their own servers and support staff. But as the Internet became established, ordinary companies often turned to Gmail and its competitors to keep their email safe, while consumers mapped their lives and personal networks out on services like Facebook. Everything started to move to "the cloud," which sounded delightfully ethereal but was, in fact, built out of serried racks of blade servers in air-conditioned buildings in Ashburn and elsewhere. The U.S. government could use the PRISM program to demand useful and specific information from these companies on particular people or topics of interest without having to trawl through vast quantities of disorganized data.

Initially, some of these companies weren't cooperative. Yahoo! refused to provide data, believing that the government's demands were unconstitutional. However, two secret surveillance courts, the Foreign Intelligence Surveillance Court and the Foreign Intelligence Surveillance Court of Review, found against Yahoo! This allowed the U.S. government to threaten that it would fine Yahoo! $250,000 a day if it didn't comply. Yahoo! capitulated, and other platform companies decided that they had to go along, too.

The STORMBREW map depicted just one aspect of the U.S. stranglehold on the "global choke points" of the global communication system. The true map included not just Verizon but other big providers, and not just network switches but the platform companies that businesses and ordinary people around the world relied on. All this information, condensed into pulses of light, was captured and fed into vast mirrors, which could then be interrogated to discern the secrets of the world.

The choke points on the map represented an irresistible opportunity. As Hayden described it years later, "This is a home game for us. . . . [A]re we not going to take advantage [of the fact] that so much of it goes through Redmond, Washington?" After the Snowden leaks, Redmond's most famous company, Microsoft, was finally able to express its unhappiness with what had happened. As Microsoft's general counsel (and current president) Brad Smith explained in 2014, "We knew what we were being asked to do. We knew what we were being required to do. We didn't know what was being done without our knowledge. And we still do not know all of that even today."

We don't know much more these many years later. The investigative journalist Patrick Radden Keefe wrote that in the age of ECHELON "the world of global eavesdropping remains, in Joseph Conrad's formulation, a blank space on the map." After a brief lightning flash of revelation, it has again fallen into darkness.

Much of the information that Snowden released remains confidential; much has surely changed since he shared his revelations in

2013. The United States enacted legal reforms that partly limited U.S. government access to the data of U.S. citizens and issued a presidential policy directive intended to reassure allies that the United States would not unduly invade the privacy of their citizens. Google and Microsoft began to encrypt their own data flows, to make it harder for the United States and other governments to secretly listen in on the backbone. Google has used its influence through the Chrome browser to encourage other businesses to encrypt their communications, too. The map of fiber-optic cables has changed, so that the United States is less central than it used to be.

Yet the NSA has maintained and expanded its focus on signal intelligence. New laws, such as the 2018 CLOUD (Clarifying Lawful Overseas Use of Data) Act, allow U.S. law enforcement agencies to compel firms to provide their information, even when it sits on servers located in foreign countries. And fiber-optic cables running through the United States are still diverted into secret rooms, where their secrets are disclosed to automated scryers.

———————

Decades and trillions of dollars later, it's easy to see how September 11, 2001, reshaped U.S. military policy. But only those who really pay attention have noticed how dramatically it transformed the nonmilitary parts of the U.S. federal government. Most important, the Department of the Treasury went from a near bystander on national security to "Obama's favorite non-combatant command." Now, intelligence gathering and economic coercion are part of Treasury's core mission.

This began on September 12, 2001, when the U.S. government started to analyze what had just happened and why they hadn't stopped it. The September 11 hijackers hadn't just used email to coordinate between the hijackers in the United States and the central organizers in Hamburg. They had sent money across international borders, using simple wire transfers that passed through the dollar clearing system and were communicated via SWIFT. As one senior Treasury official described it, "one of the great ironies of what happened on September 11 is that our enemies used the . . . increasingly borderless financial world, to strike at the heart of it." The 9/11 Commission, which was convened to discover what had gone wrong, lamented that "[t]he U.S. intelligence community largely failed to comprehend Al Qaeda's methods of raising, moving, and storing money, because it devoted relatively few resources to collecting the strategic financial intelligence that policy makers were requesting or that would have informed the larger counterterrorism strategy." The Commission concluded that before September 11, "[t]errorist financing was not a priority."

Back then, Treasury wasn't interested, either. It was happy to go after banks that laundered drug money, but it was violently allergic to the U.S. foreign policy apparatus. Treasury saw the Department of State and the intelligence community as menaces to global markets and threats to its own autonomy. In the late 1990s, when the CIA had suggested monitoring and disrupting Osama bin Laden's system for moving money around, Treasury had pushed back hard, arguing that messing with money transfers "could crumble [*sic*] US credibility and shake international confidence in the U.S. and global financial system."

Interagency turf wars suddenly seemed less relevant after September 11, 2001. When the attacks happened, David Aufhauser, Treasury's general counsel, was at a conference abroad, where international officials were congratulating themselves on their progress on stopping money laundering. As the news came in, "[we realized] . . . that perhaps we had been looking at the world through the wrong end of a telescope . . . what we . . . perhaps had not properly focused on earlier in time, was trying to capture clean money that was spirited around the world intended to kill."

Treasury had financed many wars, but it had never fought one. After September 11, Aufhauser came to believe that Treasury itself had to engage in "shadow warfare." This would require Treasury to find ways to block financial flows rather than facilitating them. The United States would strip away the pretensions to immunity of foreign banks and financial intermediaries who had "sought refuge in notions of benign neglect and professional discretion rather than in vigilance." It would constrict the financial pipelines that terrorists used to move money. Terrorists would be driven out of the world of easy electronic financial transfers and forced to smuggle "gold bullion and precious gems," until eventually they would not be able to move money at all. Officials like Aufhauser contended that America had not started this shadow war, but it would surely prevail. Its victories would be measured "in the gnawing awareness on the part of those who have banked terror in the past that the symmetry of the borderless war that they have declared now means that there is no place to hide the capital that they are underwriting terror with."

Winning the war meant mapping the tangled world of global finance, which had grown vast and unruly under the avuncular encouragement of Treasury and the U.S. Federal Reserve. Before September 11, U.S. economic officials believed that it was their job to protect and extend the freebooter's realm of unregulated international transactions that Walter Wriston and his competitors had created. Without realizing it, they had helped build a world where the problem of terrorism was "international in scope," while the U.S. economy was "deliberately open and porous." As Aufhauser testified to the U.S. Senate, "The overwhelming bulk of the assets that we seek to freeze, the cash-flow that we hope to slow, and the records that we hope to audit are beyond the oceans that surround us." So what was the United States to do?

Part of the answer was hinted at in Aufhauser's testimony if you read it very carefully. In a back-and-forth with Senator Arlen Specter, he emphasized that "the predicate for everything we do is actionable intelligence." But Aufhauser declined to explain where this intelligence came from, suggesting that they could discuss this later "in another venue that doesn't jeopardize operations and sources and methods and the like."

David Aufhauser's secret likely was that Treasury and the CIA had gained access to a horde of accurate and precise information, which allowed it to map the terrorist financial networks that it wanted to destroy. They had gotten their hands on SWIFT's records.

SWIFT was the "nerve center of the global banking industry," and its data provided the closest thing there was to a map of who was sending money, where in the world, and when. As an unnamed U.S. official described it later, SWIFT data was a "Rosetta Stone" that allowed the United States to translate an unintelligible babble of transactions into a comprehensible body of knowledge that could be parsed and searched for traces of unfriendly activity.

But SWIFT—as a matter of deliberate policy—had resisted past efforts by the United States to get its data. In the 1990s, U.S. officials, led by Robert Mueller, and an international anti–money laundering consortium had tried. Their requests were politely rebuffed. SWIFT warned that if the United States attempted to subpoena its data, it would simply move it overseas. Even so, as Lenny Schrank, the then-CEO of SWIFT described it: "We . . . began to think the unthinkable: that maybe we have some data that the authorities would want, that SWIFT data would be revealed."

SWIFT tweaked its messaging standards so that banks would need to identify the party who was originating a transaction. But it refused to cooperate beyond that. In Schrank's words: "We don't do subpoena."

After September 11, SWIFT quickly discovered that it absolutely did "do subpoena" when it had no other choice. Even though SWIFT was based in Belgium, it was vulnerable to U.S. legal and political pressure. One of its key data centers, which mirrored all its global information, was located just outside the Virginia town of Culpeper, sandwiched between the Open Door Baptist Church and an Equinix high-security facility. SWIFT's Culpeper campus enjoyed "James Bond–level security" with roughly ten-foot-high fencing and chemical weapons checks, but it couldn't easily turn away demands from Treasury. If SWIFT threatened to move its data overseas, Treasury could threaten the members of its governing board, which was run by international banks, with regulatory action. Treasury had gotten out of the business of protecting financial institutions from the U.S. security state. Now, it was eager to press them into service.

The U.S. government had considered just getting the CIA to steal the information from SWIFT, but Treasury officials persuaded the rest of the government to simply ask SWIFT for access. They got it (although the NSA seems also to have hacked into SWIFT's system independently). SWIFT's official history suggests that SWIFT only cooperated grudgingly and reluctantly, after it had been subpoenaed against its will. Both Juan Zarate, a former Treasury official, and Eric Lichtblau, a civil liberties–focused journalist, tell a different story, saying that when Schrank was told that Treasury wanted his data, his immediate response was, "What took you so long?"

Even so, SWIFT sometimes got cold feet over its arrangement with Treasury over the next few years. Their relationship had to be kept secret. SWIFT's headquarters were located in Brussels, and undisclosed data sharing was illegal under Belgian privacy law. When SWIFT's managers got nervous, high-ranking U.S. officials, including not only the Treasury secretary but Vice President Dick Cheney, National Security Adviser Condoleezza Rice, FBI director Robert Mueller, and CIA director Porter Goss, were wheeled in to reassure them.

The results were worth it. Stuart Levey, who later became the first Undersecretary for Terrorism and Financial Intelligence at the Treasury, described SWIFT's data as a "unique and powerful window into the operations of terrorist networks." Zarate said it gave "the US government a method of uncovering never-before-seen financial links, information that could unlock important clues to the next plot or allow an entire support network to be exposed and disrupted."

The arrangement stayed secret for several years, in part because SWIFT's European banking supervisors didn't want to know any more than they had to. One central bank governor told U.S. deputy secretary of the Treasury Ken Dam to "stop it" when he tried to brief the governor on the program, while another told a Treasury official, "What you have just told me, I want to know nothing about," standing up and ending the meeting. Some European security officials likely knew what was going on, but they were nearly as impatient with European privacy law as their American counterparts.

When the program was finally revealed, in a *New York Times* story authored by Lichtblau and James Risen, some European officials quietly made it clear that they didn't want to stop the surveillance. Their intelligence agencies and homeland security ministries could benefit, too. After negotiations, Europe and the United States struck a deal. The United States would continue to be able to demand data from SWIFT with new safeguards and share it with European governments, which were unable to collect the data themselves given their own strict privacy laws. Ultimately, Europe became heavily dependent on the United States for financial data and analysis.

Eventually, popular culture started to catch up. The Amazon TV series based on Tom Clancy's Jack Ryan thrillers was updated from the original books, changing the protagonist from a historian-cum-naval intelligence analyst, into a data geek who uncovers a terrorist conspiracy by poring through SWIFT data on financial transfers.

SWIFT had been transformed from a politically independent

organization, which was supposed to help protect banks from government regulation, into an all-seeing servant of the U.S. state, whose knowledge mapped out the hidden world of international financial transactions. Schrank and his colleagues were right to fear subpoenas. After SWIFT had opened the door to political demands, it couldn't be shut.

It wasn't just the financial system that was remapped. It was the U.S. understanding of what it could and couldn't do in the new world. In hindsight, as Zarate put it, "the new era of financial warfare . . . came about because we were able to view the landscape differently than our predecessors," discerning how "globalization and the centrality of American financial power and influence allowed for a new approach." It still took some time for Treasury to map these new possibilities. At first, some officials stressed the benefits of cooperation with allies, who seemed eager to help the United States fight terrorism after the attacks. Gradually, Treasury discovered that it often didn't need their help and could readily act on its own.

On September 24, 2001, President George W. Bush proclaimed that the United States intended to turn "every instrument of law enforcement, every financial influence" to "starve the terrorists of funding." Treasury lawyers helped draft Bush's executive order, "EO 13224," which put banks on notice that anyone who did business with terrorists could no longer do business with the United States. The USA PATRIOT Act, which Bush signed into law soon thereafter, provided further powers against money laundering.

Putting Treasury on a war footing required a lot of work. John Taylor, Treasury's Undersecretary for International Affairs, acknowledged later that he "knew little about disrupting the flow of funds" because his "whole approach to international finance was to *encourage the flow of funds.*" But as Bush had made clear, the new U.S. government mission was to "cut off these evil people's money . . . trace their assets and freeze them." On September 17, Ken Dam chaired a meeting with high-level department officials including Taylor and Jimmy Gurulé, the Undersecretary of Enforcement, to rebuild Treasury so that it could better fight terrorism.

There was disagreement over how exactly to do this. Taylor favored building international alliances, working collaboratively with other governments against a common threat. He set up a task force on terrorist finance, dubbed the "War Room," whose main purpose was to persuade other countries to freeze terrorist assets.

On its face, Gurulé's enforcement division looked a lot weaker. Treasury was about to be stripped of its traditional policing functions, including Customs; the Bureau of Alcohol, Tobacco, Firearms and Explosives; and the Secret Service. But it still possessed the Office of Foreign Assets Control (OFAC), an obscure unit devoted to managing sanctions policy. In the world before September 11, OFAC (whose predecessor had been created in the 1940s to stop the Nazi government from pillaging assets under U.S. control) had just been one of the many parts of the federal government devoted to specialized tasks that no one cared about outside a small community. And now, it was willing to take on a new and more powerful role—even if it made internationalists like Taylor unhappy.

After September 11, OFAC was suddenly visible and important. It had the legal authority to freeze assets unilaterally and "designate" foreign actors whom the United States wanted to cut off from the U.S. economy. Bush's new executive order extended OFAC's powers to designate foreign banks and financial actors that were "associated" with terrorism. In an industry based on reputation, designation signaled that a bank was untouchable. There wasn't any legal requirement to prove that foreign banks actively supported terrorists—the "benign neglect" that Aufhauser complained about could provide sufficient cause. In theory, designated banks could go to U.S. courts to have the designation overturned. In practice, if they hadn't gone bankrupt already as their customers and other banks fled, they would probably find that their judges would defer to a U.S. government agency's decisions about how to protect national security and fight terrorism.

Thanks to OFAC, Treasury often didn't have to work through the laborious grind of international financial diplomacy with other countries when it wanted to freeze assets abroad. Instead, it could unilaterally designate foreign banks, businesses, and institutions, even when their host countries didn't agree or didn't believe there was sufficient evidence. And when it did want foreign governments to introduce new measures against money laundering, it could use OFAC to dial up the pressure. OFAC's tool kit was irresistible to an administration that didn't much care for multilateralism. Taylor's internationalists might win brief victories in the "battle for turf," but they slowly, inexorably, succumbed to the more ruthless logic of OFAC's enforcers.

There was a simple reason why OFAC was so terrifying. When OFAC designated a foreign bank, it didn't just block it from operating in the United States. It potentially blocked it from doing business with the U.S.-regulated banks like Citibank and J. P. Morgan, which operated the dollar clearing system. After it was designated, an international bank would no longer have the correspondent account that it needed to make transactions in U.S. dollars on behalf of its non-U.S. customers. Not only that: other foreign banks that needed access to the U.S. dollar wouldn't want to have anything to do with them, for fear that they, too, would lose access to dollars.

A similar fate awaited nonfinancial businesses or individuals who were targeted by OFAC. Once they had been designated, they, too, would lose access to the international banking system. U.S.-based banks could have nothing to do with them. They would be unable to borrow money easily on international markets or trade with U.S. businesses. They didn't face quite the same existential threat as banks. Perhaps they could find non-U.S. suppliers or borrow money elsewhere. But it would still be very hard for them to operate in a global economy that was built around the financial dominance of the United States.

The United States accidentally discovered how effective this "dollar unilateralism" could be when it went after Banco Delta Asia. Based in the China-administered territory of Macau, the bank secretly provided the North Korean government with access to global financial markets. Before Treasury got involved, David Asher and William Newcomb, two officials at the Department of State, had already begun "mapping the regime's financial and business relationships around the world." They identified Banco Delta Asia as a key "financial hub" for North Korea.

Treasury official Juan Zarate had commissioned his own "financial battle map," which also highlighted the centrality of Banco Delta Asia. When he was read into State's program, he suggested that they designate Delta Asia as a "primary money laundering concern," under Section 311 of the Patriot Act, Treasury's "neutron bomb." The United States did this on September 15, 2005, blocking Banco Delta Asia from using correspondent accounts at U.S. banks. This conveyed a clear message to other foreign banks. Anyone who did business with Banco Delta Asia risked the severe displeasure of the United States.

The results were startling and immediate. Depositors started a run on Banco Delta Asia. Macau authorities shut it down and froze $25 million in assets belonging to various North Korean entities. Word spread rapidly around the financial world that North Korean money was toxic. Victor Cha, who served as National Security Council Director for Asian Affairs at the time, recounts, "It was a smash in the mouth, a slap in the face. When they first heard about the action, they just thought it was another sanction, but four weeks later they realized what had hit them. It really got the North Koreans to sit up and notice that this was a tool they'd never seen before, and frankly, it scared the shit out of them." North Korean authorities contacted Cha directly for the first time, saying that they wanted to talk. They were desperate to get the $25 million unfrozen, not because it was a vast sum of money but because they wanted to demonstrate to banks that it was OK again to do business with North Korea. However, when the State Department reached a diplomatic agreement with North Korea, it turned out to be unexpectedly difficult to give the money back. Even after the United States had struck a deal, international banks wanted nothing to do with North Korean money. The risks were just too high.

Officials like Cha simply hadn't "expected that it would have the sort of impact that it did." They had obviously hoped it would have consequences. But they didn't anticipate the shock that their action would cause to North Korea, to Asian banks, or to the global banking system.

The U.S. action sent a signal to China, too. State and Treasury officials had deliberately chosen Banco Delta Asia, because it was significant but not big enough to seriously threaten the Chinese economy. China had been sent a message. If it didn't crack down on money laundering, Macau risked being disconnected from the global financial system. China's actions suggested that it had received the message loud and clear.

The Banco Delta Asia campaign provided a blueprint for later OFAC actions. Treasury's mapmakers got busy. As the financial journalist Anna Yukhananov explained, OFAC's "targeters comb through classified intelligence reports, financial records and corporate registrations. They build charts illustrating how striking one financial node will impact other nodes." Zarate, too, emphasized how the United States focused "on finding chokepoints" "or "nodal banks." Then, it struck.

Other parts of the U.S. government started to copy the playbook, sometimes cooperating with Treasury, sometimes competing against it. The U.S. Department of Justice began to prosecute foreign banks that had breached U.S. sanctions. The district attorney for the Southern District of New York had jurisdiction over Wall Street and an eye for publicly visible prosecutions. It, too, started to target foreign banks. Private attorneys began to seek big judgments in U.S. courts against foreign financial institutions that they alleged had helped terrorists.

Over time, the United States shifted from "going fishing" for anyone who violated sanctions, to "hunting whales," as scholars Bryan Early and Kevin Preble described it, imposing massive fines on big foreign banks to create shock and awe among everyone else. HSBC (originally the Hong Kong and Shanghai Banking Corporation) had to pay nearly $2 billion in penalties for money laundering in 2012. When BNP Paribas pleaded guilty to violating Iran, Cuba, and Sudan sanctions in 2014, it had to pay roughly $9 billion. These banks had no real choice but to pay: they had little hope of overturning the penalties in U.S. courts and risked having their U.S. banking licenses and their access to the dollar clearing system withdrawn. Even a credible threat to withdraw their access might lead to their rapid collapse.

Banks' compliance departments became newly powerful. No one wanted to touch designated banks, businesses, or individuals for fear that they, too, would attract the attention of the authorities. As Levey put it, even banks that weren't obliged to follow U.S. laws calculated that "[k]eeping a few customers that we have identified as terrorists or proliferators is not worth the risk of . . . a regulatory action that may impact on [sic] their ability to do business with the United States or the responsible international financial community." Even indirect association with terrorists or other U.S. adversaries could taint and ruin a bank.

The policy had some important side benefits, as University of

Virginia law professor Pierre-Hugues Verdier noticed. Most commentators focused on the eye-watering financial penalties that big banks paid. Few paid much attention to U.S. requirements that BNP Paribas, HSBC, and others introduce extensive internal monitoring systems to ensure that they complied in the future. BNP Paribas had to create an OFAC compliance office, based in the United States "under the direct oversight of U.S. regulators," which would ensure compliance worldwide. HSBC had to do much the same in New York, "under direct U.S. supervision." These major banks—which had previously helped their clients to avoid U.S. sanctions or skirt money-laundering rules—had to operate and pay for extensive internal monitoring systems, which could report valuable information to U.S. authorities. As the Chinese telecommunications giant Huawei later discovered, these requirements could have big and unexpected repercussions.

Such successes led the United States to become increasingly ambitious. Over a decade, it gradually inched ever closer to a once unimaginable proposition: What if the United States could use its power to cut a country out of the map?

Iran became the test case. For decades, the United States had imposed stringent sanctions on the Islamic Republic, which prevented U.S. businesses from having anything to do with the Iranian economy, except under highly limited circumstances. But these sanctions were more a nuisance than an existential threat. Iran was a major oil producer—and there were plenty of global customers who wanted what it had to sell. Law professors like Anu Bradford and Omri Ben-Shahar argued that the trade sanctions the United States deployed against Iran were "futile if other countries continue to supply Iran with comparable products at a comparable price." But as two political scientists, Peter

Feaver and Eric Lorber, pointed out, sanctions and U.S. dollar power could be combined to change the game.

The George W. Bush administration had wanted to invade Iraq so that it could move quickly to topple the Iranian government, too. That didn't work out. In January 2006, Stuart Levey had a new idea. He was traveling in Bahrain when he read a newspaper article about a big Swiss bank cutting off relations with Iran and wondered whether the U.S. Treasury could get other foreign banks to do the same thing. In February, Levey pitched Secretary of State Condoleezza Rice on the idea in a U.S. government plane. Rice liked it. Treasury already knew that "major businesses simply couldn't function without access to U.S. dollars." Now, it was going to find out what would happen when it cut off access to a major country.

Levey began by blocking Iranian banks' backdoor access to dollar clearing. Countries that bought Iranian oil needed to pay for it. And because oil is priced in dollars, when a German or French customer made a purchase, their banks had to clear the transaction through correspondent banks located in the United States. Previous U.S. sanctions against Iran specifically allowed Iranian companies to conduct so-called U-turn transactions, transferring their money from one non-U.S. bank to another via the dollar clearing system. This exception acknowledged the central role of the U.S. dollar in global financial transactions, and the U.S. worry that other countries might stop using dollar clearing if it became politicized. But the exception could be withdrawn if circumstances changed.

In 2006, Treasury blocked a big Iranian bank, Bank Saderat, from using the U-turn, claiming that it had transferred money to Hezbollah. It then sanctioned other Iranian banks over the next two years, until by the end of 2008, it had blocked Iranian banks entirely from the system. In 2012, Congress passed new laws that prevented U.S. banks from providing correspondent accounts to foreign banks that dealt with Iran's central bank or other designated banks. Even national central banks were prevented from having these accounts. Under the new law, Treasury was required to take measures against any foreign bank that enabled "significant" transactions that helped Iran's energy, shipping, and shipbuilding sectors. When other countries didn't push back, as the United States had once feared, it kept increasing the pressure. By 2015, Adam Szubin, Obama's nominee for undersecretary for Terrorism and Financial Crimes, could affirm to Congress that "no Iranian banks can access the U.S. financial system, . . . not even to execute a dollarized transaction where a split-second's worth of business is done in a New York clearing bank."

These legal measures went hand in hand with a new kind of international diplomacy. Levey and other Treasury officials traveled to countries across the world—but they weren't necessarily interested in talking to political officials. Instead, they went directly to the banks. Their message was indirect but emphatic. Any bank that had anything to do with Iran—even if the relationship was nominally legal under U.S. law—risked getting stamped all over by American regulators. In an internal memo, HSBC's head of compliance, David Bagley, described for his CEO how Levey had questioned HSBC in a June 2007 meeting. Levey claimed that a particular HSBC client was providing a conduit for Iran. In Bagley's description, "Levey essentially threatened that if HSBC did not withdraw from relationships with [redacted] we may well make ourselves a target for action in the US." A U.S.-based law firm noted that the rules governing financial relationships with Iran "at times seem almost purposefully confusing." The vaguer the rules were, the more likely foreign banks were to avoid any contact with Iran whatsoever for fear that fuzzy rules would later be interpreted to their disadvantage.

When Obama replaced Bush at the beginning of 2009, he tried to build a friendlier relationship with Iran. However, Iran's brutal repression of mass protests against the regime in 2009 and its continued progress toward building nuclear weapons soured these efforts. A new generation of Treasury officials, including Szubin, began to build on the work of their Republican predecessors, using sanctions and dollar power to force the Iranian regime to give up its nuclear weapons program.

They discovered that SWIFT, too, could be weaponized against Iran. Beginning in 2008, a group of prominent U.S. policy makers led by Ambassadors Richard Holbrooke and Dennis Ross had started a private campaign, known as United Against Nuclear Iran (UANI), to ratchet up pressure on the Iranian regime. The group targeted SWIFT as complicit in providing Iran with access to global markets. As described in SWIFT's 2010 annual report, some nineteen Iranian banks as well as twenty-five other Iranian institutions had access to the messaging system.

In January 2012, UANI wrote to SWIFT arguing that "the global SWIFT system is used by Iran to finance its nuclear weapons program, to finance terrorist activities and to provide the financial support necessary to brutally repress its own people." Soon after, Congress unanimously passed an act aimed at forcing SWIFT to kick out Iranian banks, against the wishes of the administration (which was nervous about the international repercussions). The European Union responded by passing its own regulations prohibiting SWIFT from working with targeted institutions, in response to U.S. pressure and Europe's own worries about Iran's nuclear program. SWIFT complied, effectively cutting Iranian banks out of the global payments system, in what its CEO described as "an extraordinary and unprecedented step."

U.S. sanctions and the SWIFT cutoff had brutal economic consequences for the Iranian regime. It couldn't get paid for oil. Its exports dipped from a little under 3 million barrels a day to as few as 750,000 as it was forced to barter oil directly for "wheat and tea from India, rice from Uruguay, and zippers and bricks from China." Unwinding sanctions and SWIFT measures became a key bargaining point in the negotiations over Iran's nuclear program. When the United States and other powers entered into formal negotiations, Iranian foreign minister Javad Zarif made it clear that "[t]he deal will be made or broken," depending "on whether the United States wants to lift the sanctions or keep them."

If the United States had not discovered its new superpower—weaponizing the dollar clearing system against its adversaries—it is unlikely that Iran would ever have agreed to make wide-reaching concessions on its program to develop nuclear weapons. In the Joint Comprehensive Plan of Action, the United States and other powers agreed to stop applying sanctions against Iran's oil industry and banks, removing key designations, and allowing Iran to have access to SWIFT again. However, the United States didn't agree to remove its domestic sanctions.

It was nearly impossible to roll back the international measures. A policy based on creating fear, awe, and terror can't be turned on and off like a spigot. When Obama administration officials urged European banks to lend to Iran and businesses to invest there, they found that no one wanted to listen. Banks and businesses worried that U.S. authorities would change their mind again, using the vagueness of OFAC rulings and regulations to determine that they were sanction breakers, and would punish them harshly.

The United States had made itself too powerful to be trusted—it couldn't credibly promise that it wouldn't break its word to business under a different administration or a different interpretation of the rules. Stuart Levey—who had left politics to become the chief legal officer at HSBC, complained in the *Wall Street Journal* that the Obama administration was "pushing non-U.S. banks to do what it [*sic*] is still illegal for American banks." He furthermore hinted heavily that current or future U.S. regulators might decide to punish banks that entered the Iranian market. Christopher Hill, who served as the head of the U.S.

delegation to the Six Party Talks on North Korea's nuclear program, described the problem in blunt terms: Treasury had unleashed a "kind of sanctions doomsday machine that could not be turned back off."

And there were other problems. Rachel Loeffler, a George W. Bush administration official, had warned after leaving office that the new financial weapons could "lose their effectiveness" if they were overused, discrediting the United States and alienating the banks that were supposed to implement them.

Obama's Treasury secretary, Jack Lew, went farther. In a speech he gave in March 2016, shortly before he left office, he reflected on the awesome financial power of the United States and how it might end up undermining itself. Lew recognized that financial sanctions had become a "powerful force in service of clear and coordinated foreign policy objectives," arguing that "the power of our sanctions is inextricably linked to our leadership role in the world." U.S. sanctions would be ineffective if the United States were not the "world's largest economy" and if the U.S. financial system did not play "the predominant role . . . in global commerce." Yet they carried an implicit temptation and an implicit cost. Exactly because they seemed so effective, policy makers might be tempted to turn to them as a first step when facing a new crisis.

Lew suggested that this might not just make them less effective over time. It could potentially undermine U.S. dominance of the world economy. Overreach might "ultimately drive business activity away from the U.S. financial system." For sure, it would be hard to reshape the global financial system so that the United States was no longer at its center. Furthermore, other potential financial hubs have faltered, as the City of London deals with the damage of Brexit and Hong Kong finds its autonomy undermined by China. But Lew's later warning that the "plumbing is being . . . tested" to "chip away" at U.S. "centrality" aptly describes efforts by countries like Russia and Turkey to create financial ties that are concealed from the unblinking eye atop the pyramid as well as China's quiet and relentless efforts to create its own alternative global system of finance.

———————————

As in other areas, the United States had succeeded in mapping the world and hence in remaking it. But the more visible that its power became, and the more willing it was to use it, the more reason other governments and businesses had to create their own alternative maps. Maybe they could remake the networks so that they were no longer so centralized and so vulnerable to U.S. power. Maybe they could conceal themselves in the complexities of the plumbing or create their own annexes that connected haphazardly to the larger whole. Or maybe they could try to emulate U.S. power by building their own centralized networks as an alternative source of power and authority.

3

WAR WITHOUT GUNSMOKE

When Meng Wanzhou finally returned to her company's head-quarters in Shenzhen, she was greeted by a throng of deliriously happy employees. They pumped their fists, took video on their cell phones, waved, smiled, and gave thumbs-ups. It wasn't just employees who were thrilled. "Meng Wanzhou is back at work" was the number one trending topic on Weibo, a leading Chinese social media platform.

Meng Wanzhou is the chief financial officer of Huawei, China's telecommunications giant, and the daughter of Ren Zhengfei, the company's founder. She had "suffered for three years overseas" under house arrest in her Vancouver mansion, fighting extradition to the United States over charges of bank fraud. Her lawyers finally struck a deal with U.S. authorities that allowed her to return to China. When she landed, just days before China's national day of celebration, cheering crowds serenaded her at the airport with "Ode to the Motherland." Meng had draped herself in patriotism, wearing a red dress and proclaiming, "If faith has a color, it must be China red."

Huawei wasn't just an ordinary Chinese company. In its early days, it had flown the red flag with five stars over its lonely stand at a telecommunications trade fair. As it grew bigger, it was China that draped itself in Huawei's colors. A Chinese company was competing against the world's best and beating them.

But the fanfare at the airport concealed an unfortunate truth. Meng wasn't returning swathed in victory. Back when she had left, Huawei was the world's biggest manufacturer of telecommunications equipment and was poised to become the world's biggest smartphone brand, too. Most important, it was building the infrastructure for the next generation of the Internet. Over the years that Meng was trapped in Canada, the U.S. government engaged in an unprecedented campaign to systematically dismantle the company's ambitions. It blocked Huawei from buying modern semiconductors and crippled its cell phone business. U.S. officials stopped its allies from installing Huawei telecommunications equipment by threatening their access to vital intelligence.

The truth was that Huawei was now in trouble, desperately trying to reinvent itself as a producer of smart vehicles and server farms, or anything technological that didn't require the latest generation of semiconductors and wasn't directly exposed to U.S. wrath. Once, long before, Huawei had been a tiny, opportunistic trading company looking to buy and sell whatever would make a profit. Now, the vast conglomerate, with nearly two hundred thousand employees across the world, was forced once again to scrabble indiscriminately for new markets.

Meng Wanzhou's arrest signaled an enormous change in the U.S. relationship with the People's Republic of China. After two decades of ever deepening economic interconnections, the U.S. government had grown suspicious of Chinese companies in general, and Huawei in particular. Finally, it was acting on those suspicions. The U.S. government employed its stranglehold on global finance, global information, and global technology to throttle Huawei. It feared that if it didn't, Huawei would help China build its own empire of influence and control.

Finance provided the legal justification for the U.S. countermeasures. Meng Wanzhou got into trouble because Huawei had involved a global bank in its lawbreaking. Information provided the opportunity. Huawei's bank, HSBC, was forced to give the United States data that provided evidence of Meng's involvement in illicit activities. And U.S. control of semiconductor supply chains was weaponized to drive Huawei out of the markets where it made most of its profits.

Ren depicted his daughter as an accidental casualty in a much larger conflict, claiming that "under the grand backdrop of the Sino-U.S. trade war, [Meng Wanzhou] is like a small ant, . . . caught [in] the collision of two giant powers." That wasn't how many U.S. policy makers saw it. The United States feared that Huawei might undermine its own influence over the Internet, creating a system of submarine cables, base stations, and routing switches controlled by China. America's objective was not simply to limit Huawei's access to military-grade technology or redirect trade flows. It was to prevent Huawei from undermining U.S. dominance.

Even if Huawei's global reach wasn't the result of a Chinese plot (many U.S. politicians believed that it was), America knew from its own experience how quickly commercial success could be transformed into imperial power. China and Huawei saw themselves as underdogs, fighting to overcome well-entrenched opponents. China's government spoke of its defensive "war without gunsmoke" against American efforts to transform China's politics and society. Its politicians and defense intellectuals used pungent terms like "assassin's mace" to describe the stealth tactics they could use to redress the balance. Huawei, too, saw its quest for market dominance as an unequal struggle against dominant powers. The company modeled its rise in China on Mao's dictums of guerrilla warfare—first take control of the countryside and then gradually surround and subdue the cities.

The fight over Huawei wasn't an economic spat over mobile phones or cell towers. It was a new phase in a ruthless struggle between the imperium that had grasped the heart of the global economy and a growing power that considered itself as a victim of empire. America had built its underground empire half by accident. Now that it had it, it would do everything necessary to preserve it. China—whether to defend itself from American imperial aggression, build its own empire, or some combination—would in turn do what it could to preserve itself and build up a position of strength from which it could challenge U.S. dominance.

———————

In happier times, Huawei had liked to compare itself to an army. It had taken the heights of the notoriously cutthroat Chinese telecommunications market through strategy and ruthlessness. As Ren warned in an internal speech, the field of telecommunications was the "toughest and riskiest" economic sector. But "the market . . . respects only the brave. If Huawei intends to survive, it has to carve out a bloody path for itself."

Such sanguinary metaphors didn't necessarily mean all that much. Terms that were unfamiliar to English speakers weren't necessarily any more sinister than football commentators comparing a team's defeat to a massacre or a bloodbath. Still, Ren seemed more bloody-minded than most. He established Huawei University in 1998 to inculcate a "military attitude to business" in the company's leaders, approaching management training like "the indoctrination of troops." The university's core theme was that the "market is a battlefield." Its courses covered topics including "The Particularity of the Law of War and the Nature of War," "Guidelines and Strategies for War," and "Re-Reading *The Art of War*," as well as an eclectic mix of Buddhist philosophy and Western art.

Ren borrowed his ideas about business strategy from Mao Zedong, who had used unorthodox tactics to win control of China. Mao's own unlikely-seeming path to power built on the lessons of early twentieth-century irregular military leaders like Ireland's Michael Collins. Start in the countryside, the hinterlands, where no one is paying attention. Then build up your strength, surround the cities, and overwhelm them.

Huawei, too, rose from the countryside. Ren liked to talk about how he himself was raised in an impoverished and obscure part of China. He was studying at the Chongqing Institute of Civil Engineering and Architecture during China's Cultural Revolution, when Mao's student cadres sought to return China to its revolutionary heritage. They sent intellectuals "back to the land" to labor beside peasants under brutal conditions. But Ren wasn't an intellectual. He kept his head down and joined the Engineering Corps of the People's Liberation Army, where he stayed for a decade.

A few years after Ren got out of the army, he set up business in what was the small coastal city of Shenzhen. Mao was dead. His successor, Deng Xiaoping, wanted to grow a modern Chinese economy in a hurry, and Shenzhen was the forcing ground. In 1978, just before Deng defeated his rival to become the recognized leader, China experimented with new policies in the special region that later became the Shenzhen Special Economic Zone. Deng started cautiously as he consolidated power, using the more market-friendly Yugoslavian approach to Communism as an ideologically palatable alternative to Mao's crude and brutal version of Marxism. Gradually, the Shenzhen zone pioneered the market economy in a Communist state.

At first, Ren was just one among the myriad of entrepreneurs who knew that they wanted to make money in the new China but weren't quite sure how. Ren likely had better political connections than most—he had been a delegate to the 12th National Congress of the

Chinese Communist Party. But it took him some time to identify a clear business opportunity. Huawei started as a simple trading company, buying and selling children's balloons and fire alarms. When Ren's company stumbled into the business of telephone switches, he saw his chance. If China was going to escape the trap of rural poverty, it would need a modern phone system. That meant phone networks, which in turn required switches that Huawei could import and sell, eventually learning to build them itself. Over the next several years Huawei became a telecommunications manufacturer, battling against others to win customers and build networks.

Huawei described its early strategy using Mao's words: "encircling the cities" by occupying the countryside. It avoided direct fights with its bigger opponents. Instead of selling to the big cities, Ren settled on a "sequence of very targeted war plans," focusing on rural areas that were disdained by his larger peers. Huawei built deep relationships with its rural customers, connecting them into broader networks, and gradually gathered the resources and power to challenge Huawei's adversaries on their home territory.

As a book celebrating Ren explained, Huawei was like a pack of wolves. To take down a great lion, the wolves "eat into its territory from the very periphery to the core [using] various unconventional tools and . . . depending on their unmatched adaptability and market understanding to render the technical advantages of the lion irrelevant." One by one, the lions that dominated Chinese telecommunications—giant companies like Shanghai Bell, Great Dragon, and the American manufacturer Lucent—succumbed, were taken over, or were driven out of the Chinese market.

Other Chinese businesses, too, had to claw for territory in the world that America had made. These new firms desperately needed foreign investment, not just because of the money but because of the skills and knowledge that came with it. Their government helped, paradoxically, by inviting foreign businesses to come in. Chinese suppliers might start out by producing parts for Western firms, or copying their advanced technology, but they hoped to emulate their Western competitors and, perhaps, outcompete them. Eventually, Chinese businesses could turn to adaptive strategies that worked from the periphery to undermine their American competitors' technological advantages. That might enhance China's power as an accidental by-product. Most business leaders, for all their professed patriotism, cared more about making money.

America provided a model as well as a target. Ren, like many of the technology entrepreneurs who came after him, was fascinated by the United States. When asked who he was most influenced by, Ren named Mao and IBM's CEO, Lou Gerstner. If Chinese businesses were to take their rightful place in the world, they would need both to understand how U.S. tech firms had succeeded and to adapt the lessons to Chinese circumstances.

Huawei spent a lot of money on management advice from IBM and built up a strong internal culture, combining Big Blue's emphasis on corporate loyalty with Maoist self-criticism sessions. The "Song of Huawei," which was composed in 1995 as a kind of corporate anthem, spoke of reinvigorating the Chinese nation while exhorting employees to "learn the advanced technology from the US."

As Huawei grew, Ren attracted the favor of senior Chinese officials. In 1994, he met the Chinese Communist Party's general secretary, Jiang Zemin. As he described the meeting, in words that later took on an unfortunate resonance, "I said that switching equipment technology was related to national security, and that a nation that did not have its own switching equipment was like one that lacked its own military. Secretary Jiang replied: Well said."

His company may have enjoyed other forms of assistance. A former Huawei senior executive told the *Financial Times*, "Business was flattish in the first decade, and then things took off like crazy. People suspect that something must have happened to help, but it's a mystery even inside the company."

When the global telecommunications business crashed at the start of the millennium, Huawei cut jobs and diversified into cell phones. Characteristically, it also used the crisis to launch a general assault on overseas markets. As it had in China, Huawei tried first to capture the periphery before taking on the center. It targeted markets in Southeast Asia, South America, and southern Africa that were neglected by the big international telecommunications companies. Huawei rapidly acquired a reputation for supplying solid technology at rock-bottom prices.

The company owed its success to Ren's drive and ruthlessness, but it also benefited from the Chinese model of industrial development. As Julian Gewirtz explained, before he became a China director on Biden's National Security Council, Deng and others "placed limits on China's openness to exchange with the United States and on excessive dependence on the capitalist superpower." Chinese leaders feared that they might be overthrown if China embraced globalization too vigorously. They imposed increasingly onerous conditions on foreign companies' access to Chinese markets, demanding that they share their technologies with local business partners while providing a helping hand to exporters like Huawei.

This was part of a government strategy to take advantage of the economic opportunities of globalization while managing its political risks. China's military hackers often worked for businesses on the side, providing them with strategic information on their foreign competitors' core technologies. American politicians were outraged that China was turning itself into a manufacturing power on the back of foreign know-how, even though America itself, a century before, had crafted permissive intellectual property laws that allowed its own businesses to steal valuable technologies from the United Kingdom and Germany.

U.S. policy makers often depicted the Chinese economy as a threatening totalitarian leviathan, acting with a single purpose. But China, too, was riven by bureaucratic infighting, by subterranean clashes between government and business, and by ferocious competition among the firms themselves. Still, they were not entirely wrong, either. Like their American equivalents, Chinese business ambitions and political power sometimes reinforced each other.

America mostly worked outward and down, projecting power from the commanding heights of the world economy. Gradually and painfully, China clawed its way up and in, advancing from the outskirts of the global economy toward its center. In some economically strategic sectors—solar panel and battery manufacturing—Chinese companies raced ahead of foreign competitors. They lagged in others, despite big government investments. Ambitious government plans to build a domestic semiconductor industry capable of making cutting-edge chips foundered on the lack of domestic engineering knowledge and capacity. The disconnect between China's grand ambitions and its limited capabilities allowed dubious entrepreneurs to fleece local governments of billions of yuan on the promise to build cutting-edge semiconductor fabs.

Huawei's success was built on borrowed ideas, but it was real. It spent a lot of money on research and development, even if much of that money was spent on reverse engineering other companies' products. One observer who had worked with the company commented that they had "never seen anything that they make that is original technologically." Huawei was eventually sued by the network equipment manufacturer Cisco for stealing intellectual property. In 2007, it was blocked from buying 3Com by the U.S. government. Despite these attacks, Huawei kept on getting bigger.

———————

In 2012, John Chambers, Cisco's CEO, launched an offensive against Huawei, claiming that the company didn't always "play by the rules" when it came to intellectual property. His claims helped provoke American officials to start taking action. But U.S politicians weren't just worried that Huawei was stealing American know-how. They believed that Huawei was intimately connected to the Chinese government and endangered American security.

These fears grew as Huawei tried to enter the U.S. market. Some small rural telecommunications providers had already bought Huawei equipment, but when Huawei bid to upgrade Sprint Nextel's phone network, Arizona's Republican senator Jon Kyl opposed it vociferously. In a letter cosigned with other senators, he warned that Huawei and ZTE were financed by the Chinese government through export loans and subsidies, and might embed switches, routers, or software in American networks that would potentially allow "communications [to] be disrupted, intercepted, tampered with, or purposely misrouted" by the Chinese military.

Huawei tried to head off this criticism, inviting C. A. "Dutch" Ruppersberger, the ranking minority member of the House Select Committee on Intelligence, to meet Ren in Hong Kong. This backfired disastrously. Ruppersberger and Mike Rogers, the committee chairman, coauthored a report that described Huawei and ZTE as threats to U.S. national security. They argued that China could use Huawei and ZTE equipment for "malicious purposes" and claimed that technical protections could not fully mitigate the threat. The two members of Congress had independently come to the same conclusion as Jiang two decades before. Telecommunications switches were like armies—if you didn't control them, you didn't control your national security.

One former telecommunications executive told us that his company invited Huawei to bid for contracts but never intended to do business with them. The lowball bids helped this company put pressure on Ericsson and Nokia, but its executives knew that actually doing business with Huawei would invite far more trouble than it was worth. Huawei would never be allowed to break into America.

Increasingly, American officials worried about what Huawei was doing elsewhere, too. The company had expanded from its base in the developing world to serve richer countries, including many of America's allies. The United States couldn't offer an alternative to Huawei's equipment. All the big American telecommunications manufacturers were dead or had been sold off, victims of global competition. There were only three major telecommunications equipment providers in the world—Ericsson, Nokia, and Huawei—each with approximately between 15 and 30 percent of the global market.

American officials feared that Huawei was playing a double game. According to Huawei executives, Ren told his people that "[i]n China, [they should] state that Huawei strongly supports the Communist party of China. Outside China, stress that Huawei always follows key international trends." Confidential Huawei marketing material leaked to the *Washington Post* detailed sophisticated surveillance products used to trawl the Internet and mobile devices for Chinese national security and defense clients, with voiceprint identification and location tracking systems. Michael Hayden's line simply didn't exist for the Chinese government. Maintaining security at home blurred into pursuing regime adversaries abroad.

The United States feared that Huawei might help China do to the United States what the United States had previously done to China and the world. The march from the periphery was working. European firms like Ericsson and Nokia struggled to win contracts outside the United States because Huawei's base stations and network products were just too cheap. Huawei seemed set to rebuild the world's telecommunications system as everyone moved toward implementing 5G, a new communications standard for broadband cellular networks.

American officials saw that as a dire threat to national security. Pre-5G cell-phone base stations are add-ons that connect to the underlying communications networks without being part of them. When 5G is fully implemented, its base stations will be an integrated part of the global communications infrastructure. 5G's advocates predict that everything will be able to talk to everything else. That means that refrigerators, cars, security cameras, pacemakers, and robots might all be engaged in a many-stranded and invisible web of conversation running through Huawei-built base stations. The company would be an essential part of the world's core communication system, sending and receiving constant updates to and from every imaginable device. Information, money, logistics: everything would flow through Chinese-built equipment.

U.S. officials talked about immediate spying risks. The real fear was that by building the basic infrastructure for the world's 5G networks, Huawei could help China to counteract and gradually subsume the underground empire that the United States had constructed and turn it toward its own purposes. Huawei's own marketing materials highlighted its ability to track "political persons of interest." The company was actively trying to reconfigure the Internet itself, proposing new global standards that would make it easier for authoritarian countries to see what their citizens were doing. It was not a big leap to imagine that Huawei could help bring about an Internet shaped by Chinese rather than U.S. values. If the stakes were high, Huawei might be able to track and monitor adversaries or take down the entire communications systems of countries that did things China didn't want them to do.

Kevin Wolf, who was the official in charge of Obama-era controls on the export of technology, told us that "the Chinese always accused me of trying to encircle China, and [said] we were discriminating against them economically, and [trying] to hold them down." But he saw his job as having nothing to do with economic considerations and everything to do with national security. In his eyes, Huawei wasn't just an ordinary Chinese company selling phones and switches. Huawei's "size and ubiquity and relationship with the Chinese government" meant that the problems had to do with the company's "existence and opportunity" rather than its current behavior.

That was hard to communicate to America's allies, which were sometimes more interested in cheap infrastructure than theoretical-seeming security threats. The Trump administration started urging U.S. allies not to use Huawei equipment. Some, like Australia, were already suspicious of Huawei and were easy to convince. Others, like the United Kingdom, were more skeptical.

In a tense meeting of Britain's National Security Council, Britain's Chancellor of the Exchequer, Philip Hammond, persuaded his colleagues to allow Huawei to continue providing 5G technology to Britain, potentially saving billions of pounds. His colleague, Gavin Williamson, the secretary for defense, disagreed strongly but was fired after allegedly leaking key details of the meeting to the press. U.S. officials were horrified at the decision, suggesting that the U.K. was handing Huawei a "loaded gun" and allowing "China to control the Internet of the future."

American officials didn't pay much heed to British claims that the threat of Chinese surveillance was manageable. Their own intelligence services had penetrated Huawei technologies, which were riddled with vulnerabilities. What really worried them was the prospect that Huawei would allow China to build its own networked imperium, shoving the United States to one side. Keeping Huawei out of the United States didn't matter much if China could build 5G networks everywhere else in the world. The American metropolis would find itself gradually and inexorably encircled, until it finally succumbed. U.S. officials started asking how America could strike at Huawei from the heights while it still held them.

W hen Steve Stecklow began reporting on China-Iran business
relations, he didn't expect to precipitate an international crisis.
He had been part of a team reporting on surveillance technology at the
Wall Street Journal. One of their stories described how Huawei had sold
a system to Iran's largest mobile phone operator that would allow police
to track people's movements using their cell phones. Stecklow clearly
had excellent sources. After he moved to Reuters, he wrote a detailed
report on how Huawei's Chinese competitor ZTE had installed an
Internet surveillance system for Iran's national telecommunications
provider. A leaked product list suggested that some of the basic equipment that ZTE was providing had been manufactured in the United
States.

Nine months later, Stecklow wrote another article, saying that Skycom, a company that was purportedly independent of Huawei, had sold
U.S.-manufactured equipment to Iran. Strangely enough, many Skycom
employees described themselves as working for "Huawei-skycom [*sic*]"
on LinkedIn. Everyone wore Huawei company badges. A few weeks
afterward, Stecklow published a third piece, describing what seemed to
be a shell game of corporations behind corporations, in which Meng
Wanzhou had been the secretary for a holding company that owned all
of Skycom's shares.

Stecklow's articles spelled trouble for Meng. Yet the United States
was only able to act on this story because it had already transformed its
financial dominance into a tool of coercion.

Stecklow's article on ZTE spurred the U.S. Department of Justice and Department of Commerce to investigate. There was plenty for
them to find. ZTE didn't see U.S. export rules as a hard legal limit but
as an annoying hindrance. Iran offered tempting commercial opportunities: it was a mid-income country that needed urgently to build

new phone networks, and was off-limits to most Western firms. The problem was that ZTE's key products relied on American components or often worked best when they were deployed together with American equipment. If ZTE broke U.S. rules on technology exports, it risked having to pay massive fines or being banned from future access to U.S. technologies.

It's highly unusual for a major multinational company to cosplay a James Bond villain, explaining its perfidious plots in detail. Yet that is exactly what ZTE did. In an internal document flagged as "Top Secret" and "Highly Confidential," ZTE noted that it was conducting a "large amount of business" in countries that the United States had identified as "State Sponsors of Terrorism." That posed "enormous legal risk" because it was "almost impossible" for ZTE to get U.S. permission to export to these countries.

ZTE had found the solution. The "Top Secret" document provided a how-to guide on getting around cumbersome U.S. rules. First, you created a web of shell companies in Beijing, Hong Kong, and Dubai, all run by Chinese citizens. Then you got one company to purchase the U.S. technology and sell it to another, delivering it to a third, which in turn would have a contract with a local subsidiary in the country in question. This elaborate commercial roundabout would make it seem as though ZTE weren't doing forbidden business with Iran or any other country that the United States had blocked. As ZTE's how-to guide helpfully explained, the web of companies would make it "harder for the U.S. government to trace . . . or investigate the real flow of the controlled commodities."

This grand master plan went horribly wrong. In 2014, ZTE's chief financial officer was stopped in Boston's Logan Airport. His assistant's laptop reportedly contained a "treasure trove" of documents on ZTE's illicit business in Iran, including the "Top Secret" document. When the U.S. Department of Commerce charged ZTE with no less than 380 violations of export regulations, it cited the document as evidence of the company leadership's intentions. ZTE had to pay a $430 million fine (with an additional $300 million suspended penalty), to submit itself to an independent corporate compliance monitor, and to promise to discipline the employees who had been involved. Later, when it turned out that ZTE hadn't followed through on its promises, it narrowly avoided U.S. penalties that would have destroyed it.

But ZTE wasn't the main target. As Kevin Wolf told us, "[P]art of the motive of going after ZTE was to get information we couldn't get about Huawei." The assistant's laptop also held a second secret ZTE document, which was restricted to senior leaders and the director of ZTE's legal department. This briefly described another company, with the codename "F7," which it claimed provided the template for how to secretly sell U.S. technology to Iran. It was obvious to anyone who knew the telecommunications marketplace that F7 was Huawei.

The F7 document was hearsay—it didn't provide incontrovertible evidence that Huawei had broken U.S. law. Nor did Stecklow's reporting. As he acknowledged, "I've never proved that Huawei has violated U.S. sanctions." Just a few years later, Stecklow had "pretty much forgotten all about" the story. Nonetheless, his reporting and the F7 document were the initial links in the chain of events that led to Meng's arrest and Huawei's fall from the heights.

———

Meng had begun her career at Huawei in the early 1990s as one of three secretaries in Ren's fledgling telecommunications company. As Huawei grew, so did her role. Ren insisted that he did not plan to have a family member succeed him and instituted a complicated rotating leadership structure. Still, many saw Meng as the heir in waiting, and she rose to become the company's chief financial officer. This meant that along with other senior company executives, she had to think about how and whether Huawei complied with the complex rules that the United States imposed on foreign firms that used its technology.

Ruppersberger and Rogers' report had asked pointed questions about Huawei's compliance with U.S. sanctions on Iran. Both Meng and Ren appeared to have had mixed feelings about compliance. According to the *South China Morning Post*, they told employees at an internal question-and-answers session that there were "scenarios where the company can weigh the costs and accept the risks of not adhering to the rules."

On December 1, 2018, Meng stopped in Vancouver, British Columbia, en route from Hong Kong to a business meeting in Mexico City. Meng (who was known to her Canadian friends as Sabrina or Cathy) and her husband had made Vancouver their second home. Her children had gone to school there, while her husband, who goes by Carlos, had pursued a master's degree from a local university. A decade earlier, they had purchased a $4 million house. They liked Vancouver enough to move up to an estate worth over $12 million.

Meng didn't get home or make her connection. As she got off the plane at gate 65 of Vancouver International Airport, she was met by a contingent of Canadian border guards. They brought her to an interrogation room, where her electronic devices were placed in a bag designed to jam any communications and made her hand over her passcodes. At roughly two p.m., after nearly three hours of questioning, Meng was arrested by the Royal Canadian Mounted Police, on foot of an extradition warrant from the United States for alleged bank fraud.

Bank fraud might have seemed a strange charge for someone suspected of selling forbidden technology to Iran. There was a reason for it. NSA hackers had also gathered a lot of secret information on Huawei. But the United States couldn't easily use this information in court since it didn't want to disclose its intelligence sources and methods. Even more important, it wanted to extradite Meng from Canada to the United States. Breaching U.S. sanctions was not a crime in Canada, but bank fraud certainly was. To make the charge stick, U.S. prosecutors needed to provide initial evidence that Meng had deceived a bank. Happily, they could turn to HSBC, which was Huawei's international bank and had become entangled in the underground empire.

Several years earlier, the U.S. Department of Justice had charged HSBC with helping the Sinaloa drug cartel to launder $881 million in narco-trafficking profits through the U.S. financial system. The bank agreed to pay $1.9 billion in fines. It also entered into a multiyear "deferred prosecution" agreement, under which it would avoid criminal prosecution (and probable extinction) so long as it cooperated with an independent monitor, which would scrutinize the company's dealings with suspicious clients and compliance with money laundering laws.

HSBC's executives didn't much like being supervised. According to a sealed report by the monitor, they engaged in a policy of "Discredit, Deny, Deflect and Delay" to frustrate auditors, who were trying to work through HSBC's books to identify potential wrongdoing. It soon came to light that HSBC's foreign exchange desk had engaged in improper trading and that HSBC management hadn't wanted to discipline the responsible traders. U.S. prosecutors began considering criminal charges against the relevant unit of the bank. That, in turn, might have led to the unwinding of the agreement to defer prosecution and the possible collapse of HSBC.

According to Reuters, HSBC tried to persuade the U.S. government to drop the threat of prosecution by providing information on its dealings with Huawei. HSBC hired a prestigious law firm to investigate its former dealings with Huawei, conducting over one hundred interviews and poring through hundreds of thousands of emails and years of financial transactions. It provided the findings of this investigation to the U.S. Department of Justice in a series of meetings in 2017.

These meetings were supposed to persuade U.S. prosecutors that HSBC was cleaning itself up and documenting its past misdeeds. They also, whether deliberately or accidentally, served up Huawei on a gilt platter with fork and whetted carving knife.

Back when Stecklow's stories were published, HSBC had asked Meng to explain what lay behind them. According to the United States, Meng gave HSBC a PowerPoint presentation describing Skycom as no more than a business partner of Huawei's and assured bank officials that Huawei strictly complied with U.S. laws and regulations. That gave U.S. Department of Justice prosecutors what they needed. If what Meng had said wasn't true, then she had arguably misled Huawei's bank to maintain access to "international banking services . . . including U.S. dollar-clearing." And that could be interpreted as fraud. Prosecutors claimed that HSBC (which in the Huawei indictment was labeled "Financial Institution 1") "cleared more than $100 million worth of Skycom-related transactions through the United States," exposing it to "civil or criminal penalties." But the United States stuck to its side of the implied deal. It was Meng, not HSBC, who was under indictment.

After Meng was charged, her lawyers claimed that she did not present a flight risk. Nonetheless, Judge William Ehrcke demanded over $7 million bail for her limited release. After posting bail, she was required to stay under constant surveillance by a security detail and shackled to an electronic bracelet to force compliance with an eleven p.m. and six a.m. curfew. This didn't stop her from enjoying many of the privileges of the rich, including high-end shopping trips and exclusive restaurant meals. It did prevent her leaving Canada.

The United States' global financial imperium wasn't just the rationale for arresting Meng. It was the means, too. Without the empire, foreign banks like HSBC would not have been so willing to satisfy U.S. demands. With it, they needed access to the dollar-clearing system in order to survive. When HSBC was under threat of extinction, it was willing to do whatever was necessary to appease American prosecutors. In a world where the United States didn't have this power or didn't exercise it, Meng would have likely been able to enjoy the break in her trip and continue onward, never dreaming that the United States might dare to interrupt her journey.

After Meng's arrest, Chinese media claimed that HSBC had deliberately "conspired" with the U.S. Department of Justice to set a "trap" for Huawei. Articles in government newspapers suggested that Meng's indictment was the culmination of a long, drawn-out plot by the United States and HSBC. Both had purportedly been working together since at least 2012 to entrap China's most important telecommunications company.

They were right about America's intent, if not HSBC's. Senior U.S. officials certainly wanted to take Huawei down. However, they were dead wrong about the careful long-term planning. U.S. officials had had to improvise even more than usual because they needed to contend with the formless chaos at the heart of their own government. Donald J. Trump was the president, and his attitude to China shifted depending on his whims, peeves, and whomever he had spoken to last. Remarkably, a new weapon of empire emerged from these officials' desperate efforts to make do, in a chaotic and unpredictable administration. Intellectual property—which Wriston had once hoped would liberate businesses from government—was reforged into fetters and shackles.

When he wanted, Trump could ruthlessly defend American security interests. In February 2020, he reamed out Boris Johnson, the prime minister of the United Kingdom, venting his fury in an "apoplectic" phone call at Johnson's refusal to block U.K. phone companies from buying Huawei equipment. Trump's spleen went beyond angry words. His unofficial hatchet man for Europe, the U.S. ambassador to Germany, Richard Grenell, tweeted that Trump had "just called me from AF1 and instructed me to make clear that any nation who chooses to use an untrustworthy 5G vendor will jeopardize our ability to share Intelligence [*sic*] and information at the highest level." The clear implication was that if the U.K. persisted in buying Huawei equipment, it would be kicked out of the exclusive "Five Eyes" club of countries that the United States was willing to share top-level secret intelligence with.

But Trump was erratic. While he wanted to punish China, he was also desperate to negotiate a trade agreement that might convince American voters of his command of the art of the deal. Trump's ferociously hawkish national security adviser John Bolton later described Trump's desire to strike a trade deal with China as a "black hole" "twisting all other issues around" itself, including Huawei.

Trump kept on hinting that he saw the U.S. measures against Huawei as a bargaining chip that could be cashed in for trade concessions. Equally, he didn't want to be publicly taken for a fool. He could respond viciously when allies like the U.K. failed to follow the U.S. line, even if they were led by people like Johnson, whom he personally liked. His short temper, showiness, and impulsiveness meant that hawks like Bolton could manipulate him toward policies intended to crush Huawei and shield U.S. national security interests but made it very hard for them to keep him on target.

Trump hadn't been entirely pleased with Meng's arrest when he was told about it. At the 2018 White House Christmas dinner, he complained to Bolton that Huawei was China's largest telecoms company and described Meng as "the Ivanka Trump of China." According to Bolton, he kept on hinting that Huawei could be a useful bargaining chip in trade negotiations.

In May 2019, the U.S. Department of Commerce's Bureau of Industry and Security took the serious step of putting Huawei and several affiliates on the so-called Entity List. Kevin Wolf heard that it had "come about . . . during the China trade talks" because "Trump wanted more leverage to put pressure on the Chinese to buy grain from Nebraska or whatever." Listing Huawei had broader consequences. The Entity List identifies foreign businesses that the United States considers to be national security risks. U.S. businesses can only sell U.S.-made technology or products to these companies if they have a special license from the government.

That potentially hit Huawei hard, since the company relied on U.S. intellectual property to make its phones. Trump's commerce secretary, Wilbur Ross, explained in his press statement that the goal was to "prevent American technology from being used by foreign-owned entities in ways that potentially undermine U.S. national security or foreign policy interests." All this went down well with the boss. According to Bolton, Trump told his people that the press statement was "a fucking great statement. It's beautiful."

But Trump kept on trying to come to a deal with China. When he met Chinese President Xi Jinping during the G20 Summit in Osaka, Japan, they seemed to reach a compromise on Huawei. President Trump delayed imposing further tariffs on Chinese goods and tweeted that he had "agreed to allow Chinese company Huawei to buy products from [our High Tech companies] which will not impact our National Security." However, Trump didn't have the attention span to follow through, allowing officials like Ross and Bolton to mostly "re-reverse" Trump's "loose comment."

As hawks tried to weaponize the Entity List against Huawei, they kept running up against its limits. It applied only to U.S. products and U.S intellectual property. Nebraska senator Ben Sasse wanted to argue that the Commerce Department List could "effectively disrupt our adversary" because "Huawei's supply chain depends on contracts with American companies." The problem was that Huawei might find alternative foreign suppliers.

As Wolf described it, the Trump administration "was trying to . . . import the export control system to act as a sanction against an individual company for largely unstated objectives." Secondary sanctions were so effective because they worked outside the United States, thanks to the global power of the U.S. dollar. Export controls, in contrast, did not "legally affect foreign made items, even if they were made by U.S. technology or U.S. companies" outside the United States. The result was "a system that [favored] the competitors of U.S. companies, and [had] no impact on Huawei."

As we later discovered, our own ideas inadvertently helped show the way to a solution. In 2019, we wrote an academic article on what we called "weaponized interdependence," explaining how the United States was turning the interdependent networks of global finance into a tool of coercion. Writing that article helped us flesh out the ideas that later turned into this book. And it turned out that it helped others flesh out their ideas, too.

While we were finishing writing this book, another scholar, Tufts historian Chris Miller, published a definitive history of semiconductors and U.S. power, *Chip War*. When one of us bought the book on publication day, and started reading, he was startled to discover that we were part of the story that we were telling. Miller described how our article had been written to warn the United States of the dangerous consequences of weaponizing the world economy. But he also described how a senior Trump administration official took a very different meaning from them.

When the United States wanted to tighten the restrictions further, it used the core idea of our article—single choke points can be used against adversaries. As Miller told us by email, "I almost fell out of my chair when my interview subject told me they'd read your weaponized interdependence article and thought it was a good playbook to implement." He described in his book how the official mused: "weaponized interdependence. It's a beautiful thing."

Very likely, Trump officials would have figured out the value of choke points without our article. Anyway, what was more important was the particular choke point that they discovered—an obscure precedent from the dawn age of export controls, which allowed them to turn U.S. intellectual property into a global equivalent of the dollar clearing system, weaponizing the semiconductor supply chain against Huawei. For decades, the United States had claimed jurisdiction over foreign banks that touched the U.S. dollar and used its control of dollar clearing to discipline them. Now, it claimed jurisdiction, too, over foreign-based technology companies that significantly touched U.S. intellectual property, even indirectly.

Already, Department of Commerce rules allowed it to block the export of foreign products if more than 25 percent of the intellectual property came from the United States. In 2020, the department used the cumbersomely titled "foreign-produced direct product" (FPDP) rule to extend these restrictions much farther. The department claimed jurisdiction not just over products that included U.S. intellectual property but products that had been built using products or processes that relied on U.S. intellectual property. As Wolf put it, "trillions of dollars of transactions, trillions with a 'T'" were affected by a rule "that was buried in 9 point font in a footnote at the bottom of a 320 page Entity List."

This seemingly arcane footnote had very specific consequences for semiconductors. Even if the United States wasn't actually manufacturing semiconductors at the scale that it had in the 1990s, it maintained its grasp on the intellectual property that foreigners and multinationals needed to make them. Since U.S.-controlled companies like Cadence dominated semiconductor design, and U.S. technology played a key role in producing them, Huawei would have a very hard time buying modern semiconductors without U.S. government permission.

Thanks to the ingenuity of his officials, Trump's chaotic approach to policy gave birth to a new economic weapon. Equally it complicated the weapon's use—his tweet after meeting Xi was, by definition, official U.S. government policy. Department of Commerce officials had to figure out how to license some U.S. technology to Huawei and ended up providing billions of dollars' worth of licenses. Businesses were still able to sell to Huawei, so long as they secured U.S. government permission and didn't assist its ambitions in 5G and cloud computing. That allowed Huawei to survive but not to prosper. It could no longer aspire to take the commanding heights of the world's technology economy by building its own world-spanning alternative network.

Huawei had taken defensive measures, accumulating a massive stockpile of semiconductors before the ban came down. The company had even chartered a special cargo plane to airlift home a last shipment days before the final deadline. Even so, its phones began to fall behind their competitors as it started to run out of the newer chips. By the first quarter of 2021, its global market share of mobile phones collapsed from a high of 20 percent to 4.

Huawei could buy less advanced chips designed by companies like Qualcomm, but only on U.S. government sufferance. The new rules reeled TSMC in, too. The U.S. government had spent much of 2019 lobbying Taiwan to stop TSMC from selling semiconductors to Huawei. The new rule allowed it to turn the thumbscrews directly on the Taiwanese company, which controlled over 50 percent of the global semiconductor market and was a generation ahead of its nearest competitor, the South Korean company Samsung. TSMC had a near monopoly on manufacturing the most advanced chips (sub-10 nanometers) with over 90 percent of global production. In 2019, Huawei accounted for $5.4 billion of TSMC's revenue, making it TSMC's second-largest customer after Apple. After the United States announced the new rule, TSMC had to choose between selling its most advanced chips to Huawei or having access to the American technology needed to develop and produce them. The choice was painful, but it wasn't difficult.

When TSMC fell into line, the U.K. government had an excuse to start excluding Huawei from contracts. Ian Levy, the technical director at the U.K. National Cyber Security Centre, warned, "We think that Huawei products that are adapted to cope with the [Department of Commerce rules] are likely to suffer more security and reliability problems because of the massive engineering challenge ahead of them, and it will be harder for us to be confident in their use."

Nearly three years after Meng Wanzhou's arrest, the U.S. Department of Justice announced that it had reached an agreement with her lawyers. Meng admitted that Huawei had controlled Skycom, that Skycom had offered to sell "embargoed" equipment to Iran, and that she had made "untrue statements" to HSBC. In return, the United States agreed to defer the prosecution and dismiss the charges if she continued to abide by the law over the next four years.

The United States didn't exact hundreds of millions of dollars in fines from Huawei or demand a long-term monitoring agreement. There wouldn't have been much point. By the time that Meng arrived in Shenzhen, Huawei was already subject to draconian restrictions. Unless some technological miracle happened, or U.S. pressure relented, Huawei's global ambitions would wither away.

Huawei thought miracles were a more likely bet than a U.S. change of heart. In a conversation with Huawei researchers in August 2021, Ren stressed the need for "more theoretical breakthroughs, especially in the fields of compound semiconductors and material science." China had launched a new research program, to develop novel semiconductor materials, which it hoped might revolutionize the industry and steal a march on the United States and its allies. This was a very high risk strategy, but as Ren said, "If we pursue only what's practical, we may forever lag behind."

Huawei could still sell to the periphery and redoubled its efforts in the emerging markets overlooked by the West. Countries that weren't as closely tied to the United States as the U.K. were still willing to buy their base stations from Huawei. Some even preferred to. As a Russian "government insider" put it, "We're either going to be bugged by the US or by China, so we need to choose the lesser evil." But Huawei had no very obvious way to build strength in the markets it would need to take the metropolis. It suffered setback after setback as its European rivals—Nokia and Ericsson—won more and more 5G contracts.

In the 1980s, Walter Wriston had hoped that the global diffusion of intellectual property would undermine the rules that caged businesses behind national borders. Instead, U.S. intellectual property turned out to be a long and nearly invisible fishing line, with shiny lures and baited hooks that foreign businesses snapped at and swallowed. As the United States started to draw it in, Huawei and China realized how much their fortunes depended on an increasingly hostile power. The lion had rounded on the wolves and was driving them back to the outskirts of its territory.

Just a few years before, Huawei had been central to China's global technology ambitions. Now, it had become a cautionary tale about China's vulnerabilities. The United States could use its choke hold on the channels through which global communications, finance, and technology flowed to hold even the most powerful Chinese companies hostage.

China saw itself as besieged and endangered, too. President Xi Jinping had already noted in a 2018 speech, "Our situation in which key and core technologies are controlled by others has not fundamentally changed." He called for a new Long March "to start over again," building up the strength that China needed to confront the old empire squatting behind its fortifications atop the commanding heights of the new economy. China's government wanted to identify technological "choke points" that could be used to strangle Chinese companies. China's Ministry of Commerce announced its own Unreliable Entity List, which would limit market access to firms that threatened Chinese national security. A secretive committee began to vet foreign technology, identifying opportunities to replace American exports with locally supplied goods. Xi approved a three-year plan to rebuild China's science and technology system, to promote "self-sufficiency and self-empowerment in technology" and a five-year economic plan that elevated technological self-reliance into a core goal and promised to "fight tough battles" for key technologies. The government radically stepped up its efforts to support semiconductor manufacturing, announcing an additional series of investments totaling $118 billion.

But it wasn't clear that China could become self-reliant, let alone find the opportunity to build its own empire of technology. Chinese semiconductor companies, like the Semiconductor Manufacturing International Corporation (SMIC), based in Shanghai, were still unable to make sophisticated semiconductors at scale. Increasingly, the United States and its allies denied them access to the Western design software and equipment that they would need to master manufacturing. Local suppliers weren't able to help, either. *Nikkei Asia* quoted a manager of one of China's biggest local design toolmakers, Empyrean Technology, complaining that "asking us to fully replace Synopsys and Cadence is like coming to carmakers and asking to build rockets." Still, China is unlikely to give up. President Xi appointed his trusted adviser and vice-premier, Liu He, to oversee the self-reliance strategy. As Liu explained, "For our country, technology and innovation is not just a matter of growth. It's also a matter of survival."

China was also vulnerable to spying and subversion. The Snowden leaks demonstrated that the United States was using its central position in global communications networks to gather strategically valuable information. This startled Chinese leaders into focusing more closely on the vulnerabilities that came together with foreign technology. Terms like "information security" appeared far more often in state newspapers than before as journalists came to terms with the surveillance programs revealed by Snowden, while specialist journals like *Government Procurement Information* argued that China's institutions needed to "completely extricate ourselves from being subject to the influence of foreign enterprises and foreign powers" and to "replace imported products and services with independent and controllable domestic hardware and software services, . . . and safeguard the security of the core interests of the country and military."

The deeper problem that Xi confronted was that China had no financial structures like the ones that had allowed the United States to compel HSBC. Even worse, while China was deeply vulnerable to U.S. pressure, the United States was not nearly so vulnerable to it.

When the United States sanctioned Hong Kong's then chief executive Carrie Lam for human rights violations, as the official who ran Hong Kong and had become the face of its anti-democracy crackdowns, she found that she couldn't get a bank account in a Chinese bank. The U.S. power to designate individuals, businesses, and institutions meant that Chinese banks were terrified of violating the sanctions against her. Lam had to be paid her salary in cash. She hoarded actual piles of money in scattered heaps around Government House, the colonial-era mansion with two swimming pools that serves as her official residence. But when China retaliated by sanctioning Gayle Manchin (then chair of the U.S. Commission on International Religious Freedom), U.S. banks didn't feel the need to take notice. Manchin professed herself "flattered" by China's attention, but since she had no plans to travel there, it didn't affect her life in any material way.

That was why the Chinese government tried to insulate itself from the global financial infrastructure. Speaking at an industrial forum in Beijing, former finance minister Lou Jiwei warned that rising U.S. nationalism and dollar dominance could push China and the United States into a new "financial war." Analysts and former financial officials called on the Chinese government to prepare for the "nuclear option"—"that the United States could expel China from the dollar settlement system."

Some Chinese thinkers hoped that China could build its own financial networks, to protect itself in the future, and perhaps to retaliate. As Russian firms tried to avoid sanctions after the invasion of Ukraine, they started using yuan rather than dollars to make and receive payments. In 2015, China had created analogous institutions to SWIFT within CIPS (Cross-Border Interbank Payment System), its own international payment system. By 2021, official figures claimed that CIPS was processing $12.68 trillion worth of transactions. Those numbers were likely exaggerated, and represented less than a tenth of the amount that SWIFT processed. Even so, a unit of the Bank of China advised Chinese banks to switch their settlement services from SWIFT to CIPS, warning that "a good punch to the enemy will save yourself from hundreds of punches from your enemies. . . . We need to get prepared in advance, mentally, and practically."

Even if it couldn't control the plumbing of the global economy, China still had one weapon that it could deploy—market access. There was growing demand for access to China's domestic market, where hundreds of millions of consumers were joining the global middle class and where manufacturers were hungry for machine tools, raw materials, oil, coal, and a myriad of other commodities. The policy instruments that it had developed to control globalization could also be used to selectively punish businesses, and even countries that displeased China, albeit at a cost.

When Norway's Parliament awarded the Nobel Peace Prize to Liu Xiabao, a Chinese dissident, China restricted imports of Norwegian salmon. After the Obama administration indicted five Chinese military officials for cyber spying, the Chinese government banned the use of the most recent version of Windows on Chinese government computers.

China's problem was that these instruments were self-limiting. Restricting Norwegian salmon imports probably didn't hurt China very much, but it didn't hurt Norway much, either, so long as others bought the fish. More serious measures might end up damaging China as much as the state it was targeting. When Australia called for an investigation into the origins of coronavirus, China retaliated with trade sanctions that limited or blocked imports of important Australian goods. But China declined to ban the most important import from Australia—iron ore—because its companies desperately needed it. Even after China blocked government-owned power generators from buying Australian coal, they quietly started importing it again several months later, when the economy hit an energy crunch. Other sanctions had relatively little effect because Australian exporters were easily able to find other markets. China could only hurt other countries by hurting itself, and sometimes it couldn't hurt them much.

Weaponized markets still had their uses. Midsize countries might prefer to avoid actions that would offend China, such as hosting the Dalai Lama. Businesses were more vulnerable to Chinese displeasure than governments, especially if they were dependent on China. When China targeted a London lawyers' chambers that had given advice about human rights abuses in Xinjiang, other U.K. barristers stayed quiet for fear that they would be hit next. The National Basketball Association lost a "substantial" sum that NBA commissioner Adam Silver estimated at roughly $400 million, after Chinese TV stopped broadcasting basketball games. China had retaliated against a team manager who had tweeted in support of the pro-democracy Hong Kong protests.

Still, China couldn't really hurt the economy of even a midsize country like Australia without hurting itself, too. Unlike the United States, it didn't control any of the key choke points in the subterranean machineries of the world economy. In the late 1990s, when the Internet and global finance were taking off, China had barely begun to reconnect with the world and had little time to shape how the world's infrastructure evolved.

Judged by the size of its economy, China was a global power. Judged by its influence over global economic networks, it was at best an also-ran. The United States could use its underground empire to pass the painful costs of coercion onto allies and enemies. When it wanted to exclude Iran from the world financial system, it wasn't America that paid the price but non-U.S. banks, which were required to implement U.S. laws that mulcted their pocketbooks or face massive fines and possible destruction. When the United States decided to deny Huawei access to semiconductors, all that Huawei and China could do was retrench and hope that they could overcome America's technological advantage by developing their own resources.

Once more, they both had to fall back on Mao's logic of irregular war against a stronger opponent. As one of Huawei's suppliers told *Nikkei Asia*, "If the U.S. crackdown is like bombardment with the most advanced fighter jets, Huawei's counter-efforts are definitely like guerrilla-style campaigns."

4

WAKING INTO WINTER

On March 1, 2022, something unexpected happened. The president of the European Commission gave a historic speech.

The Commission, based in Brussels, Belgium, is the executive body of the European Union (EU). In the 1980s and 1990s, it helped weave together a new Europe, guiding its squabbling governments into the Single Market and breaking down economic barriers between countries. A few years later, Irish punts, Portuguese escudos, German deutsche marks, and French francs were transmuted into a single currency, the euro. It was Thomas Friedman's story of globalization writ small. Bitter national enmities would give way to free markets and open borders in a triumph of commerce and international law—all guided by the technocrats of the Commission.

By 2022, that vision had receded into the barely imaginable past. Now it wasn't the Commission but big countries like Germany and France that set the agenda. Anyway, Europe just wasn't in the business of dramatic transformations anymore.

When Russia invaded Ukraine, it was as though the clock had struck midnight in a fairy tale. Europe's delightful illusion of security through commerce evaporated in a billow of gun smoke. Pundits expected that Europe would continue its slide into irrelevance, issuing indignant statements of condemnation and perhaps announcing a few ineffectual economic measures, as Ukraine was brutally dismembered and devoured next door.

Instead, Ursula von der Leyen, a protégé of former German chancellor Angela Merkel and the sitting president of the European Commission, announced what sounded like a new beginning for Europe. "At the speed of light," the EU was adopting "three waves of heavy sanctions against Russia's financial system, its high-tech industries and its corrupt elite." Europe was banning key Russian banks from the SWIFT network, choking off the supply of Airbus parts to Russian airlines, and freezing the accounts of Russian oligarchs. Most shockingly, it was blocking Russia's central bank's access to the money it held in Europe, paralyzing "billions in foreign reserves" that Moscow had thought were safe from political interference. Over the following days, Europe and the United States added measure after measure, cutting Russia out of key aspects of the global economy. For decades, the EU had slumbered and dreamed of a world without power politics. Now, it had woken.

Waking up was one thing. Making economic war was quite another. The EU project was built to open markets up, not weaponize them. And the EU itself was vulnerable and divided. Europe could feel the bear clawing at its vitals, but Germany's economy depended on Russian gas. So did Hungary's—and Hungary's president was a fan of Vladimir Putin.

That Europe was able to respond at all, though, was thanks to changes set in motion years before Russia's invasion. Here, the spur to Europe's transformation was surprising. It wasn't fear of Russia or even worries about China that first caused Europe to rise from its long historical torpor. Instead, it was the threat posed by the United States of America.

———————

A few years ago, no mainstream European official would have thought that the United States was dangerous. The relationship between the EU and the United States was too fundamental to be questioned. The United States and the EU would sometimes disagree on policy or have temporary spats: that happened between friends. But one would never fundamentally threaten the other.

Indeed, modern Europe was in part an American construction. The heady ambitions of European federalists, who wanted to create a United Europe after the disaster of World War II, had coincided with the practical desire of the United States to get its allies to cooperate on rebuilding their economies. This didn't lead, as some federalists had hoped, to a European superstate, but to a succession of organizations with confusing acronyms, begetting each other like unmemorable biblical patriarchs: the ECSC, the EEC, the EC, and finally the EU.

The initials shifted, but the dream remained the same: building economic cooperation as an alternative to the conflict that had plagued Europe. Germany and France—the EU's two largest founding countries—had been bitter antagonists for nearly a century, alternating between brutal wars and wary peace. Their common membership in the EU was supposed to make war unthinkable. Both committed themselves, alongside the other founding countries, to build an "ever closer union" that would transform the war-torn continent into a pacific zone of market relations.

The EU had been founded on a story about peace through markets. It didn't have to think about war because its important members were also members of NATO and could take shelter beneath America's nuclear umbrella. Anyway, trade provided its own kind of security guarantee. Why would other countries hurt their own economies by making war on their trading partners?

Occasionally, America's willingness to protect was at odds with Europe's enthusiasm for trade. During the Cold War, the Reagan administration wanted to deny the Soviet Union's access to hard currency. But European countries like Germany needed stable energy supplies and wanted to buy Soviet gas and oil. They were even prepared to help Gazprom, the Soviet gas producer, build a pipeline to transport Siberian gas to Western Europe.

A precocious Harvard undergraduate, Antony (Tony) J. Blinken, wrote a senior thesis that he quickly turned into a book, explaining how the United States believed that the pipeline gave assistance to the enemy, while Europeans claimed that it would improve the chances of peace. The United States wanted to destroy the Soviet Union through "economic warfare," but prominent Europeans wanted to transform it instead. They believed that the pipeline would help integrate Russia into the world economy, changing its politics and moderating its behavior.

The Reagan administration imposed economic sanctions on the European businesses constructing Russia's gas pipeline and even hinted that the United States would "reconsider military commitments to Western Europe" if the Europeans didn't cooperate. But the Europeans held firm, openly flouting U.S. sanctions and daring the United States to retaliate. They were furious at America's interference with "European owned, operated and even state-owned companies." Reagan blinked, fearing that the sanctions would hurt American businesses more than European sanction busters. The pipeline was completed only a few months later than scheduled.

All this was forgotten when the Cold War ended, and the EU fervidly embraced the new global economic order of open trade. Europe relied on economic interdependence to make peace, taking continued American protection for granted and assuming that its self-interest and global economic openness were one and the same thing. As the Germans put it, the idea was to achieve *Wandel durch Handel*: to transform the world through trade.

Pieties and profit went hand in glove. Trade ostensibly drew the Chinese economy closer to the Western model while fattening the wallets of German car producers and machine manufacturers. Gazprom's pipeline drew Russia closer too, but it also provided cheap energy and raw materials for manufacturers like the German chemical giant BASF. Germany and France—the EU's two dominant states—thought that it was perfectly reasonable to give Gazprom and the Russian oil giant Rosneft partial ownership of Europe's energy infrastructure, ignoring protests from Poland and Ukraine. Shared interests would surely entangle Russia further with Europe. Although Europe relied on Russia for gas, Russia depended on Europe for money. If Russia ever stopped supplying gas to Europe, it could only hurt itself, forgoing profit and abandoning expensive infrastructure.

Perhaps the magic of commerce could indeed transform a rough and threatening beast into a mannerly courtier. But behind the fairy tale lurked a less edifying story about the sordid lust for gold. Cold War *Ostpolitik*, a policy aimed at gradually transforming Russia and Eastern Europe through trade and political ties, often degenerated into a tangle of self-serving relationships that enriched well-connected European politicians. Gerhard Schröder, the former Social Democratic chancellor of Germany, was notoriously eager to help Russian companies build Europe's energy infrastructure. A year before he lost the chancellorship, he told his biographer that he wanted to "make money" when he left politics. Russian energy giants like Gazprom and Rosneft happily helped him achieve his ambition, paying him generously for his connections.

The EU relied on America for security, Russia for energy, and China for trade. These dependencies didn't trouble it particularly. All that European officials could see was the flatland of peaceful commercial exchange, stretching to infinity in two dimensions. Everything beneath the surface—the growth of America's underground empire; the subterranean resurgence of Russia's territorial ambitions; China's increasing authoritarianism—was as invisible as if it were happening on another plane of existence.

When European politicians worried about the dominance of Silicon Valley, it was because EU companies were getting squeezed out of the market. European politicians hoped that the euro might eventually displace the dollar, but they did not see the dollar clearing system as a major strategic threat. Why would the United States use it against them? When Europeans worried about global trade and supply chains, they focused on economics, not security risks. EU officials didn't care about the geopolitical risks of relying on Russian gas. They worried instead that market concentration of energy suppliers might hurt economic competition. Managing competition among energy companies was the kind of job that could be turned over to the European Commission, which was no longer molding a new Europe but decreeing obscure changes to phytosanitary regulations (don't ask) in offices with off-white walls and blandly sinister official art. In truth, the Commission still had great power—energy markets were, after all, important—but mostly over dull-seeming things that few outside Brussels cared about.

The EU found it hard to even think about its collective security interests. Its so-called Common Foreign and Security Policy was a halfhearted afterthought to the individual interests and policies of its member states. The Commission worked relentlessly to wall off the areas it controlled—trade and the Single Market—from dangerous foreign policy concerns that might give member states like France an excuse to intervene in the economy. When security issues arose, such as the scandal over the NSA's ECHELON surveillance system at the turn of the millennium, EU officials mostly shrugged. As the Austrian privacy activist Max Schrems told us in 2016, the "basic issue" was that "the European Union doesn't have any jurisdiction over national security." There was no European OFAC. Sanctions decisions had to be made unanimously by all twenty-seven member states and were implemented by the governments' own national bureaucracies (which often lacked the resources to do it properly). When other countries used trade weapons or supply chain attacks to undermine EU security, the EU's first instinct was not to fight back, or even to defend itself, but to petition the World Trade Organization to set things right.

At its worst, the EU's faith in globalization led it to ignore existential risks. But at its best, it inspired initiatives to draw the poison from bitter and protracted disputes, as when the EU brokered the 2013 deal in which Iran agreed to limit its nuclear ambitions. European officials had hoped that an agreement would stanch the suppurating wound that was the U.S.-Iran relationship. That would allow European businesses to set up shop in Iran without having to worry about American sanctions, and perhaps build foundations for a tentative U.S.-Iran peace. By doing well, the EU might also do good. The Europeans didn't just help at the margins. In the words of then Secretary of State John Kerry, Catherine Ashton, the EU's High Representative for Foreign Affairs was a "persistent and dogged" negotiator. She played a "decisive role" in bringing together the final agreement, the so-called Joint Comprehensive Plan of Action (JCPOA).

The JCPOA was the last great exercise in building peace through trade. Under the JCPOA, Iran returned to SWIFT, while the UN lifted the restrictions that it had imposed on Iran. The United States still wouldn't allow its own companies to go to Iran, but it did agree to waive the "secondary sanctions" that targeted foreign businesses. In return, Iran agreed to limit its enrichment of nuclear fuels, although it insisted on "sunset clauses" that would ease these restrictions after some years.

The EU hoped that the JCPOA would draw the United States into a healthier relationship with Iran and that Iran would feel less need to build a nuclear weapons program if it felt less threatened by its enemies. The deal became a symbol of Europe's diplomatic prowess and newfound global relevance. As the EU itself demonstrated, peace and friendship could be built on trade and interdependence.

———————

When Donald Trump was elected the forty-fifth president of the United States, Europe began to stir fretfully in its slumber. Yet as Peter Wittig, who served as Germany's ambassador to the United States, told us, people weren't terribly worried at first. They assumed that the office would shape the man. Trump was volatile, but he was also vulnerable to flattery. Over the first several months of the Trump administration, a succession of European leaders visited Washington to pay homage.

Europeans did expect trouble over the JCPOA. At a Tea Party rally in 2015, Trump and his rival for the Republican nomination, Senator Ted Cruz, had sparred over which of them hated it more. Cruz announced that any future president should "rip to shreds this catastrophic deal," while Trump described the deal in different appearances as the "worst," "terrible," "bad," "horrible," and "laughable."

Still, when Trump became president, he didn't withdraw immediately. Unlike Cruz and other Republicans, Trump wasn't opposed on principle to an agreement with Iran. His detestation was rooted in personal pique. Trump hadn't negotiated the JCPOA himself and was convinced that his unparalleled mastery of "the art of the deal" would allow him to strike a better bargain. In January 2018, Trump renewed the waivers on U.S. secondary sanctions, although he threatened that he would terminate the agreement in 120 days if the Europeans did not agree to "fix the deal's disastrous flaws."

Informal talks between Europe and the United States foundered on the deal's sunset clauses, which permitted Iran to restart nuclear enrichment after roughly a decade. Brian Hook, who was the State Department's lead Iran negotiator, told us that his European counterparts agreed that the deal was flawed, but their "pride of authorship" prevented them from solving its problems. Hook's European counterparts respected him more than they did some other Trump officials, but they disagreed with this analysis. It seemed to them a miracle that a workable deal had been reached at all, and they couldn't believe that the United States was so willing to throw it away. In April 2018, Macron visited Washington, DC, hoping to persuade Trump to accept a more sweeping but vaguely detailed new arrangement. Trump didn't bite.

Just weeks later, the Trump administration unilaterally blew up the Iran deal. U.S. economic sanctions against Iran snapped back into place. Although Iran was the target, European firms were in the crosshairs, too. By reintroducing sanctions on foreign companies, the United States was forcing its allies to stop honoring a deal that the United States itself had negotiated and signed. Macron had predicted that the United States would open a "Pandora's box" if it pulled out of the JCPOA. Fears and horrors tumbled out in multitudes over the next several years, but they were followed by little hope.

This time, the United States had no reason to back down. Its control of global finance had grown vastly since Reagan was president, allowing it to shift the pain from American exporters to European companies. Despite fervent lobbying, the Europeans couldn't persuade the United States to agree to carve-outs for their companies, leading the French energy giant Total to pull out of a $4.8 billion deal to develop Iran's South Pars oil field. Other European companies fled, too. As Karine Berger, a former French politician, explained, Europe had a "major problem." "[F]rom an economic point of view, there [was] no solution" to the difficulties European companies faced. Their choice was to either abandon Iran or cut themselves off from U.S. dollars and U.S. business. It wasn't a difficult call. The head of the Danish logistics giant Maersk put it bluntly: "With the sanctions the Americans are to impose, you can't do business in Iran if you also have business in the U.S., and we have that on a large scale."

In theory, EU legislation blocked European companies from complying with U.S. sanctions. In practice, European companies could easily work around the law. If they simply claimed that they were stopping their business in Iran for reasons unrelated to sanctions, regulators had no stomach to prove otherwise. An EU official claimed that the EU's blocking legislation had "signaling value" but admitted that it was really up to companies themselves to decide what to do.

In August 2018, the Trump administration—responding to pressure from Republican senators like Cruz and anti-Iran lobby groups like the Foundation for Defense of Democracies—started talking about getting Iran kicked out of SWIFT again. Secretary of the Treasury Steven Mnuchin didn't want to press the issue without European consent, but officials like National Security Adviser John Bolton embraced what they dubbed a "maximum pressure" campaign against Iran. An unnamed administration official started leaking against Mnuchin, claiming that he was "making Trump into Obama," while the "Europeans [were] clowning the Americans" and "publicly gloating" together with Iran over Mnuchin's hesitations. Very possibly, it was a coincidence that Bolton badmouthed Mnuchin later, when he wrote his memoirs. Mnuchin ended up "advising" SWIFT to disconnect sanctioned Iranian institutions, and in November SWIFT announced that it was cutting Iranian banks off in keeping with its "mission of supporting the resilience and integrity of the global financial system as a global and neutral service provider," maintaining the thin legal fiction that it wasn't responding to U.S demands.

Europe scrambled to create new financial channels to Iran that weren't vulnerable to U.S. pressure. Eventually, three big European countries agreed to build a completely new financial institution together, for the sole purpose of keeping the Iran relationship on life support. Germany, France, and the United Kingdom (which was pulling out of the EU) set up INSTEX (Instrument in Support of Trade Exchanges), an institution designed to support Iran trade through a complicated barter system that avoided any direct relationship with the U.S. dollar.

The United States hinted that it might sanction the European government officials who ran INSTEX, but it needn't have bothered. INSTEX concluded its first transaction in March 2020, helping export medical goods to Iran. After that, it didn't do much of anything. As one financial industry figure described it to us in late 2021, there was a "very bad smell in the room" at INSTEX, a lot of "finger pointing," and not much else going on. Some European officials "likened [INSTEX] to a laboratory, where you can . . . try out weird things," and it did start developing "unusual workarounds for different parts of the financial system." But it wasn't able to do much on its own, and the EU was unwilling to take the transformative steps that would allow it to really set up a viable alternative to U.S. dollar power. As then European High Representative Federica Mogherini lamented, it was hard to counter "the weight of the US in the global economy and financial system." For European industry, the "bitter Iran experience" came to symbolize the EU's impotence.

Slowly, the Europeans came to understand that Trump's hostility went beyond Iran. The Trump administration wasn't just bargaining for European concessions, as other administrations had. On his good days, Trump thought of Europe as a lackey to be thrashed into submission. On his bad ones, it was an adversary to be crushed.

When Trump was asked to identify the United States' biggest foe in summer 2018, he responded, "Now you wouldn't think of the European Union, but they're a foe." In a *Meet the Press* interview, when Trump was asked about European worries over the Iran deal, he bluntly responded that he didn't "care about the Europeans." Trump said privately that he wanted to pull the United States out of NATO, which he saw as a racket set up to milk America for Europe's benefit.

This new America was frightening and potentially hostile, and Europe couldn't do much about it. Decades before, European governments had been able to force America to back down when their fundamental economic interests were at stake. Now, they were reduced to supplications and impotent complaints. Europe had awakened to discover that it had been transformed while it was asleep from an ally to a mere outlying province of a greater empire. Its financial system and its businesses had been press-ganged into service by a United States that was breaking bad.

European officials had woken up, but they struggled even to find the words to describe what had happened to them. Their particular dialect of globalization was fit only to articulate Europe's selfish needs and desires in terms of the open global economy. Now, that economy's master was driving its allies like cattle before a goad. So what could Europe do in a world where America no longer had its back? The initial answer—as so often in the EU—had the ambiguity of the Delphic oracle, if Apollo had descended on his votary in a stupefying cloud of bureaucratic catchphrases.

Competing buzzwords like "geostrategic Europe," "strategic autonomy," and "strategic sovereignty" spread like contagions across Brussels, Paris, and Berlin, swapping DNA and rapidly mutating as they reproduced via think tank policy briefs and politicians' speeches. According to Franziska Brantner, a rising foreign policy thinker in Germany's Green Party, all this fighting over words was not "toxic quibble," as others had described it, but was instead the "way that political actors try to conceal deep, substantial differences and their consequences." Bureaucratic white papers were their own kind of stories, and officials fought over which one was the right one to tell. At stake was the meaning of Europe, its relationship with the United States, and whether it should stick with its commitment to open markets or use them itself as tools of coercion.

One apparently inoffensive buzzword, "strategic autonomy," provoked particularly bitter disagreement. This catchphrase had been coined in 2016 by the European External Action Service, the EU's embryonic foreign service, to hint that the EU should develop its own military machine rather than solely depending on America. After the collapse of the JCPOA, European officials extended strategic autonomy to frame economic questions, too. Should the EU stick with its free market philosophy? How could it act independently of a United States that was suddenly untrustworthy? How might it act against the United States if European interests demanded it?

France's president Macron argued that Europe needed to embrace strategic autonomy in both economic and military affairs. But the term repelled German chancellor Angela Merkel, who was instinctively committed to a strong relationship with America. As a former defense official in Merkel's party explained, "the security and defense establishment in Germany does not like . . . the term 'strategic autonomy' at all." It feared that Macron and the French government wanted a world where "Europe [takes] care of its own security, without the United States." In a 2017 speech at the Sorbonne, Macron deliberately avoided the provocative catchphrase but did little else to soothe German suspicions. He argued that the EU had sheltered itself for too long from the rest of the world, on the theory that "security was not its business. This was performed by America." It needed to develop "European sovereignty" if it wanted to protect its citizens and be relevant to them. It had to be able to defend itself, "in complement to NATO."

Even in Germany, things were changing. It was no surprise that Macron's Minister for the Economy and Finances, Bruno Le Maire, wanted the EU to develop its "economic sovereignty" and avoid becoming "a vassal that obeys and jumps to attention." What was remarkable was that one of Merkel's key ministers publicly agreed. Germany's Federal Minister of Foreign Affairs, Heiko Maas, wrote an essay for a prominent German newspaper arguing that the United States and Europe had started drifting apart from each other long before Trump. He claimed that it was time to build a more independent European Union, with "payment channels independent of the U.S., and an independent SWIFT system." Europe could serve as a "counterweight" to the United States and the "pillar" of a new international order.

Such ideas were far too radical for Merkel, who quickly dismissed Maas's essay as a mere "expression of opinion." She suggested that she hadn't been consulted and that she sharply disagreed, especially on the proposal to remake SWIFT.

However, Maas had not been talking off the cuff. His proposals reflected the work of a task force that had been quietly assembled inside Germany's foreign ministry to write the Federal Republic's first ever "America strategy." Postwar Germany had never needed such a strategy, but then, no U.S. president had considered it an enemy. As a senior German foreign policy official described it, the task force was engaged in nothing less than "an overhaul of German foreign policy, since the key assumption being called into question is the total reliance we have on the friendship with the U.S."

Even after Merkel's hostile response, the German foreign ministry continued thinking about the unthinkable. It had to take care to cover its tracks. With the support of France's foreign ministry, it commissioned the European Council on Foreign Relations, a prominent think tank, to write a report advising how Europe might respond to U.S. financial coercion. The report was coauthored by two young policy intellectuals, Ellie Geranmayeh and Manuel Lafont Rapnouil (who left soon after to take over the French foreign ministry's planning office). As a former senior German official described it to us, the two ministries "didn't want to have a direct footprint," but they wanted to put the topic of European autonomy "on the table."

The report had a bland title, "Meeting the Challenge of Secondary Sanctions," but explosive implications. Geranmayeh and Rapnouil argued that the United States might very well continue to engage in economic aggression that would undermine European interests. Europe had to prepare to respond aggressively itself, building its own coercive instruments to counter American financial power. The EU didn't just need to understand the United States' dominant role in global financial networks. It needed to act on this understanding, reducing its vulnerabilities, while "showing a determination to leverage" its own power "for Europe's benefit." INSTEX could become the "keystone of a European trading system that [ran] in parallel to conventional, US-connected routes," insulating European businesses again from U.S. meddling.

Blockchain technologies and a stronger euro might allow the EU to better resist U.S. pressure. Importantly, the EU should equip itself to retaliate against U.S. coercion, targeting American banks and businesses by freezing their assets or denying them licenses to operate in the EU. These suggestions were radical, and Geranmayeh and Rapnouil hoped that their mere existence might deter U.S. overreach so that the proposed tools would never have to be used.

The report helped spur the European Commission to rethink its own role. The Commission had long seen itself as a guardian of free market exchange. The "four freedoms" promised in the EU's founding treaty—free movement in goods, services, money, and people—were its adenine, thymine, guanine, and cytosine, genetic building blocks whose combinations spelled out the code of the greater organism. But a few months after the publication of Geranmayeh and Rapnouil's report, Ursula von der Leyen became the new Commission president. Unlike her predecessors, she wanted the EU to evolve, balancing its commitment to open trade with a new focus on national security, perhaps even developing its own economic weapons.

Von der Leyen hadn't prospered in her previous job as Germany's Minister of Defense (which was notoriously "the graveyard of German ministers"). However, she had become convinced of the need for a real European security strategy. Von der Leyen was born in Brussels, the daughter of a senior Commission official. As defense minister, she toured other European capitals, arguing for more European security cooperation and a common European army. It was Macron who suggested she would be a good president for the Commission. He, too, wanted the EU to start taking defense seriously and hoped that von der Leyen could win her country's support for a stronger and more politically independent Commission. Merkel (who had been her mentor in German politics) agreed to nominate her, providing her with a chance to return to Brussels to remake Europe and her own career.

When von der Leyen was appointed, she announced the need for a "geopolitical Commission." She didn't really explain what "geopolitical" meant, ducking arguments with other Commission officials who had spent decades building a defensive wall around its core responsibilities of trade and the Single Market.

As Pierre Haroche, a French political scientist, explained, such Commission officials worried that rhetoric about geopolitics and strategic autonomy was a Trojan horse, concealing the forces of economic protectionism and state intervention that they had fended off for decades.

Any construction that they let through their defenses might break open and allow the enemy to rush out and overwhelm the defenders. These officials did what they could to defend against the old enemy. In a widely reported speech, Phil Hogan, the European Commissioner for Trade, announced that the EU's trade policy would henceforth be guided by the concept of "open strategic autonomy," under which the EU would act more forcefully and assertively within the rules of the global trade system, protecting them as well as it could from Trump's attacks. By adding a single adjective, Hogan watered down the notion of strategic autonomy so that it subordinated national security to trade rather than trade to national security. His magnificently ambivalent catchphrase was immediately ridiculed. Alan Beattie, the *Financial Times'* trade correspondent, quickly created a new trade philosophy name generator, which allowed readers to mix and match random policy buzzwords. Still, it provided a banner under which the forces of free trade might rally against the enemy.

Rhetorical fights turned into policy battles. It was increasingly hard to assert with a straight face that open trade was the universal solution to Europe's problems. When the coronavirus pandemic hit, the EU's member states realized that they depended on Chinese manufacturers for personal protective equipment (PPE) and American drug companies for vaccines. The just-in-time supply chains that Europe relied on had become existential vulnerabilities. Everyone started hoarding, and the EU's member states fought one another for scarce resources like medical masks and ventilators. After weeks of chaos and mutual accusations, they agreed that they would no longer block one another from buying PPE. Instead, they would defer to the Commission, which would retain the power to block exports to the rest of the world.

Talk about strategic autonomy became the language in which European officials discussed Europe's vulnerabilities. Soon, they weren't just talking about America. A senior Commission official told us that "strategic autonomy in economic terms . . . was the vulnerability we had with regards to PPE, with regards to certain ingredients, all the dependencies in our supply chains, which . . . come from China."

Old worries about Trump and new fears of China forced Commission officials to start thinking more practically about what a geopolitical Commission could do. As the European Council on Foreign Relations had recommended, they began work on a so-called anticoercion instrument, a new legal framework that would allow the EU to take "countermeasures" against outside threats, whether they came from America, China, or some other country again.

Even the most hardened trade zealots were convinced that the Commission needed new powers. It couldn't turn to the World Trade Organization anymore, because Trump had sabotaged the WTO's legal appeals process. Sabine Weyand, one of the Commission's most senior trade officials, had a very personal understanding of how trade might trump war. She had grown up in a border town between Germany and France. After Trump, she was willing to acknowledge that "[e]veryone is looking at their dependencies: they are vulnerabilities, not trade links." That meant that Europe had to change: "We cannot watch on as others weaponize trade. We need to be able to respond."

Weyand and other officials hoped that mere readiness would be enough to right the balance again: "If the instrument works, we will not have to use it." As another Commission official told us, the expectation was that "you would have something that would be strong enough to deter a conflict." Like Geranmayeh and Rapnouil, these officials hoped that the mere existence of a deterrent might defang outside threats and perhaps even help revive the old system of multilateral trade that Europe had benefited from for so long.

Maas's proposals for an independent European financial system, as well as Geranmayeh and Rapnouil's more radical suggestions, were quietly pushed to one side, perhaps to be considered again if things deteriorated badly. As usual, Europe wanted to keep its options open as long as possible. The ambiguities of language helped those who were still committed to free trade to find a compromise with those who wanted a sharper geopolitical transformation of Europe.

But it wasn't all games about language. Before Trump, no European official would conceivably have announced, as Weyand did, that the Commission wasn't just mapping Europe's vulnerabilities to other powers but had started looking for the "reverse dependencies . . . where others [are] dependent on us." A small group of Commission officials was quietly delegated to find weaknesses in the economies of other powers, which the EU could exploit if it needed to.

Europe had begun to think and talk about strategy. It could see the urgencies of American sanctions and vulnerable medical supplies, but another vulnerability was so vast as to be nearly invisible. Countries like Germany didn't just depend on American finance and Chinese export markets, but on Russian energy supplies. Gazprom's pipelines were supposed to bring Russia closer. But what would happen if they were used instead to choke Europe's economy?

———

Many years after she had launched her political career, Franziska Brantner, the Green Party's Europe spokesperson (and later Parliamentary State Secretary for the Federal Ministry for Economic Affairs and Climate Action) remembered how "suffocating" it had felt to grow up in Germany's post–Cold War political system. It wasn't just that nobody wanted to rock the boat. The consensus between Germany's two dominant political parties, the Christian Democrats on the center-right and the Social Democrats on the center-left, stifled real debate. As Brantner saw it, Germans had plenty of interesting ideas, but most of them didn't get mainstream discussion. That helped explain how Germany sleepwalked its way into dependence on Russian gas and oil.

The modern German economy was built on the back of Russian energy supplies. After the Cold War, Germany and other northern European countries kept on looking for new ways to get Russian gas. Gazprom kept looking for new ways to get it to them, circumventing Ukraine, which wanted to siphon its own cheap supplies from the pipeline connecting Siberia to Western Europe. First came the Nord Stream 1 pipelines, which connected Russia and Europe along the bottom of the Baltic Sea. Then there was the South Stream pipeline, which was supposed to go under the Black Sea but was never built. The European Commission blocked it in 2014, fearing that it would undermine market competition. That reportedly provoked Putin to yell in an EU-Russia summit, "If I hear one more word about competition, I'm going to freeze your you-know-whats off."

Such threats were ignored. German manufacturers needed cheap gas for energy. So did German households. That was all that anyone really needed to know. Germany's centrist political consensus depended on a pervasive willed ignorance about what powered Germany's manufacturing economy and how it might be weaponized. Even Putin's American admirer, President Trump, talked contemptuously about how gas meant that Germany was "totally controlled by Russia."

Germany's Green Party attracted activists and aspiring politicians because it was willing to challenge such fantasies, pushing not just on energy, but on environmental politics, gender issues, and other causes, too. In its early years, that made for bitter internal fights between Greens who wanted to attack the consensus from outside and those who were willing to work within the system. But as the Greens won political office—as junior coalition partners to the Social Democrats in the 1990s, and then as the dominant party in the state government of Baden-Württemberg—the moderates took over. They still clung to many of the Greens' founding goals, including getting rid of nuclear power. But they were willing to work with other parties to get there.

Mainstream German politicians saw Russian gas as the solution, but the Greens thought it was the problem. It kept Germany addicted to fossil energy, delaying the transition to a carbon-free economy. It benefited Germany and a few other rich northern countries at the expense of their European partners. Finally, it made Germany dependent on an increasingly vicious autocracy. Greens had no time for slogans like *Wandel durch Handel*, which they saw as a convenient justification for shoving human rights and democracy concerns aside in the pursuit of profit.

So long as the Greens were out of government, they had little power to change things. In 2015, Gazprom formed a consortium with big, well-connected European energy companies to build Nord Stream 2, a second set of pipelines to carry gas under the Baltic Sea. It seemed that the fix was in. Sigmar Gabriel, one of Schröder's long-standing cronies, was Germany's Minister for Economic Affairs and Energy. In public, he argued that Nord Stream 2 would create a "different and better relationship with Russia." In private, he assured Putin that the South Stream debacle wouldn't be repeated. This time Gabriel would stop European authorities from "meddling" with the pipeline. The Nord Stream 2 contracts were specifically designed to block the European Commission from intervening.

Merkel claimed that Nord Stream 2 was a purely "commercial project," and her Christian Democrats worked with Social Democrats like Gabriel to push it through. When Alexei Navalny, a prominent Russian opposition politician, was mysteriously poisoned, the Greens filed a motion in Parliament calling on the government to stop Nord Stream 2. All the other parties ganged up to vote against them. As the *Financial Times* noted, opposing the Greens' motion was one of the very few occasions on which "Merkel's CDU/CSU, the Social

Democrats, the hard-left Die Linke and the hard-right Alternative for Germany had ever agreed on anything." The other parties in Germany simply didn't want to listen when the Greens said that Nord Stream 2 was "splitting Europe," alienating countries like Poland and Ukraine.

Ukraine's complaints fell on deaf ears in Europe. As the *Wall Street Journal* explained, they eventually found a more enthusiastic audience in the U.S. Congress. At first, Vadym Glamazdin, who worked for Ukraine's national energy company, Naftogaz, had tried to lobby Trump administration officials. He couldn't even get them to answer his letters. Then Glamazdin went to Congress instead, working with a lobbyist to figure out, "What do the Russians need [to build Nordstream 2] that they don't have?" A think tank researcher stumbled on a hidden vulnerability. A Russian energy expert had admitted in an online forum that Russian ships would find it hard to lay the pipelines for Nord Stream 2.

The Ukrainians had found their choke point. They could propose specific actions to U.S. senators who not only detested Gazprom but wanted to help U.S. energy companies. Thanks to the "fracking" revolution, U.S. natural gas output had grown by nearly 70 percent, making the United States the biggest gas producer in the world. Ted Cruz, like Donald Trump, mixed fawning admiration of Russia's purported cultural virility with hostile skepticism toward Europe's Russia policy. He also represented Texas, a gas-producing state. Cruz loved Glamazdin's ideas and started building a political coalition to stop Russia from building more pipelines to Europe. He wanted Europe to buy U.S.-produced "freedom gas," which would be chilled, liquified, and shipped across the Atlantic in tankers.

By the time that Cruz got involved, the pipeline was nearly built. However, the last few miles of the undersea pipeline had to traverse a basin near the Danish coast, where tons of chemical and conventional munitions had been dumped during World War II and the Cold War.

That meant that the pipeline had to be very carefully positioned. All-seas, a Swiss-Dutch engineering company, had developed proprietary technology that allowed its ship to lay three to five kilometers (between two and three miles) of pipeline a day, even under these dangerous conditions.

Cruz and his colleagues targeted Allseas in draft legislation, which was incorporated into the U.S. 2020 National Defense Authorization Act, calling on the U.S. State and Treasury Departments to identify any "vessels that engage in pipe-laying at depths of 100 feet or more below sea level for the construction of the Nord Stream 2 pipeline project." As Cruz and Senator Ron Johnson gleefully told Allseas' CEO, Edward Heerema, any firm found to be violating the law could be subject to "crushing and potentially fatal legal and economic sanctions." Allseas quickly got the message and sent its ship home. Cruz and his Senate colleagues moved on to other targets, including insurance firms, the pipeline's certifier, and the employees of the German port of Mukran, which was supplying the pipes.

Even those who were hostile to Nord Stream 2 thought that U.S. politicians were overstepping by threatening similarly "crushing legal and economic sanctions" against port stevedores in a struggling eastern German town. While Merkel's response was characteristically understated, saying, "We do not approve of this practice of extraterritorial sanctions," the Green Party's foreign policy spokesperson described the letter as an "economic declaration of war" and wanted German companies to be protected from the "Wild West methods of Washington." Heiko Maas proclaimed Germany's belief that "European energy policy is decided in Europe, not the US," neglecting to mention that the project had been designed precisely to avoid European oversight. He furthermore warned that "a strategy of burned bridges" would push Russia into China's arms.

American greed and threats may have been counterproductive.

Brantner had opposed Nord Stream 2 "long before Trump decided that he didn't like the project" because it didn't make sense in terms of "our climate objectives . . . and our European ambitions and solidarity." Brantner told us that "it was quite tragic that Trump came out so forcefully against Nord Stream, too. Because then we were cornered . . . 'oh, you're just with Trump.' And you just want to have his liquefied gas. And I think, . . . it would have been easier to win the arguments against NS2 had not Trump become so forcefully against it."

After Trump lost power, the Biden administration still worried about Russian gas, but it worried about relations with its allies, too. Tony Blinken, who had written so many years ago about European energy politics, was no longer a young Harvard prodigy. Now, he had been confirmed as Biden's secretary of state. Despite continued pressure from Cruz, who held up confirmation hearings for the director of the CIA and other key officials, the United States agreed to put the Nord Stream sanctions on ice in return for a German promise of $175 million in green technology aid to Ukraine and an agreement to punish Russia if it tried to weaponize the pipeline against Ukraine or Europe.

The Nord Stream 2 pipeline was completed in September 2021, but its final regulatory approval was delayed by German officials. Merkel was retiring from politics, and her party, the Christian Democrats, lost power in Germany's elections. The new government was led by the Social Democrats, but it also included the Greens, as well as the smaller pro-market Free Democratic Party.

Green ministers in the new government described the pipeline as a "geopolitical mistake" and warned that the pipeline might never carry gas if Russia escalated hostilities in Ukraine. Such statements fed Russian worries that Germany and the EU would prevent Nord Stream 2's completion.

Russia had already begun to weaponize its gas supplies in the summer, stopping Germany from fully refilling its gas reservoirs after an unusually cold winter. Russia's state-owned news agency spelled out the implied message, for those too obtuse to understand it. "During the assessment of any move by the corporation on the European market one should always bear in mind one crucial fact: Gazprom must finish construction of the Nord Stream 2 pipeline." Gazprom would withhold its supplies to "accustom" Western partners to the unfortunate reality that their energy security depended on Russian cooperation.

Even as Russia moved toward invading Ukraine, many German politicians clung to their delusions. Social Democrat chancellor Olaf Scholz warned that Germany would punish Russia, but he persistently declined to say whether he would cut off Nord Stream 2, while his defense minister suggested "we should not drag [Nord Stream 2] into this conflict." Leaked internal government documents said that Germany wanted an energy exemption from any sanctions against Russia.

The United States insisted otherwise. At a summit, President Biden threatened that "if Russia invades . . . there will be no longer Nord Stream 2. We will bring an end to it." A few days later, the Green economics minister, Robert Habeck, reiterated that Nord Stream 2 would not be approved if Russia invaded Ukraine, saying that "[t]hese days, energy policy is always geopolitical." Hours after Russia invaded, Habeck announced that he was halting the certification of Nord Stream 2, putting the project into deep freeze.

We don't know what would have happened to these pipelines if Russia hadn't invaded Ukraine. But they—and Europe's relationship to Russia—might still have been in trouble.

A diplomat with decades of experience in European energy politics told us that the EU hadn't really worried in previous confrontations that Russia would cut off the gas supply. After all, Russia could expect decades of continuing profits from its relationship with Europe. But by 2022, this relationship was on the verge of breaking down, even without the threat of war.

The EU had initiated an extraordinarily ambitious plan to move toward a post-carbon economy. If it succeeded, Europe would no longer have much need for Russian fossil fuels. In the diplomat's description, Europe's peace through trade with Russia depended on a "repeated game," in which Europe had a long-term interest in buying gas and Russia had a long-term interest in selling it. Now that seemed set to unravel.

That was why Russia had insisted on completing Nord Stream 2. Russia was desperate to lock Europe in, hoping that immediate business needs would beat vague aspirations to do something about long-term climate change. It was too much to claim that the Ukraine invasion was "the first Climate War," as this diplomat did. Putin's motivations went far beyond energy. He wrote long and delusional screeds about a greater Russia that would include Ukraine and saw Ukraine's faltering integration into Western Europe as a threat to his own power. If Ukraine succeeded in becoming a successful democracy, Russians might start asking questions about their own ruler.

But even if climate change didn't start the war, it made it cheaper and easier for Russia to deploy gas as a weapon. If Europe was moving away from gas and coal anyway, why not weaponize gas supplies while it was still vulnerable? There was no longer any indefinite long-term stream of future profits that might be endangered. The chain of relations that produced peace through interdependence had been broken, whether Europe realized it or not.

And who knew: perhaps the Europeans would give in when they were forced to realize how much they depended on Russian gas. The old consensus was gone. No one could believe anymore that Russian gas was a merely commercial solution to Europe's energy needs. The question was who would win. Could the Greens' imagined future—in which Europe no longer depended on fossil fuel autocracies—prevail? Or would Europe be forced to concede its dependence and fall further under Russia's influence, as Putin clearly hoped?

———————

In the days after Russia's invasion, the answers to these troubling questions were still unclear. At first, it seemed too late to do anything. Pundits all assumed that Russia was going to win the war. Ukrainian resistance would collapse, and Russian tanks would roll into Kiev. Europe's economic response would be a sideshow at best and a debacle at worst. But Ukraine held on, and Europe and America's economic response was far more comprehensive than anyone expected. That was in part perversely thanks to Trump, who had woken Europe from its dreams four years before, not with a kiss but with a blow.

Before war was declared, U.S. secretary of state Tony Blinken had warned that the United States would deploy a "range of high-impact economic measures that we have refrained from using in the past," and he praised the solidarity of America's allies. Yet it wasn't certain how far that solidarity went. A leading financial newspaper, *Handelsblatt*, reported that the German government had refused to countenance cutting Russia out of SWIFT.

On February 24, 2022, when over a hundred thousand Russian troops invaded Ukraine, the EU had to decide whether it was serious about geopolitics. It didn't have troops, but it did have economic power. Would the EU apply real sanctions? If Germany didn't lead, the rest of the EU was unlikely to follow. EU sanctions required the unanimous support of all twenty-seven members. As one anonymous official said before the invasion, the risk was an outcome that is "not the highest common denominator but the lowest in terms of what a member state can stomach."

It turned out that the United States had been secretly working together with the EU to coordinate possible sanctions since November. As a State Department official later told the *Financial Times*, top U.S. officials spent "an average of 10 to 15 hours a week on secure calls or video conferences with the E.U." The Commission played a crucial coordinating role, working back and forth between the United States and the national capitals of Europe, slowly and painfully creating agreement over what to do. When the sanctions were announced, the United States was unusually willing to allow Europe to take the lead, repeatedly waiting for the Europeans to announce what they were doing before it followed suit.

That was why von der Leyen's March speech was historic. The sanctions were far more sweeping than any that the EU had ever contemplated before. Germany's willingness to "sacrifice" Nord Stream 2 meant that other member states had to step up, too. There wasn't the usual horse trading over concessions. When Italy said that it wouldn't veto a decision to use SWIFT, Germany, too, abandoned its objections. Measures that had seemed wildly controversial only a few weeks prior to the invasion were rapidly adopted, only to be eclipsed by even more extreme seeming punishments.

At times, Europe and the United States seemed almost to be competing to see who could designate Russian banks and oligarchs the fastest. Roman Abramovich, a Putin confidante who made a $12 billion fortune during Russia's transition from Communism, was forced to sell his ownership of the British soccer club Chelsea. Igor Sechin, the owner of Rosneft, had sent his eighty-eight-meter yacht, the *Amore Vero* (True Love), to the French harbor of La Ciotat for repairs in January. On March 2 its crew tried to flee, "taking steps to sail off urgently, without the repairs." The yacht was seized. In May,

Italian authorities seized a yacht that allegedly belonged to Putin himself.

Some of the more moderate sanctions had been foreseen. But no one expected the most radical measure, a comprehensive attack on Russia's central bank reserves, which was outlined, negotiated, and implemented in just seventy-two hours. Russia's Central Bank had spent the last decade amassing some $600 billion in reserves to protect itself from U.S. sanctions. When the EU and United States took action, the bank suddenly and unexpectedly found itself unable to access much of its money.

Apart from some gold bullion, these reserves were mostly denominated in dollars, euros, and sterling. They didn't exist physically—just as entries in the ledgers of other central banks and international institutions like the Bank for International Settlements. That allowed the United States and EU to block access to them, provided they acted fast enough. Again, von der Leyen's staff at the Commission played a crucial role. Bjoern Siebert, her chef de cabinet (principal deputy), hashed out the details of how to prevent Russian access to its money in long encrypted calls with Treasury Secretary Janet Yellen, former European Central Bank president Mario Draghi, and other European officials, hurrying to get the details right before the markets opened on Monday.

European politicians trumpeted that Europe had finally become a geopolitical force. Josep Borrell, who had succeeded Mogherini and Ashton, proclaimed in May 2022 that "this is the moment at which the European Union behaves like a geopolitical actor . . . using the language of power." At the same event, Alex Stubb, the former prime minister of Finland, spoke of how the EU had learned to act speedily and decisively: "[Q]uite quickly, the European Union moved from a . . . regulatory superpower to an actor. . . . It was an actor in the euro crisis, but it took a few years. It was an actor in Covid, but it took a few months. When the war came, it actually took only a few days." Now, "with the leadership of Josep and Ursula von der Leyen . . . the Commission today is a geopolitical Commission, just like they promised [it] would be."

The heady excitement of von der Leyen's speech didn't last long. Geopolitical blitzkrieg quickly degenerated into the unrelenting grind of trench warfare, as the EU and Commission struggled to implement the measures that they had agreed in haste. The Commission still kept negotiating for new sanctions, but the more that Europe acted against Russia, the more obvious its reliance on U.S. power and its vulnerabilities to global trade became.

Europe still couldn't take charge of its own story. Europeans didn't worry that Biden would turn their dependency on U.S. power into a weapon against them. But that dependency hadn't gone away. It became ever more obvious as the EU tried to wage economic war against Russia.

The EU was poorly equipped for this kind of conflict. It had only just begun thinking about economic coercion and using adversaries' weaknesses against them. The EU's member states needed U.S. intelligence to implement sanctions. They didn't know who owned which bank account, and which ships were trying to evade controls. The more that the EU sought to build its own sources of power and authority, the more it realized that it needed what the United States had: information, institutions, technical expertise, and power over global markets. In a nod to these limits, former Danish prime minister and former NATO Secretary-General Anders Fogh Rasmussen suggested that protection from economic coercion be added to the list of NATO security guarantees, "to produce the same deterrence and solidarity in the economic realm among democracies that NATO produces in the security realm." Europe could help the United States but it still couldn't stand on its own.

The Commission's financial services chief, Mairead McGuinness, told the *Financial Times* that she was open to creating an EU OFAC that could oversee sanctions and coordinate policy among the member states. As she euphemistically described the problem, "In some countries there's a strong infrastructure on sanctions implementation and others not so much." Chancellor Scholz conceded that Europe "simply can no longer afford national vetoes" in foreign policy "if we want to be heard in a world of competing major powers." But other European countries didn't want to give up their right to block foreign policy measures that they didn't like.

Even if Europe built up the institutions, others could still use its dependencies against it. Politicians quietly worried about what might happen in America's 2024 elections. As one European told us, borrowing a term from the Arnold Schwarzenegger Terminator movies, a second Trump administration would be "T2": far more powerful, lethal, and sophisticated than the original. If Trump or someone like him won, Europe would have to adapt to a world suddenly turned chilly and bleak again.

Russia hoped it could threaten Europe with a cold and bitter winter. In summer 2022, Russia shut down the Nord Stream 1 pipeline for "maintenance." Southern European countries, which didn't need Nord Stream and had endured endless lectures on debt during the 2010–2012 European economic crisis, were impatient with German calls for solidarity. Spain's minister of energy, Teresa Ribera, remarked pointedly that "contrary to other countries, Spain hasn't been living beyond its means in energy terms."

Russia wanted to worsen these tensions. In a July 2022 televised address, Putin argued that sanctions hurt the countries imposing them more than they hurt Russia, and that there would be "catastrophic" consequences if the United States and Europe pressed further. He clearly hoped that the economic trauma of a gas embargo would fracture the coalition of countries ranged against him. When Hungary's foreign minister visited Russia to press for peace and beg for gas, Russia's minister of foreign affairs, Sergey Lavrov, congratulated him. Lavrov claimed that a "battle is ongoing. The European bureaucracy wants to subjugate all and everyone, the national governments. It wants to dictate conditions and to buy out any dissent."

There were opportunities as well as dangers. The Greens hoped that the crisis might further accelerate the shift to a post-carbon economy. The Commission argued that the best response to Russian coercion was a "massive scaling up and speeding up of renewable energy," easing regulations that had slowed the construction of solar facilities and wind farms. These changes and investments would not just protect European security but mitigate climate change, too.

A different Europe might be possible, one whose alternative to war was not free trade and open markets but green energy and self-sufficiency. Even before the war, Europe had begun to impose tariffs on high carbon intensity products like steel and cement. Now the European Commission wanted the authority to use trade sanctions against countries that failed to implement their commitments under the Paris Agreement. That might change Europe's relationship with the Biden administration, which had begun to view climate change as a national security threat. As the financial commentator Edoardo Saravalle proposed, the EU might use "green sanctions" to target activities that increased global warming.

But such changes would take years, and Europe first had to somehow survive through a winter without warmth. Habeck started bringing coal plants back online, despite the Green Party's long-standing resistance to fossil fuels. He delayed the shutdown of nuclear power plants, enraging protesters and many of his own voters. Once, the

Greens had coalesced around their opposition to nuclear power. Now, their leaders wanted to keep nuclear power plants in operation because the alternative was so much worse.

Even if Europe surmounted its problems with Russia, it would have to start thinking about China, too. Big companies like Volkswagen could manage being cut off from Russia, but they panicked at any suggestion that they might have to do without access to Chinese markets. Germany's Green foreign minister, Annalena Baerbock, warned business that "interdependence also involves risks" and called for Germany to reexamine its "business first mantra" with China. But the climate transition that she and her colleagues wanted would be far harder—perhaps even impossible—if it couldn't import Chinese solar panels and batteries.

These tensions would surely grow as the United States and China drew farther apart. If it wanted to please the United States, Europe would have to deny China access to the sophisticated goods and machines that its government and business leaders desperately wanted, incurring the risk of retaliation. But if Europe grew closer to China, it would inevitably antagonize the United States.

Von der Leyen's vice president, Margrethe Vestager, was blunt in explaining how Europe had created this dilemma for itself. As she put it, "[W]e have had a hard awakening into the era of weaponized interdependence." Some said Europe was naïve, but Vestager believed that "we were just greedy." She and other Europeans "now [saw] the stark limits of a production model based on cheap Russian energy and cheap Chinese labor" and "must take the lessons learned."

Those lessons would not be easy. Could Europe find unity around shared security rather than open markets? Might the internal tensions between France and Germany, big member states and small ones, northern and southern Europe, or eastern versus western, widen into fractures under these new stresses? And how might China and other outsiders respond to Europe's efforts to transform itself into a geopolitical power?

Once upon a time, Europe had dreamed it could enjoy the friendship of its protector and trade with everyone else, all at once, while staying blessedly protected from harm. It had finally fully awoken, cold and alone, on a bare hillside in winter. There wasn't going to be any easy happy ending.

5

HOOK'S CAPTAIN

On August 26, 2019, an Indian oil tanker captain got a surprising email. It promised him several million dollars if he did just one simple thing. The message wasn't written by a scammer pretending to be an exiled Russian oligarch, who needed just a couple of small details about the captain's bank account. As the *Financial Times'* Demetri Sevastopulo discovered, it came from the State Department's point person on Iran, Brian Hook.

Hook and his colleagues in the Trump administration thought that the Iran sanctions were not being properly enforced, allowing Iran to continue selling its oil on global markets. Taking matters into their own hands, Hook and his team had started "mapping out . . . the pressure points." One target was shipping. Iran had to transport oil to its customers, which often required it to work with non-Iranian shipping companies. If U.S. sanctions stopped these companies from getting insurance, for example, liability risks might stop their tankers from docking at ports. Any ports that allowed tankers with Iranian oil to dock could themselves be sanctioned. By mapping out the oil transportation industry and attacking the weak links, Hook believed that the United States could squeeze Iran more effectively.

Hook had discovered another pressure point, the oil tanker captains. His email promised that the captain would get his millions if he only steered the tanker to a port where it could be impounded. The email included a State Department phone number that the captain could call to check if he was worried it was a scam.

Hook quickly followed up with a second, more threatening message, informing the captain, "With this money you can have any life you wish and be well-off in old age" but "If you choose not to take this easy path, life will be much harder for you." If the captain refused Hook's offer, the United States would sanction him personally, overturning his life and profession. If he accepted, he would get millions of dollars, but at what cost? Iran's government is notoriously unforgiving of those who betray it (its agents regularly assassinate dissidents abroad). The captain and his loved ones might not enjoy their newfound wealth for long. For days, the tanker circled in the ocean as the captain pondered his choices. Finally, when he didn't respond, Hook decided for him, contacting him again to tell him that he was designated under U.S sanctions laws.

The captain's dilemma was the dilemma of global business in miniature. Industry had spent decades building international markets in the name of efficiency and profit. The U.S. government had transformed these economic networks into chains and shackles. As America's allies and adversaries try to protect themselves or build empires of their own, business leaders are being conscripted into these new battles.

This creates a whole new kind of political risk for business. The networks that facilitate global commerce—information, production, and money—have themselves become a source of corporate vulnerability. As other governments discover the pressure points, it's hard for business to stay neutral. Companies have been penned into ever narrower zones of choice, navigating the choppy waters between contending leviathans, each of which could smash them with a casual slap of its tail.

As clashing powers—the United States, China, Europe, and even Russia—press companies into their service, businesses struggle to respond. Some firms choose one side, some the other. Some hesitate, circling in the sea until their decisions are forcibly made for them, while others, like Walter Wriston decades before, plot voyages into uncharted waters, hoping to build piratical realms beyond the reach of sovereigns. For decades, businesses thought that political risk meant developing countries rewriting the rules or seizing their assets. Now, they are coming to understand that powerful, wealthy countries present the greatest risks. Those that fail to realize this may capsize.

In 2001, Brad Smith was appointed general counsel at Microsoft after pitching the company's board with a PowerPoint deck that had just a single slide with a single phrase: "It's time to make peace." Over the next two decades, Smith and Microsoft discovered the tangle of complexities lurking behind that simple slogan.

Microsoft had encountered the power of government far earlier than its competitors a few hundred miles to the south, in Silicon Valley. In the 1990s, U.S. Department of Justice antitrust enforcers had decided that Microsoft had become too powerful and proposed breaking it up into three competing companies. Microsoft narrowly escaped this forcible dismemberment but realized that it needed to change course, and quickly.

That was why Smith had crafted his slide. Microsoft's founder, Bill Gates, had once prided himself "on how little time we spent talking to people in the federal government." Now, Microsoft's continued survival depended on making peace with a hostile power. It had to discover how to work with regulators rather than against them. Over the following decades, Smith (who eventually became Microsoft's president as well as general counsel) succeeded in turning Microsoft from a notorious scofflaw into a company that prospered by working together with the government. The threat of breakup receded into historical memory.

This took time, work, and money. Microsoft gradually accumulated the diplomatic capacities of a small nation. It set up government relations teams everywhere it did serious business, using Smith's charm and his bosses' clout to build close relationships with government officials. Microsoft used these relationships to its own advantage and the disadvantage of competitors like Google. Very often, Microsoft endorsed greater government regulation of technology, so long as the technology belonged to Microsoft's enemies. Very often, it succeeded.

Like a minor government, Microsoft had to deploy influence while maintaining neutrality. What could it do when the great powers that shaped its world—the United States, EU, and China—disagreed, demanding that Microsoft did different and incompatible things? Where possible, Microsoft finessed the ambiguities, seeking to persuade all sides that it was acting as they wanted. When that didn't work, it could try to persuade the powers to resolve their disputes. Sometimes, the best way for Microsoft to make peace with regulators was to help them make peace with each other.

As the United States reinvented surveillance after September 11, 2001, Microsoft had to call on these diplomatic skills to navigate the treacherous straits of the EU-U.S. relationship, all clashing rocks on one side, all grasping tentacles on the other. The EU publicly required that multinationals like Microsoft respect the privacy rights of its citizens, even if it sometimes preferred not to know what the NSA was actually up to. The United States quietly insisted that U.S. businesses provide it with sensitive data, whether the Europeans liked it or not. Microsoft's privacy policy became increasingly precarious as some parts of Microsoft weren't allowed to know what other parts were doing. It wasn't surprising that the whole thing eventually fell apart.

In December 2014, the privacy activist Casper Bowden gave a talk in Hamburg, to tell a big crowd why Microsoft had effectively fired him. Bowden was speaking on the main stage of the annual conference of the Chaos Computer Club, a legendary hacker collective that had somehow grown into an unruly organization, which regularly attracted ten thousand attendees to its meetings.

Bowden had excellent reason to feel pleased with himself. After years of desperately trying to get people to listen to him, he finally had an audience. Long before most other people, he had figured out that the United States was able to listen to nearly everything that Europeans were saying to one another. He just hadn't been able to get anyone to care.

Before he had become Microsoft's chief privacy adviser, Bowden had been a privacy activist and independent expert, providing advice on technology issues to the U.K. Labour Party. Activism wasn't much of a livelihood—as one of Bowden's comrades described it to us, the U.K. privacy community consisted of a few people arguing with each other in a pub. Bowden was very good at what he did, dissecting the details of privacy invasive technology and regulations with forensic rigor. Still, he was prickly, and he got into fights too easily and too often. His hot temper was forgiven by his friends. They knew that his frustrations were inseparable from his commitments.

That was why they were bemused when he first joined Microsoft in 2002. He just didn't seem the type. Bowden's new job involved telling Microsoft's "National Technology Officers"—its informal ambassadors to governments and politicians around the world—how to think about privacy issues. But he was a dubious fit with the corporate culture of his new employer. After he was hired, Bowden would still yell at his activist friends that they weren't "going hard enough" after Microsoft on privacy.

As he became more worried about the American government, he found it increasingly difficult to work for an American company.

Onstage in Hamburg, Bowden told his audience that he hadn't had access to secret company information. Instead, he had "deduced" the existence of a massive American surveillance apparatus "from open sources and deciding to read the American laws." As European governments and businesses turned to the cloud, they had put all their data on servers that were run by U.S. companies like Microsoft, often on U.S. national territory. That potentially provided the U.S. government with legal access.

According to Bowden, the problem came to a head when he addressed an internal meeting on cloud computing in 2011. He described how he told Microsoft's national ambassadors, "If you sell Microsoft cloud computing to your own governments . . . the NSA can conduct unlimited mass surveillance on that data." Microsoft wanted to seem neutral to its customers, but it was enabling the United States to paw through their most sensitive information. As Bowden described it, his talk was greeted with dead silence. When the meeting broke for coffee, he was threatened with being fired. Microsoft let Bowden go without cause two months afterward. Years later, when Microsoft described its willingness to defend "fundamental privacy rights," Bowden recalled how he had been "fired" and dismissed Smith's "posturing" as "nauseating cynicism."

Bowden's next couple of years were spent traveling, trying to get foundations, activists, and politicians to pay attention to U.S. surveillance. No one wanted to listen. Just before the Snowden revelations broke in the summer of 2013, Bowden tried to persuade businesses to take the problem seriously. As he recounted it, "Basically, they laughed at me." When the Snowden files were made public, they showed that Bowden had been mostly right. U.S. intelligence agencies were indeed able to demand data from U.S. companies, with no real protections for the privacy of European citizens.

Bowden was obsessed with legal and technical details and willing to ask the awkward questions that may have finally cost him his job. Those traits helped him piece together a story that was hiding in plain sight, but they also hampered him from convincing others of its importance. He tried to change the world through angry tweets and interminable Power-Point presentations bristling with abstruse legal terminology.

Yet had he spoken with the tongues of angels, he would still have had a difficult sell. Businesses like Microsoft didn't want to open up the mess to public inspection. Even if they had wanted to, they were forbidden under U.S. law. Nor were Microsoft's European government customers going to make it confront the truth, unless they were forced to. Europe's economy depended on U.S. information companies. Nearly everyone who knew anything had strong self-interested reasons to look away.

Microsoft, Google, Amazon, and their competitors only changed their minds when Edward Snowden forced the debate by providing journalists with his trove of secrets. It was far harder to pretend that nothing was happening after Snowden revealed the vast extent of U.S. surveillance. Bowden still lacked the rhetorical skills to get attention for his cause. He died of cancer in 2015, vindicated but, as ever, disappointed in the world.

Others took up the fight. Max Schrems, a charismatic young Austrian lawyer and privacy activist, realized that the Snowden revelations might allow him to drive a wedge between Europe and the United States. In October 2015 he persuaded Europe's highest court to strike down the main EU-U.S. agreement that allowed businesses like Facebook to transfer personal data across the Atlantic, on the grounds that it was breaching EU privacy law and handing this data to U.S. surveillance agencies.

This had potentially catastrophic consequences for U.S. e-commerce firms, which stored their European users' data on U.S.-based servers.

Eric Schmidt, the CEO of Google's holding company, feared that the court's decision might break the global Internet, destroying "one of the greatest achievements of humanity." Brad Smith seemed less alarmed, at least in public. Even if the "old legal system [had] collapsed" along with the agreement, its foundations had crumbled away a long time before. Cloud computing had gone global. It was time for the law to catch up.

Later, however, Smith admitted that "all hell broke loose" when the court issued its judgment. Smith and other senior Microsoft officials had good reason to worry about the Snowden revelations. As Bowden suspected, Microsoft was indeed giving the U.S. government information on foreign nationals. Between 2011 and 2021—the only years for which there is public data—the U.S. government used its national intelligence powers to demand that Microsoft give it information on anywhere between 24,000 and 39,000 user accounts a year. But Microsoft couldn't explain this to the public without breaking U.S. law. The Department of Justice had decided that even the fact that Microsoft was handing over the data was classified.

When Edward Snowden released his files, Smith discovered that things were even worse than he had thought. Strong circumstantial evidence indicated that the NSA was working with GCHQ, its British counterpart, to tap into Microsoft fiber-optic cables that intersected in the United Kingdom. Apparently, the United States was grabbing data from Microsoft without any warrant, on the theory that the Fourth Amendment didn't hold outside America's borders.

Looking back years later, Smith said that the Snowden revelations helped create "a chasm between governments and the tech sector to this day. Governments serve constituents who live in a defined geography, such as a state or nation. But tech has gone global, and we have customers virtually everywhere."

The global commercial peace that had existed before Snowden depended on everyone pretending that the chasm wasn't there. Now that everyone knew that everyone knew, Smith and other business leaders had to re-create peace in a world of governments and national territories.

Although Smith did not explicitly say so, the biggest problem was the United States. Years before, NSA director Michael Hayden and his colleagues had inscribed an invisible boundary, separating the United States of America, where government was bound by laws and citizen rights, from a lawless outside world where the NSA could grab information it thought was in America's interests. Now, not just foreign terrorists but American multinationals found that they fell outside the zone of protection.

And as Microsoft's business evolved into providing cloud services, it found that ever more of its business was on the wrong side of the line. Microsoft was no longer a purveyor of office software, sold on floppy disks or CD-ROMs and shipped across the globe. Its business services were bundled together with virtual access and storage, allowing non-U.S. governments, businesses, and organizations to access a comprehensive suite of applications that integrated everything they did. By December 2021, Microsoft's cloud services were earning some $22 billion in quarterly sales, accounting for almost half of the firm's total revenue.

Yet even if the cloud seemed to exist nowhere and everywhere at once, U.S. companies like Microsoft were bound by U.S. law. American authorities demanded data on foreigners, threatening harsh penalties for American companies that did not comply, while ordering them to keep their compliance secret. These authorities also believed themselves entitled to seize industrial quantities of data from these companies overseas, without warrant and without informing the businesses, let alone the users, of what was happening. That made life nearly impossible for Microsoft and its competitors. How could foreign governments and foreign businesses trust Microsoft to keep their data private in the future?

Microsoft's first response, like Google's, was to try to shield itself against its home government's snooping. Despite their rivalry, both companies urgently needed to press back against U.S. government surveillance to protect their overseas business. They began to encrypt the torrents of information that rushed along cables between their data centers, making it far harder for the NSA to tap it.

When Schrems's court action succeeded in 2015, Smith tried to turn it into an opening for a more lasting and lawful peace. He argued that the rights of the constituents who elected Europe's and America's governments overlapped with their needs as customers of cloud services. Constituents reasonably wanted their privacy rights and their civil liberties to be protected, no matter where their data was. The obvious solution was for governments to agree that citizens' rights should travel with their data. European citizens would have the rights they were guaranteed under European law even if their data was stored in the United States. The converse would be true for Americans' data if it was stored in Europe. If the U.S. government wanted information on European citizens, it would have to ask European governments, and vice versa.

This proposed peace treaty didn't suit U.S. national security agencies at all. When Europe and the United States started to negotiate a new arrangement, U.S. intelligence agencies grudgingly agreed to voluntary limits on intelligence gathering and a U.S. official to deal with European complaints (the European Court of Justice found this inadequate and eventually struck down the new deal, too). They didn't want to be limited by any international agreements, and their European counterparts (who survived on the scraps of U.S. intelligence) quietly concurred. National security surveillance remained a lawless world, a war of all against all.

Government surveillance started slowly tipping over into sabotage. In 2010, researchers noticed that a new "worm" (a program capable of spreading across networks), which they called Stuxnet, was infecting machines around the world. It turned out that a joint U.S.-Israeli hacking project, aimed at slowing down Iran's nuclear program, had gone feral, infecting computer systems it was never supposed to touch.

Obama had hesitated to authorize the program, fearing it would create a dangerous precedent. Whether because of the precedent, or more likely because they were going to do it anyway, other countries, including China, Russia, and North Korea, started attacking their enemies' computer systems, and sometimes their friends', too. Government-sponsored hacking blurred at its edges into a vigorous underground criminal economy, where hackers hired themselves and their software out to steal money, and where people's financial information was bought and sold as a mass commodity. Russia reportedly offered carte blanche to criminal hackers attacking foreign systems, so long as they were prepared to help the government when asked. The United States demurred at such illegality, but it was quietly willing to pay top dollar on the gray market for new and undocumented hacking techniques. After North Korea was sanctioned, it used cyberattacks to raise hard currency, including the notorious SWIFT heist and the WannaCry ransomware (which briefly forced TSMC to close down its plants).

Businesses like Microsoft found themselves in a new world of trouble. They weren't just stranded between clashing legal obligations. They had become easy targets in a universal war. As Smith told the RSA Conference in 2017, cyberspace was "the new battlefield," but it was a "different kind of battlefield," which was "owned and operated by the private sector." When Sony made an unflattering movie about North Korea's leader, government-backed hackers retaliated by

breaking into Sony's servers and dumping a treasure trove of commercially sensitive information onto the Internet. Other companies were
bombarded with increasingly sophisticated attacks (some of them, like
WannaCry, based on leaked NSA tools and techniques).

Government-backed hackers from Russia sometimes respected
their own national boundaries (their programs might be designed not
to infect systems with Cyrillic alphabets), but they certainly didn't
respect the lines the United States had drawn. Instead, they took the
war to the world economy. When Russian military intelligence started
invading Microsoft's platform for juicy information on its customers,
Microsoft's leaders hesitated over what to say in public. They feared that
Russia "would retaliate against [their] business interests and employees." Indeed, after Microsoft indirectly referred to the hacking at an
open event, Russia demanded that a Microsoft employee who needed
a visa go to the Russian embassy, two thousand miles away, for an
interview. The employee got his visa without any fuss but was handed
an envelope containing two documents indicating Russia's indignant
denial and displeasure. It was to be hand-delivered to Microsoft executives in Redmond to ensure they got the message.

Smith and other leaders didn't want to face off against governments, but Microsoft was buffeted back and forth between U.S. officials
who were angry that Microsoft wasn't helping America's cause and foreigners who saw Microsoft as a U.S. government pawn. A Trump adviser
told Smith that since Microsoft was an "American company," it should
"agree to help the U.S. government spy on people in other countries."
How those other countries might retaliate was presumably Microsoft's
problem. After the Snowden revelations, the Chinese government
banned government use of Windows. It eventually made Microsoft produce a special Chinese edition of Windows, in cooperation
with a government-owned technology group.

Microsoft desperately wanted all this to stop. Yet demilitarizing the battlefield was far more difficult than soothing regulators. What was needed—as Smith saw it—was nothing less than a remaking of the global rules of war and peace.

That sounded ridiculously ambitious, but Smith and his colleagues were working from an established model. In an internal meeting, Smith mentioned that the International Committee of the Red Cross (ICRC) had brought governments together to create the Geneva Conventions, which protected civilians in times of war. His colleague, Dominic Carr, immediately responded that it might be time for a new Convention, under which governments would promise not to use cyberattacks against civilian targets. Microsoft was a private company—but the ICRC, too, had been a private organization. It had been able to persuade governments to change the laws of armed conflict. Why couldn't Microsoft do the same?

Microsoft decided that it wanted an international Convention declaring that cyberattacks against civilian targets were off-limits. That would fulfill a clear humanitarian aim in ways that suited Microsoft. Contrary to the Trump official's belief, Microsoft's fundamental commitment wasn't to America but to its customers and shareholders. Most of Microsoft's customers were civilian targets. So was Microsoft itself. When Smith publicly proposed a "Digital Geneva Convention," he argued that companies like Microsoft, which held the world's information, should become a "trusted and neutral Digital Switzerland." In return for immunity from attack from governments, they would commit not to help governments in their attacks.

The term "digital Switzerland" implied that tech companies were themselves a new kind of world-spanning country, even if they lacked territory of their own. That didn't go unnoticed. When Denmark's foreign minister remarked that tech companies had become "a nation of sorts," Smith half-demurred, but he argued that the analogy "underscored a key opportunity. If our companies are like nations, then we can forge our own international agreements." The technology sector needed to "come together as the ICRC did in 1949." Microsoft and its peers could provide an alternative to rising nationalism, protecting customers everywhere, and refusing to attack them anywhere, "regardless of the country from which we come," and "the government that may ask us to do so." Smith hoped that geopolitics would stop devouring technology, if only the technology sector was allowed to withdraw from geopolitics into the kind of strict neutrality that Switzerland had maintained when it declined to join either the Allies or Axis powers during World War II.

These sweeping proposals attracted some political interest, even if they didn't transform the world. Leaders including France's Macron and New Zealand's Jacinda Ardern signed on to a nonbinding "Paris Call for Trust and Security in Cyberspace." After consideration, the Biden administration signed on, too, in late 2021. Businesses—including Facebook, Dell, and Oracle—agreed to a Cybersecurity Tech Accord, although Amazon and Google declined involvement.

When Russia invaded Ukraine in 2022, governments like Switzerland rethought their neutrality, implementing new sanctions. Microsoft's understanding of peace changed, too. In 2015, Microsoft had pressed for the EU and United States to reach agreement over surveillance, so that companies like Microsoft could live in peace and sell to both. In 2017, it had wanted to transform the laws of war and peace, declaring the global technology sector to be neutral and off-limits. Now, Microsoft abandoned neutrality to take one side in a bloody war.

This new approach was described in two carefully authored blog posts by Smith and Tom Burt, Microsoft's vice president for customer security and trust. It was restated more bluntly by Smith in a remarkable keynote speech at Microsoft's 2022 Envision Conference in London.

Smith's presentation seemed to have been broadcast from a different world than two other headline speeches, which respectively described the U.K. economic landscape and touted new technologies to enable "seamless customer experiences." In his description, the new weapons of war moved "at the speed of light." Microsoft personnel sitting in Redmond, Washington, were manning Ukraine's front lines. The first "shell to be fired" in the war had been a Russian cyberweapon, FoxBlade, intended to destroy three hundred server systems across a dozen Ukrainian governmental and sectoral organizations. The security specialists in the Microsoft Threat Intelligence Center (MSTIC, pronounced "Mystic") had been the first to see it being deployed. With access to some twenty-four trillion daily signals from devices running Microsoft products globally, MSTIC had an extraordinary overview of cyberspace, helping it shield Ukraine against waves of attacks.

Smith returned to the idea of a digital Geneva Convention, under which technology companies would protect civilians, playing a "fundamentally defensive rather than offensive role." But instead of reaffirming neutrality, he explained that Microsoft had forged "a closer relationship with the Ukrainian government and the national security advisors and team there." Smith didn't mention that his colleague Tom Burt had contacted Anne Neuberger, Biden's deputy national security adviser for cybersecurity, who had asked him to share the code of Russia's malware with Estonia, Latvia, Lithuania, Poland, and other European governments. As the *New York Times* later described it, Microsoft "had begun playing the role that Ford Motor [Company] did in World War II, when the company converted automobile production lines to make Sherman tanks."

As the war accelerated, Microsoft did even more. When the Ukrainian government's servers came under attack, Microsoft moved sixteen out of seventeen ministries to the "cloud outside Ukraine." Smith compared Russia's cyberattacks to the World War II air raids of the Blitz, which had driven the U.K. government into deep underground bunkers. It was as if some alternative-world Switzerland had not simply abandoned its World War II neutrality but used miraculous technologies to transport

Winston Churchill's government into an impregnable castle in the sky, where it could manage the war and conduct its ordinary affairs above the altitudes traversed by Nazi bombers. The Digital Geneva Convention's aim of protecting "civilians and enterprises" was magically transformed into the mission of defending a country and sustaining its government in a "hybrid war."

Naturally, Microsoft declined to extend any similar courtesy to Russia, the aggressing power. Microsoft had suspended sales in Russia in March. It still provided support to hospitals, schools, children, the elderly, and companies trying to deliver pharmaceuticals to the public, but the Russian government was left to fend for itself.

Instead, Microsoft offerred to help hold Russia to account. Smith invoked the Nuremberg trials, where Nazis were prosecuted after World War II, pledging that Microsoft would make sure that "history can remember what happened here," providing its technology at no charge to identify shattered Ukrainian hospitals, schools, and water towers. He called on the Microsoft community to support NATO and work together to support Ukraine. In a follow-up report, he argued that the war pitted Russia, a "major cyber power," not just against an "alliance of countries" but "a coalition of countries, companies, and NGOs," all engaged in the collective defense of free expression and democracy.

When Smith had first become Microsoft's chief lawyer, he had argued that prudent business strategy required that the company make peace with governments. As governments began to weaponize markets, not just regulate them, Microsoft found it increasingly hard to keep professing neutrality. That led it to experiment with ever more ambitious attempts to remake the laws of war, and finally, to participate openly in a war against an aggressor. Smith boasted about how Microsoft's tools and software suites, created for business purposes, provided critical defensive advantages. The Ukraine conflict was a real-time marketing demonstration that Microsoft products were invaluable, and perhaps even indispensable. Smith claimed that even LinkedIn, Microsoft's professional networking platform, had become a military resource, allowing Microsoft security personnel to quickly find and contact the chief information officers for Ukrainian organizations that were about to be attacked.

―――――――――――――

LinkedIn wasn't only useful for wartime defense. Shortly before the Ukraine war began, the Taiwanese semiconductor giant TSMC put up a help wanted notice on the service: "As our business continues to grow globally in scale and complexity, we are looking for a Business Intelligence Analyst who is interested in translating geopolitical and economic changes to impact on IC [integrated circuit] industry supply chain."

The bland language belied the urgency of TSMC's plea. TSMC's leaders had reason to fear that geopolitics would devour their company.

TSMC had been founded as a bet on the globalized economy. Open markets and rapid communication allowed semiconductor companies to find their niche, specializing in one aspect of production rather than trying to do everything in-house. Companies like TSMC focused narrowly on the things they could do well, making sure they did them better than the competition. TSMC was a "pure play" fabrication (fab, for short) company, manufacturing semiconductors that were designed elsewhere. It could focus more easily on production improvements than integrated manufacturers such as Intel, squeezing out little innovations as well as big ones in regular increments.

In 1998, TSMC's founder and then CEO, Morris Chang, laid out TSMC's strategy in an internal document. He believed that if TSMC built deep relations with customers, learned what they wanted, and properly integrated sales and engineering, it would become the biggest silicon foundry in the world, more or less as a matter of course. To do this right, TSMC needed to solve two problems.

First, it needed to build trust with its customers, the technology companies that ordered specialized chips from TSMC. These companies competed furiously with each other—TSMC might make processor chips for many different phone manufacturers, each struggling to win or protect its own market share from the others. Each customer had to work closely with TSMC, providing highly sensitive information about their technological needs and business strategies to a company that also had close relationships with their most bitter adversaries. That was why Chang believed that TSMC had to credibly guarantee that it would keep their proprietary information secret.

TSMC would have to seem completely even-handed. Chang's strategy document mandated that if TSMC provided a special "one-time" deal to one of its customers, it would offer "similar deals" to the customer's direct competitors in the same field, to avoid any impression of favoritism. Such strategies allowed TSMC to become what the *Wall Street Journal* described as the "Switzerland of semiconductors," working impartially with competitors like NVIDIA and Qualcomm to build their chips.

Second, TSMC needed to tech up, catching up with its competitors' ability to produce sophisticated semiconductors, and eventually beating them. TSMC started by catering to niches that bigger competitors like Intel didn't care to compete in. It grew by combining its own know-how with the information it got from customers from around the world. That allowed it to enter new markets. Customers didn't just bring economies of scale, allowing TSMC to produce more cheaply. They brought economies of knowledge, providing TSMC with an unrivaled understanding of what companies needed and what they didn't, and where TSMC's increasingly formidable research budget ought to be spent.

Technical progress in the semiconductor industry involves building smaller architecture chips (measured notionally in nanometers) that need less electricity and have greater processing power. TSMC progressed until it was working at the cutting edge, where it dominated the production of high-end semiconductors. Its rivals had a hard time keeping up. Samsung, the one firm that Chang said he really feared, found it difficult to persuade key customers to trust it because it made phones and other products as well as chips. Its customers saw it not just as a supplier but as a potential rival. Intel—which didn't have the same deep customer relationships as TSMC—began to fall behind.

TSMC planned to start building 3-nanometer chips in 2023, and 2-nanometer production in 2025. Meanwhile, Intel struggled to produce 7-nanometer chips. Apple—one of Intel's biggest customers—had already turned away from Samsung in 2011, when Samsung began to compete with the iPhone. In 2020, Apple announced that its new Mac computers would use Apple-designed processors. Naturally, it would outsource production to TSMC. The veteran chipmaker AMD, which had spent decades nipping at Intel's heels, stopped building semiconductors altogether and started relying on TSMC instead.

By December 2020, an activist shareholder was demanding that Intel consider dumping its manufacturing operations to focus on design. As an industry analyst told the *Financial Times'* Kathrin Hille, the industry had become "incredibly dependent" on TSMC. Two decades before, there had been twenty foundries. Now, "the most cutting-edge stuff is sitting on a single campus in Taiwan."

The analyst's claim of a "single campus" was a slight exaggeration—but only slight. Even as TSMC worked with international customers, it remained an intensely local company. TSMC had been set up with the help of the Taiwanese government and was deeply integrated into Taiwan's economy and education system. It wasn't just that Taiwanese engineers were willing to work harder than their U.S. equivalents, and for less pay. It was that some aspects of innovation didn't travel very well. Taiwan's semiconductor industry was "centered around a small industrial park south of Taipei." As Dan Wang, an expert on Asian technology production, explained, manufacturing semiconductors depends on a deep accumulation of "process knowledge"—an intimate understanding of what works and what doesn't, which is difficult to explain to those who are not already embedded in the culture. While TSMC made sporadic efforts to build foundries elsewhere, none of them took deep root.

At first, that seemed less like a weakness than a strength. TSMC's Taiwanese home base helped find new customers as China began to develop its own technology industry. TSMC's carefully developed reputation for impartiality allowed it to work at least as easily with Chinese companies as with U.S. ones. After all, Chinese companies were closer geographically, culturally, and linguistically. TSMC built up a particularly close relationship with Huawei, which became its second-largest customer after Apple, accounting for 15 to 20 percent of its global revenue.

Yet as geopolitical tensions increased, TSMC's position became ever more difficult. The People's Republic of China saw Taiwan as part of its national territory and politicked to bring it back to the bosom of the motherland, whether through gentle persuasion or ruthless force. Just as TSMC played Switzerland in the technology sector, engaging with competing technology companies without committing to any, it played "Finland: a sometime friend to both feuding giants" as the United States and China started eyeing each other warily.

When the Trump administration turned the underground empire's weapons against Huawei, TSMC was collateral damage. U.S. rules restricted TSMC from exporting latest-generation chips to its second-biggest customer if they used or were made with U.S. intellectual property. The global chip shortage in 2020 meant that TSMC's earnings didn't suffer, again demonstrating the company's market dominance. But how would TSMC fare if China and Taiwan were reunited? What would the United States do if the world's most important manufacturer of advanced semiconductors was governed by its adversary?

In the 1990s, as semiconductor manufacture had gone global, the U.S. Department of Defense had followed suit. The U.S. military had an insatiable appetite for semiconductors. It increasingly relied on chips produced in the Asia-Pacific region, although it kept its most "trusted" supply relationships on U.S. territory. But as Taiwanese producers gradually became a key "part of an increasingly globalized US defense chip industrial base," the U.S. Department of Defense became increasingly nervous. When TSMC began to outdistance its competitors, the United States began to worry about how much U.S. national security systems depended on just one manufacturer, on one island, under the shadow of a threatened Chinese invasion.

TSMC's chairman, Mark Liu, argued that war was unlikely because the world economy depended on Taiwanese semiconductors. U.S. defense intellectuals were more pessimistic. In 2021, two of them wrote an article for the U.S. Army War College Quarterly, *Parameters*, advocating a "broken nest" strategy, under which the United States would destroy TSMC's facilities in the event of a Chinese incursion. They hoped that this threat would help deter China from invading Taiwan.

All of this was horribly uncomfortable for TSMC, especially as it realized that Biden, too, was worried about producing critical technology on an island claimed by China. The company that Chang founded had thrived so long as national security strategists paid no attention to its success. Now, it had become a global economic choke point that great powers wanted to use and deny to others. Every business wants to be economically irreplaceable. Few want to be so irreplaceable that their factories might be blown up in a preemptive strike.

Even worse, TSMC's competitors started to capitalize on its

political difficulties. Intel had hired a new CEO, Pat Gelsinger, after its disastrous failure to keep pace with TSMC's technology. Gelsinger quickly announced that Intel would start edging into TSMC's core business, providing foundry services for companies that designed their own semiconductors. He also started to talk pointedly about how dangerous it was for the United States to rely on a Taiwan-based company for its core technology, suggesting that America needed to secure its chip supplies domestically.

U.S. politicians had already started trying to bring semiconductor manufacturing home. The same day that Trump restricted TSMC from supplying Huawei, TSMC announced it was going to build a $12 billion fab in Arizona, which would make 5-nanometer semiconductors.

That made Gelsinger very unhappy. He wanted the United States to subsidize only companies with "deep American roots" and pointed out that TSMC was keeping its cutting-edge technologies at home in Taiwan. Gelsinger spent much of 2021 in meetings with officials in the United States and Europe, pressing them to support homegrown companies like Intel. As he put it in a public interview, "[W]here the fabs are is more important to the next couple of decades, than where the oil reserves are." His and others' efforts persuaded the United States and Europe to announce major legislation to subsidize domestic semiconductor production. But Western governments wanted to hedge their bets, too, offering money to companies like TSMC that had a technological edge over their competitors.

TSMC would likely have preferred not to play this game at all. A TSMC "insider" said that it had "decided to move forward with the plant [in Arizona] because the U.S. government implored us to do it." As Liu explained elsewhere, TSMC was only building the plant because of "political nudges on our customers." Liu himself believed that "semiconductor localization [in the United States] will not increase supply-chain resilience" and might even hurt it.

TSMC certainly had no principled objection to subsidies. It owed its existence to the largesse of the Taiwanese government. But this new game of targeted subsidies presented problems. Intel wanted geopolitics to reshape the market because it needed an edge against a competitor with better technology. For just that reason, TSMC wanted as little geopolitics as possible. The more that U.S. and European politicians focused on the dangers of locating production in Taiwan, the more likely they would help TSMC's competitors or demand that TSMC change where and how it made things.

The pandemic complicated all of this again. In 2020 and 2021, coronavirus combined with geopolitical tensions to hit semiconductor production. Complex supply chains broke down, as factories shut down to deal with surges in infection. Businesses cut back on their orders for chips because they expected consumers to pull back, only to face enormous shortages when demand remained robust. Huawei and other Chinese companies laid up huge stockpiles of semiconductors before U.S. sanctions hit, tying up production lines. All this generated massive shortages across the entire economy. Cars had become mobile computers with wheels. Every electronic device needed semiconductors. The unfortunately named "Chipageddon" meant that supply chains—and making sure that each country got what its economy needed—became part of the everyday political conversation.

Barely a month after Biden was sworn in as president, his administration ordered a hundred-day review of four critical supply chains: semiconductors, batteries, pharmaceuticals, and rare earth minerals. Biden told the public that "we've seen how a shortage of computer chips . . . has caused delays in production of automobiles that has resulted in reduced hours for American workers." Now, "we need to stop playing catch up after the supply-chain crisis hit . . . we need to prevent the supply chain crisis from hitting in the first place." His executive order called for "[m]ore resilient supply chains . . . facilitating greater domestic production, a range of supply, built-in redundancies, adequate stockpiles, safe and secure digital networks."

On March 15, 2021, the Department of Commerce's Bureau of Industry and Security (BIS) invited comments from the semiconductor industry. The hundred-day review called for the creation of a "data hub" in which the Department of Commerce would lead an "effort to bring together data from across the federal government . . . to track supply-and-demand disruptions and improve information sharing between the federal government and the private sector." The Biden administration announced that it was asking businesses like TSMC to "voluntarily share information about inventories, demand, and delivery dynamics" to help the administration "understand and quantify where bottlenecks may exist."

There was a big stick behind the soft-spoken request. As Biden's commerce secretary, Gina Raimondo, explained, "What I told [semi-conductor firms] is, 'I don't want to have to do anything compulsory but if they don't comply, then they'll leave me no choice.'" If firms like TSMC didn't provide the data, the Biden administration would invoke its powers under the Defense Production Act. Nor was the administration just demanding that TSMC provide information on its own activities. The data it wanted would allow it to peer into the intimate details of TSMC's customers' business.

Providing this information would endanger the trust relationship at the heart of TSMC's business model. How would its customers react if they knew it was sharing their information with the U.S. government? Chinese firms were particularly likely to be upset, but other companies, too, might worry.

TSMC's initial response was to play for time. The company emphasized that it had already taken "unprecedented actions," including its planned fab in Arizona, to address global semiconductor shortages. A week later, the company's chief lawyer, Sylvia Fang, made it clear that

TSMC didn't want to provide detailed information, reassuring customers that "we definitely will not leak our company's sensitive information, especially that related to customers" and that "customer trust is one of the key elements to our company's success." Ultimately, TSMC handed over a tranche of information, while publicly stating that its customer secrets were protected. It didn't publicly explain how it had managed to protect secrecy while providing the information that the United States demanded.

China's state media treated TSMC's acquiescence as a form of treachery. A *Global Times* editorial argued that "the data that TSMC and other chipmakers are required to provide will . . . seriously compromise the commercial interests and business secrets of mainland semiconductor industries." The United States didn't just want to identify supply chain bottlenecks. "It is crystal clear that obtaining the sensitive data may be just the beginning of the US wielding its hegemony stick in the semiconductor industry, and its ultimate goal is to take control of the advanced manufacturing capacity to revitalize its domestic semiconductor industry." Chinese academics warned that the data could "potentially help Washington impose sanctions on Chinese companies in a more precise way." Nonetheless, TSMC kept to its policy. Given its dependence on U.S. intellectual property, U.S. suppliers, and the U.S market, it had no other option.

These dilemmas were not apparent to everyone. *New York Times* columnist Thomas Friedman praised TSMC's trust-based model of production, depicting it as the alternative to China's oppressive approach to technology. If Xi just appreciated the ecology that TSMC had created, he would see that "seizing Taiwan just to get hold of TSMC . . . would be a fool's errand."

Just a week later, Morris Chang commented briefly on globalization. He didn't refer to Friedman's column but to Friedman's famous pronouncement that the world was "flat" because of globalization. "Well,

Tom," Chang announced, with politely withering understatement, "the world is not flat anymore." Gelsinger (who Chang considered "discourteous") and his allies said that South Korea and Taiwan were unsafe. They wanted to return to an era when the United States produced 42 percent of the world's semiconductors. Chang countered that it wasn't possible to turn back the clock. Reestablishing a complete semiconductor supply chain in the United States would be impossible, even if the United States paid hundreds of billions of dollars in subsidies.

Chang's frustrations were understandable. TSMC had to forgo some of its home advantages, building a semiconductor fab on U.S. soil. It had to provide confidential information on its customers, endangering relations of trust that it had spent decades assiduously building. And it had to play on a table that was increasingly tilted to its disadvantage by geopolitics, scuttling its carefully nurtured image of neutrality. Chang's sharp complaints about Friedman were likely fueled by his own nostalgia for a world in which his company could just focus on technology and markets, without having to worry about the U.S.-China confrontation. As the company's LinkedIn ad signaled, this world had disappeared forever. Chang himself lamented that "those good days when we can serve everybody in the world, those good days are gone. I just hope that they don't get any worse."

On March 30, 2015, Vitalik Buterin was in London, warning a small audience about the dangers of economic centralization. It was a chilly day, but the twenty-two-year-old was dressed in a striped T-shirt and cargo pants. He began by updating people on where things stood with Ethereum, the software project that he had started. It still hadn't launched but would soon. Then his real talk began.

Buterin told his fellow crypto enthusiasts how projects like Ethereum, which decentralized things to the blockchain, could transform the economy and help the world from going bad. "Crypto" is short for "cryptography," the science of encoding information so that it is difficult or impossible to access without a mathematical key. Crypto people weren't just fascinated with codes for their own sake. Many thought that crypto could undermine government power or even get rid of governments altogether.

As Buterin said that day, there was a "bit of a cult" around "decentralizing all the things." Most crypto people worried about concentrations of power and believed that math and technology offered answers. But he warned that the radically decentralized world that some libertarians dreamed of was unlikely. What was worryingly plausible was a dystopian "singularity" in which the base layer of the economy became a centralized means of control.

Buterin explained that every complex society had "base layer services"—fundamental institutions and infrastructure like roads, electricity, and policing, often provided by government, which everything else relied on. Now private businesses had taken charge of a new set of base layer services, like the Internet, payment processing (PayPal), and commoditized sharing (Uber and Airbnb). Most base layer services were networks and tended to get centralized over time, concentrating power. That was a problem. As Buterin described it to us years later, there are two reasons to decentralize: "One is you want it to be decentralized, to make it harder for the government to shut down. And the other is you want it to be decentralized, to prevent the operators from . . . deciding on their own to cheat users." Government and corporate power reinforced each other, as governments could more easily compel big centralizing businesses to do what they wanted.

Buterin wanted to rebuild society's plumbing on a different base layer using blockchain technology, the cornerstone of currencies such as Bitcoin (which used crypto to create a new kind of money). Blockchain is supposed to facilitate networks with decentralized authority, where no one is really in control. Unlike Bitcoin, Ethereum was not just a digital currency but an all-purpose machine that could support a multitude of services. It even allowed people to set up their own decentralized autonomous organizations, or DAOs, using programmed rules that would distribute money, art, or information in specific predefined ways once particular conditions were fulfilled. That led some to dream of a world where central intermediaries—banks, art dealers, clearinghouses—were completely replaced by decentralized computing systems, all using Ethereum to implement transactions.

While Buterin used very different language, he had identified the dangers of the underground empire—how society's plumbing becomes centralized, providing an opening for power and coercion. Buterin and others hoped that blockchain might be a solution. Blockchain-based currencies and social systems might eliminate intermediaries and immunize the base layers of society against the temptations of empire, stopping governments and businesses from controlling people's lives.

These political aspirations risked getting swamped by financial temptations. Six years after Buterin gave his talk, Ethereum had a total notional value of $483.4 billion. Early investors boasted about their yachts and Lamborghinis. Buterin himself didn't succumb. Although he became a billionaire for a while, he was happiest writing blogposts explaining how little you could travel with and still be comfortable (a forty-liter backpack, basic tech, eight T-shirts, shorts, tights, and underwear).

Crypto had attracted grifters from the beginning, even though its most respected figures were more interested in changing the world. As Silicon Valley investors piled in after them, they wanted to fund companies that would become essential to the crypto economy, allowing them to make vast amounts of money. Entrepreneur after entrepreneur discovered that the best way to turn a profit in a decentralized economy was to figure out ways to centralize parts of it again.

———————

The blessing and the curse of the crypto community was that it worried about government from the beginning. Most business and finance people didn't care about politics unless they absolutely had to. Their obliviousness helped the underground empire take root and grow.

In contrast, crypto had the politics baked in. If the quarrelsome tribes of crypto could agree on one thing, it was undercutting the government's monopoly on issuing money and its power to keep track of it. That was what had brought them together.

That ambition had taken root long before crypto was crypto. Friedrich von Hayek, who invited Walter Wriston's father to join the Mont Pèlerin Society, had famously argued that private currency would curb government profligacy and inflation. Wriston himself anticipated that global "electronic currency" would tame governments. But it was when the Internet and cryptography went mainstream that people properly started trying to realize Hayek's vision.

The Internet seemed to provide the first truly decentralized means of global communication. Libertarians proclaimed that the Internet undermined the government's power to censor information and that cryptography made financial transactions unintelligible to government. As the "Cypherpunk Manifesto" grandly announced, cryptography would "ineluctably spread over the whole globe, and with it the anonymous transactions systems that it makes possible." As everyone moved into the invisible economy, the government's tax base would shrivel into nonexistence.

These dreams inspired fiction and business plans (the two sometimes merged into each other). Neal Stephenson was now a famous science fiction author. His near-future novel, *Cryptonomicon*, depicted how good crypto, an amenable island state, and a convenient hoard of World War II gold might bring a new world into being. Peter Thiel, who co-founded PayPal and funded an early fellowship for Buterin, wrote later that *Cryptonomicon* was "required reading" for the early PayPal team, all of whom were "obsessed with creating a digital currency that would be controlled by individuals instead of governments." As Thiel later admitted, none of them really knew much about money, but their "grand mission" was "to create a new internet currency that would replace the U.S. dollar." PayPal's office kept a "World Domination Index" of user growth and pitched venture capitalists with a slide claiming that the company could capture some of the profits that the U.S. government made by issuing dollars.

Toppling the sovereign was just too hard. PayPal gave up its ambitions to dominate the world, becoming an ordinary (if lucrative) payments company. It found out that disobedience had consequences. In 2015, PayPal reached a $7.7 million settlement with OFAC for its involvement in hundreds of sanctions violations. When Russia attacked Ukraine in 2022, PayPal cut off access to Russian accounts without demur.

It was even harder to topple the old monarch without anointing a new ruler. A truly libertarian currency would need more than a tech-friendly island nation and a heap of gold bars. It would have to stop the new currency's owner from doing the same bad things as the governments she had replaced.

That meant solving a fundamental political problem. Monarchs could tell people what to do and back up their threats. As *Snow Crash*, an earlier Stephenson novel noted, Louis XIV had a slogan engraved on his cannons, *ultima ratio regum*, "the last argument of kings." The threat of violence was the foundation of sovereign power. It allowed kings to decide how much currency was issued, what happened when banks went into default, and how to solve disagreements over who owed what money to whom. Equally, it created problems. A sovereign could use threats and force to expropriate their subjects' gold. She could pay for wars or crises or palaces just by issuing more money, at the risk of driving up inflation.

Libertarians wanted money without kings, queens, or centralized power. But if no one was giving the orders, how could you create the necessary consensus over what money was, who owned what, and what to do when debts were not paid? It was hard to see how to do this for digital money, which was cryptographic fairy gold, magicked out of hope and mathematics in equal proportion. Perhaps ordinary money was a fiction, too, but it was a fiction that everyone had already acquiesced to. How could you get people to take a cryptographic currency seriously? How could you stop people from cheating by duplicating crypto coins (which were no more than strings of numbers), unless you had some centralized accounting system that kept track of who owned what?

These were the problems that Bitcoin was designed to solve. It used an ingenious mathematical trick to create what Satoshi Nakamoto, the pseudonymous inventor of Bitcoin, described as the first "decentralized, non-trust-based system" of money. Nakamoto combined the blockchain—a tamper-resistant decentralized online ledger book that could keep track of who had paid what to whom—with a system for minting new coins. This combination made it very hard for people to cook the books, requiring them to use powerful computers to solve increasingly complex and thoroughly useless mathematical guessing games to "mine" coins. Mining was incredibly inefficient. Eventually, mining Bitcoin used up as much energy as a middling-size country. Nakamoto's invention spun gold not out of straw but out of wasted computing power.

For libertarians, the possibilities cascaded like varicolored scarves from a magician's sleeve. Cryptocurrencies like Bitcoin could create the broad consensus that money and financial markets needed to work without centralizing power. They could perhaps stop inflation (Bitcoin was designed to be deflationary). Crucially, they could replace trust in governments with clean and predictable mathematics. The whole messy world of political economy—of figuring out complicated ways to stop government and global finance from using their power to hurt you—seemed to vanish in a puff of logic. Individuals could create and maintain their own financial realms without lawmakers or tax collectors.

If Bitcoin was fairy money, Ethereum was a veritable magician's wand. In Buterin's description, it was a "decentralized computer, . . . with tens of thousands of nodes all around the world, talking to each other." You could use it not merely to send and receive electronic coins, but to write programs that could replace middlemen. Why use a lawyer to enforce contracts when contracts could enforce themselves through Ethereum? Perhaps you could push government out, too. As Gavin Wood, one of Ethereum's developers, explained, the decentralized computer allowed you to create and run a programmed entity that "cannot care as to whether its actions might be interpreted as legal . . . or illegal." Businesses like PayPal were real organizations, run by real people, who could go to jail if they did illegal things. But as Wood pointed out, decentralized entities that lived only on the blockchain had no human operators and could keep going forever after receiving their initial programming instructions. These "forces of nature" and "combinations of mathematics" couldn't be intimidated out of doing whatever they had been told to do. Nor could they be shut down, without shutting down the blockchain itself.

The first DAO was created on Ethereum in 2016. It was a distributed venture capital fund, allowing its investors to vote under preset programmed rules on whether to fund proposals that others submitted to it. Although it attracted nearly $100 million in investments, just under 15 percent of the Ethereum currency then in existence, it quickly ran into trouble. Its primary creator, Christoph Jentzsch, began to fear that he had conjured up a "Sorcerer's Apprentice," an apparently compliant servant that would quickly become uncontrollable.

He was right to worry. The DAO went bad quickly. People began to point out flaws in its design. Then, someone discovered a mistake in the DAO's code, which allowed them to start bleeding its investors dry, in $5,600 increments.

Stopping this wasn't straightforward. Ethereum's core developers and the DAO didn't have courts to declare who owned the funds or a police force to seize them. Nor could they just stop the program from running or change its code. They actually had to rewrite Ethereum's blockchain, rolling back the transactions that had allowed the thief to steal the money. Lacking the last argument of kings, they persuaded the community of Ethereum users and developers to "fork" the project, moving to a new blockchain. This led to seemingly endless angry debate, but a majority eventually signaled grudging approval in a vote. Ethereum survived, but it was as if a country had been forced to hold a referendum to rewrite its constitution and history books to manage the aftermath of a bank robbery.

As the crypto ecosystem grew, charlatans and mountebanks appeared as if from thin air, drawn by the heady odor of ripe chump. In June 2016, thousands of enthusiasts came to the Wembley Arena in London to hear Ruja Ignatova, the self-declared Cryptoqueen, speak about her OneCoin project. It was a scam that didn't even have a blockchain. Ignatova wrote to a partner that her plan was to "take the money and run and blame someone else for this." After pulling in what prosecutors claimed was over $4 billion in investments, she disappeared. She is now on the FBI's ten most wanted list.

More conventional entrepreneurs appeared, too, hoping to make money in what Gavin Wood had dubbed Web3—an even more decentralized iteration of the Internet. In the 1940s, conceptual artists had competed to "sign" unexpected things like the sky or to issue "certificates of authenticity" declaring that a human being was an artwork. Blockchain-registered nonfungible tokens (NFTs) turned this artistic joke into a business model, buying and selling digitally signed certificates of authenticity for an image, a tweet, or an event. Celebrities and nouveaux riches crypto moguls were prepared to pay millions of dollars for algorithmically varied "Bored Ape" NFTs.

Many aspiring crypto billionaires looked to Peter Thiel's advice in his book *Zero to One*: find a niche and build a monopoly. There were plenty of niches. As the cryptographer Moxie Marlinspike warned, very few Web3 users had direct contact with the blockchain. They relied instead on intermediary companies like OpenSea, the dominant NFT marketplace; Coinbase, a central exchange for cryptocurrencies; or MetaMask, a commonly used Ethereum wallet. Businesses depended on infrastructure providers like Alchemy and Infura. Stablecoins like Dai and Tether were an interface between cryptocurrencies and the regular world of finance. Stablecoins provided a cryptocurrency anchor to traditional currencies or a mathematically sophisticated cryptocurrency equivalent. Like Eurodollars, they were an accounting fiction tethered to real money. As Buterin explained to us, stablecoins provided essential continuity in a world where the value of cryptocurrencies rose and fell unpredictably. If you wanted to make a long-term contract, denominating it in stablecoins allowed you to mitigate the risk of currency fluctuation. Stablecoins, too, became central elements in a supposedly decentralized system.

The result, as Marlinspike said, was that "from the very beginning, these technologies immediately tended toward centralization through platforms . . . and . . . most participants don't even know or care it's happening." Like Jay Adelson two decades before, Web3 disrupters quickly found themselves creating new choke points, either deliberately or despite themselves. In an online conversation with Buterin, Nikil Viswanathan, Alchemy's CEO, professed surprise that his customers really wanted a "centralized pipe to decentralized blockchain data." Less than two years later, he saw his company's value triple to $10 billion in just three months. As one writer bemoaned, "Most web3 firms are for-profit businesses, and so are the VCs backing them . . . VCs are built to build monopolies, and monopolies want control."

Notoriety brought greater scrutiny from regulators. Worries about U.S. action had plagued the founding of Ethereum. The people who set the first DAO in motion had been advised to use ShapeShift, a cryptocurrency exchange that was designed deliberately to hide transactions. While ordinary banks were required to abide by "Know Your Customer" laws, crypto companies often ignored them. ShapeShift declined to identify its customers until the *Wall Street Journal* accused it of allowing criminals, including the authors of North Korea's Wanna-Cry ransomware operation, to launder their proceeds.

Some in the community wanted not just to circumvent U.S. regulations but to actively help others undermine them. In 2022, Virgil Griffith, who had helped Buterin in the early days and played a powerful role at the Ethereum Foundation, was sentenced to five years for traveling to North Korea to provide advice on using cryptocurrencies to counter sanctions. In retrospect, it was a bad idea for him to be photographed in a North Korean–style uniform in front of a whiteboard, where he had drawn a smiley face and written "No sanctions yay."

But as crypto grew, it found it ever more complicated to keep working around or evading the law. U.S. regulators and politicians could crush cryptocurrency projects that looked like threats. A relatively junior Facebook employee, Morgan Beller, had persuaded Facebook's vice president, David Marcus, to build a blockchain currency. When Marcus sat down with Mark Zuckerberg, CEO of Facebook, they discussed how "Facebook could succeed where PayPal, Marcus's old employer, had capitulated: realizing the libertarian dream of a pure, borderless Internet money." Facebook's Chinese competitors had profitably combined social media, marketplace, and payment system into a coherent whole. Perhaps Facebook could do this but for the world rather than a single country.

That had obvious political implications. If Microsoft wanted to become a neutral Switzerland, Facebook had far bigger aspirations: rewriting the operating system of the world economy to put itself in the driving seat.

U.S. and European regulators feared that Zuckerberg would replace the U.S. dollar and euro with a private-sector global currency. In an early informal conversation, U.S. secretary of the Treasury Steven Mnuchin reportedly told Marcus, "I hate everything about this." When Facebook and its partners formally announced their new currency, Libra, in June 2019, Bruno Le Maire told the French Senate that "he was resolutely against Libra becoming a 'sovereign currency' that could compete with state currencies." Fabio Panetta, a member of the European Central Bank's executive board, emphasized the risks of stablecoins like Libra replacing sovereign money. Politicians also worried that "a digital coin that is beyond the control of any government could facilitate money laundering and finance terrorism." When it met with U.S. officials, Facebook seemed completely unprepared to answer tough questions about national security.

Marcus and Facebook were quickly forced to abandon their grandiose aspirations. They headhunted Stuart Levey to lead the Libra initiative. Levey knew sanctions from both sides: he had gone from being the Undersecretary for Terrorism and Financial Intelligence in the 2000s to working as chief legal officer at HSBC during the Meng crisis. His most important job at Libra was reassuring U.S. officials that they didn't have to worry about the currency. Libra was renamed Diem and was redesigned to make it dependent on the U.S. dollar and financial system. A team of crypto engineers "worked feverishly to build a system that could monitor transactions for signs of money laundering or sanction breaking." It wasn't enough. The Biden administration signaled that it opposed the currency. In December 2021, Levey pulled the plug. Marcus had already resigned.

Crypto companies still tried to cajole governments into embracing the revolution. Big crypto went to Washington, pouring millions of dollars into lobbying. Andreessen Horowitz, a major Silicon Valley venture capital firm, published a "how to" guide for governments that wanted to "see the potential of web3," suggesting that they would fall behind if they didn't "unlock the potential of DAOs" and "embrace the role of well-regulated stablecoins." The venture capital firm had invested heavily in both. For example, it put $15 million into MakerDAO, the DAO behind Dai, which approximated the U.S. dollar using an exotic synthesis of Ethereum and other cryptocurrencies. Dai was wildly successful and became the fourth-largest stablecoin in existence. By December 2021, there were over four thousand DAOs, with $13 billion held collectively in their vaults.

U.S. regulators remained suspicious. In November 2022, the Securities and Exchange Commission (SEC) instituted proceedings against American CryptoFed DAO, which had claimed that it was the first legally licensed DAO in the United States. SEC chair Gary Gensler described stablecoins as "poker chips" in a Wild West casino. Many DAOs looked suspiciously centralized, if examined closely, providing a majority of the voting power to insiders and investors like Andreessen Horowitz. Then again, Bitcoin itself had been much more centralized in its early days than anyone had known. A couple of DAOs set themselves up deliberately to frustrate government influence by throwing away the keys. They could set up their business services as programs running on Ethereum but then tell the software not to accept any future updates. The result was code that would keep on running as long as Ethereum existed, providing services that no one could change, control, or stop.

Some crypto people accepted that governments and collective choice had a role. Buterin told us that he understood that governments would still be able to regulate, so long as there were networks. But it was reasonable to create a counterbalance because "basically, we're seeing private actors . . . get deputized into enforcing restrictions that are far more restrictive than any democratically agreed upon law." Buterin aspired to help make technologies that would give people more control over their individual and collective lives, pushing for new "soulbound" tokens that would make it easier for people to identify who they were and what they had done, and to build communities from the ground up.

Others still yearned for a libertarian utopia, where governments would no longer be able to tell people what to do. By 2022, their aspirations sprang from bitter resentment as much as hope. Silicon Valley didn't like it that politicians and journalists no longer venerated information technology founders and venture capitalists as leaders and prophets. Their unhappiness spilled over into the politics of crypto.

Balaji Srinivasan, for example, had been a partner at Andreessen Horowitz and Coinbase's chief technology officer. He wrote a book, explaining how networks of individuals (led, naturally, by far-seeing innovators like himself) would replace traditional governments. Srinivasan argued that the Bitcoin/Web3 ecosystem was contending for domination against the two centralizing powers—the Chinese Communist Party with the renminbi, and "NYT/USD," the sinister combination of forces swirling around the U.S. dollar and his personal bête noire, the *New York Times*. As nonaligned countries like El Salvador swung against the two power-hungry leviathans, Bitcoin and Ethereum might provide the foundations of a new decentralized world. The old "Pax Americana," based on the U.S. dollar and the king's cannons, would be displaced by a "Pax Bitcoinica" founded on code.

Srinivasan's self-published vision was terribly written (perhaps he thought editors were part of the NYT/USD cabal) but influential. Many other technology leaders agreed that East Coast media, regulators, and money were a Borg-like collectivity, masking its ruthless will to dominate beneath woke nostrums. Peter Thiel had once suggested that Bitcoin was "in part . . . a Chinese financial weapon against the U.S." By 2022, he seemed to have changed his mind. He ended his headline speech at the 2022 Bitcoin conference by denouncing those on an "Enemies List" to a cheering audience. Bitcoin's "real enemy" was environmental, social, and governance standards (ESG), a "hate factory" that was more or less identical with the Chinese Communist Party. Thiel called on his listeners to "go out from this conference and take over the world."

But it was OFAC that declared war on crypto a few months later, by designating Tornado Cash, a "mixer" that it claimed had been used to launder over $7 billion's worth of cryptocurrency, including $455 million stolen by North Korean hackers. Mixers were services that accepted cryptocurrency from many different sources, scrambled it all together so that it was hard to trace which money had come from where, and returned it where it came from, minus a fee. Crypto people saw mixers as enhancing privacy. Buterin had used Tornado Cash to donate money to Ukraine. But the U.S. government thought Tornado Cash was like a business that indiscriminately rented thousands of identical white vans to bank robbers and ordinary citizens alike. The mixer helped criminals to get away with their proceeds, and the more legitimate users there were, the easier it was for the heist artists to blend in with them.

U.S. officials had been worried about mixers for some time. Back in 2020, a Department of Justice official had said that "seeking to obscure virtual currency transactions in this way is a crime." In May 2022, OFAC had designated another mixer, Blender.io. A senior Treasury official had warned that crypto firms could no longer "keep their heads in the sand about blatantly suspect wallets." Some crypto companies were willing to work with law enforcement. Coinbase, for example, had a contract selling tracking information to the U.S. Department of Homeland Security. John Kothanek, its vice president for global intelligence, told a congressional committee about Coinbase's "Know Your Customer" program and urged the Department of Justice to "prosecute individuals and entities involved in facilitating illicit activity, even when that activity is located abroad."

So why were Coinbase and other crypto companies outraged when OFAC targeted Tornado Cash? The problem was that Tornado Cash's most important elements were coded instructions, running on top of Ethereum's blockchain and no longer under the control of any human being. Its cofounder, Roman Semenov, said that Tornado Cash had been "specifically designed . . . to be unstoppable." The code that ran its services had been deliberately instructed not to accept any updates. It couldn't be changed or stopped, and would keep working as long as Ethereum existed. Tornado Cash had apotheosized into one of Gavin Wood's "forces of nature."

That meant that OFAC wasn't just designating an organization or people working for it. It was designating an inextricable part of Ethereum's working software. In the words of Jon Stokes, a prominent crypto commentator, "U.S. Treasury can't turn off Tornado Cash without turning off the entire Ethereum blockchain." Sanctioning it was supposed to be "technically impossible."

Eight years before, Wood had argued that the sorcerer's apprentice would be unstoppable once it got going. Blockchain-based combinations of mathematics were "alegal"—they didn't care whether they were enabling law breaking or not—and they couldn't be punished or taken down. Governments would have to "start getting real" and recognize that they couldn't really control everything anymore. If they didn't, in Wood's colorfully jumbled metaphor, they "risk[ed] running into the age of dinosaurs and pissing up against the wind."

If Wood and Semenov were right, then the decentralized world that Srinavasan and Thiel hoped for was possible, perhaps even likely. The forces set off by the sorcerer's apprentice would be unstoppable. It didn't matter if crypto became more centralized so long as the central functions were carried out by unstoppable code running on Ethereum or other blockchains. DAOs like Tornado Cash would just sweep sanctions and sovereign authority away, like so many thousands of self-propelling brooms. If Wood and Semenov were wrong, the dream of unstoppable code was just another Mickey Mouse fantasy about the unstoppable power of electronic currency. Now, as in the past, governments would be able to use their central levers of control to compel finance to do its will.

Anonymous individuals started "dusting" celebrities, sending them tiny amounts of money from Tornado Cash so that they were in technical violation of the law. Tether, a huge but wildly controversial stablecoin, founded by a former child actor and controlled by an Italian plastic surgeon, declined to act on OFAC's designation without more specific guidance. Coinbase, despite its government connections, decided that the Tornado Cash designation was a step too far. It funded a lawsuit claiming that OFAC was illegally restraining free speech by clamping down on code. OFAC responded by clarifying that celebrities who had been dusted wouldn't get into trouble and that people could republish Tornado Cash's code so long as they didn't use it for illicit purposes.

Like Coinbase, Rune Christensen, the founder of MakerDAO, which issued Dai, had once wanted crypto to comply with regulators. He had fired employees who disagreed on the need for "government compliance and integration . . . into the existing global financial system." Just a few weeks before the Tornado Cash crisis, MakerDAO voted to extend a $100 million line of credit to a traditional community bank. But now, Christensen wanted to cast off.

In a long essay, wobbling back and forth between despair and halfhearted optimism, Christensen argued that public anger and the "post-9/11 paradigm" of financial regulation had closed the window of opportunity for decentralized crypto. Scams and scandals meant that ordinary people saw "the crypto bro as the one type of person that's even worse than the wall street banker bro." Regulators believed that either you're a "fully compliant, regulated bank, or you're a terrorist." There was a high probability that global authorities would come after Dai, and no way that Dai could comply with their demands: it, too, had been designed so that "it could never possibly become a tool of financial surveillance and control."

No compromise was possible. Christensen argued that the crypto community had to return to the days of the "cypherpunk movement," when "governments first tried to ban encryption and enforce a hellish dystopian future" without privacy. Crypto had to break its connections to the regulated financial system. Dai would move away from "real world assets," cut its dependencies on currencies like Circle that were working with the regulators, and "free float" into a new and better world.

Christensen and others like him were the heirs of Walter Wriston, though they probably had never heard of him. They dreamed that they might still head away from the world of landlocked sovereigns into illimitable oceans, where they could sail where they liked, beholden to no one but themselves.

But others stayed moored. They felt they had no choice if they wanted to avoid shutdown and keep making profits. Circle, Alchemy, and Infura quickly cut off their connections to Tornado Cash, accepting that they were vassals of the sovereign. Many other crypto companies rushed to figure out what they needed to do to comply with Treasury regulations. After all, as the CEO of Binance, a prominent cryptocurrency exchange, said after Russia invaded Ukraine, "The OFAC sanctions are not a joke . . . if you don't do this well, you end up in jail."

Once, business leaders dreamed that companies would create their own independent realms on the high seas, far from the grasp of sovereigns. Today's businesses are more like Hook's captain, boxed in by the demands of jealous states, drawing circles in the ocean. Some, like TSMC, have tried to equivocate, remaining as impartial as they can, while tacitly recognizing the authority of one monarch or another. Others, like Microsoft, have abandoned their ambitions for neutral independence and have come to embrace one side. Wriston's truest inheritors—the libertarians who created cryptocurrencies—still hope for something better, even as their zeal for decentralization spawns endless forms of recentralization, bringing back monopoly and government control under new guises.

After decades of imagining that they lived in a decentralized, borderless world, businesses again find themselves constrained by governments. Some still hope to escape the base layers of the global economy and the centralized networks of finance, production, and information that the United States controls, but it is difficult to see how.

6

THE EMPIRE OF WIND AND LIGHT

When Facebook's Libra project was announced, Vitalik Buterin happened to be in China. He had been talking to experts who were interested in blockchain. Suddenly, he saw a new explosion of interest in creating a Chinese digital currency. It was driven not by excitement but by fear.

In Buterin's description, the Chinese "pattern-matched Libra to Sputnik," comparing the Libra announcement to the historical moment when the USSR leaped ahead of the United States in the space race. China's experts were frightened that a U.S.-based company might have control of the first truly global currency. They told Buterin that if the United States "are going to overtake us, we have to do it now." Wang Xin, who directed the central bank's research bureau, warned in a speech that Libra could "create a scenario under which . . . there would be in essence one boss, that is the US dollar and the United States." China's premier Xi Jinping demanded that the bank hurry up China's own Central Bank Digital Currency (CBDC) project, to create a digital yuan before it was too late.

Of course, Libra was not sponsored by the U.S. government. Mark Zuckerberg didn't want to render unto Caesar but to become him, and his project turned out to be a "dead end." Chinese government experts still thought that Facebook was laying the groundwork for another attack by the country that had targeted and crippled Huawei and was trying to stop China from developing its own advanced semiconductors. Chinese leaders already worried that the United States would deploy its vast financial power to make Chinese firms bend to U.S. policy. Libra would provide America with an even bigger cudgel.

After China accelerated its CBDC project, it was America's turn to worry. Unlike Bitcoin and Ethereum, China's digital yuan would be centralized and managed by the government, potentially providing unparalleled insights and control into the affairs of its users. What if it became the cornerstone of a new global infrastructure of digital currencies, supplanting the existing U.S. dollar–dominated system? What if China copied the United States and weaponized finance against its enemies? What if China could use the digital yuan to mount attacks that America had never even dreamed of?

Soon foreign policy commentators started talking about America's "Sputnik moment." The White House said that the government needed to start researching a possible U.S. CBDC with "urgency." The U.S. Federal Reserve was more cautious, but as Lael Brainard, the Federal Reserve's vice-chair, told Congress, "[W]e should not take the dollar's global status as the dominant payment currency for granted." In June 2022, the Federal Reserve chairman, Jerome Powell, said that a U.S. CBDC was "something we really need to explore as a country."

Perhaps China would have tried to adopt a CBDC if it hadn't felt threatened by Libra. Perhaps U.S. politicians would have started pushing for one, too, if they hadn't worried that China might get there first. Perhaps. In our time line, the story of centralized digital currencies was of one power's anxieties feeding on another's in a chain reaction. Neither China nor the United States saw that there were limits to the other's ability to weaponize its economy. China didn't really understand that America's businesses had their own political aspirations. U.S. commentators wildly overestimated the appeal of a Chinese government–controlled digital currency. It wasn't even popular in China: few Chinese citizens wanted to use the pilot version, despite government subsidies.

As the underground empire became increasingly visible, its consequences became less predictable. The United States hadn't lost its power, but power was no longer enough to determine what would happen next. The United States found itself making ever bigger interventions. As they grew, so, too, did the likelihood of unexpected consequences. But American officials, like their Chinese equivalents, had difficulty understanding how their own actions helped feed the widening gyre.

One of China's great weaknesses in building its own empire was that other countries, businesses, and ordinary people couldn't trust it: it took advantage of them whenever it suited. But the more the United States used its financial power, control of technology, and central position in global networks to exert control, the more it risked falling into China's trap. If countries and businesses believed that the United States would deploy its power ruthlessly against them, then they might see little difference between it and its adversary. The underground empire would lose many of its attractions and have to rely on brute force. When it pressed the rest of the world to cut ties with Huawei, the United States became more like its adversary; by emulating China, the United States risked strengthening it.

There was an even bigger danger. If the U.S. strategy succeeded too well, it might drive China to belligerence rather than preventing it. Pundits wrote op-eds and white papers asking whether China could build the plumbing for an alternative global economy where it controlled the choke points. They rarely asked whether China might instead decouple and secure itself by violence, as aggressive powers had done in the twentieth century when they faced similar threats.

The Sputnik moment spiraled into a nuclear arms race that might have destroyed human civilization during the Cuban Missile Crisis. After that crisis, the great nuclear powers started working together to manage the risks of confrontation. Today, a new spiral of economic confrontation is slowly gathering strength. It might tear the global economy apart or even pull the world into actual war. If we don't want to be drawn inexorably down into the maelstrom, we need to map the spiral, start working to moderate its seemingly irresistible force, and perhaps even learn how to make it work for common purposes.

From outside, the underground empire seems like a relentless machine of domination, the product of decades of careful engineering. From inside, it looks quite different, a haphazard construction lashed together from ad hoc bureaucratic decisions and repurposed legal authorities. It still holds, somehow. The United States understands the world economy far better, and can manipulate it more easily, than its allies and adversaries. Yet as the contradictions mount, the risk of catastrophic failure grows.

Those who speak on behalf of the empire talk a good game. Politicians' speeches and officials' memoirs make its history seem like a continuous string of anticipated successes. Some tell a very different story in private conversation. Ultimately, America's underground empire wasn't the product of any grand master plan. Instead, it emerged half by accident, as officials tried to deal with one damn problem after another.

When the United States slapped at North Korea by designating Banco Delta Asia, no one expected it would show the way to sever Iran's access to global finance. The Iran sanctions themselves seemed to bump up against the ceiling of the possible; unique, and unprecedented measures to address a unique and unprecedented problem. That ceiling has become the floor on which even more ambitious structures of domination have been built.

Along the way, mistakes were made, some with long-term consequences. When the NSA didn't just demand secrets from U.S. technology companies but stole them wholesale from fiber-optic connection points, it provoked a sharp counterreaction. Companies like Microsoft and Google started encrypting the information that flowed from one data center to another. The NSA could still demand information under the law, but it couldn't see anything anymore in its secret mirrors unless it somehow got the key or discovered a hidden mathematical back door. Google didn't just encrypt its own communications, but did everything it could to encourage others to do the same, as nonencrypted websites were downgraded in Google search results.

At roughly the same time, the global system of fiber-optic cables—the plumbing of the information economy—began to rearrange itself. Chinese companies like Huawei joined the consortia that were laying down alternative underwater cables in the Indo-Pacific. These didn't necessarily converge on the old centers of the network, located in the United States and its allies. The old guard of telecommunication companies that had dominated for so long were pushed aside by Google and Microsoft, which laid their own private data cables.

And firms like Google didn't have as much to gain from collaborating with the U.S. government as AT&T and its sisters because their core business wasn't as vulnerable to U.S. regulators. That said, the U.S. government could often still make them do what it wanted. In 2020, the U.S. Department of Justice blocked a Google cable from landing in Hong Kong. It worried that the cable "would advance the PRC [People's Republic of China] government's goal that Hong Kong be the dominant hub in the Asia Pacific region," making it easier for China to intercept U.S. traffic. At a minimum, the United States now had to govern more through blunt force rather than with the willing cooperation of business. And it risked that businesses might reconfigure their economic relations so as to skirt and thereby undermine U.S. power.

Other miscalculations could be fixed. Years before Russia's 2022 invasion of Ukraine, when the Trump administration sanctioned Oleg Deripaska and his company, Rusal, it discovered that it had inadvertently removed a key component of Europe's economic apparatus. Rusal was a giant aluminum producer and processor, and Deripaska a key Putin ally. As William Spiegelberger, who had once directed Rusal's international law office, later recalled, Russian business leaders believed that "Trump is the president. . . . What are the odds that something is going to happen?" Trump didn't want to punish foreigners who might have helped him win, but he was constrained by the Countering America's Adversaries Through Sanctions Act (CAATSA), which he had reluctantly signed in 2017.

Russia's economy tottered when the United States designated Deripaska and his companies, alongside six other Russian oligarchs. But the measures threatened Europe, too. Rusal's alumina refinery on Aughinish, an unremarkable peninsula jutting into the Shannon Estuary in County Limerick, Ireland, turned out to be a hidden choke point, "creating a supply bottleneck in the EU and Germany." Europe's car factories, machine manufacturers, and builders all relied on smelted aluminum, which in turn relied on the facility in Aughinish. The United States had excellent financial maps of the world but only a fragmentary understanding of physical supply chains. It had seriously miscalculated the consequences of its actions.

European ambassadors sent a joint letter to Senate Leader Chuck

Schumer, warning that the economic fallout of the sanctions risked supply chains being "rerouted to China." They got a surprisingly sympathetic response. Dan Mulhall, Ireland's ambassador to the United States, thought that getting a hearing from OFAC "would be much more difficult than it was." He recounted how on a Friday, he "got a call from the people at the [Aughinish] plant saying that the gas supply would be cut off on Monday." Mulhall phoned OFAC, which issued a "statement of comfort" that afternoon to reassure the supplier that it would not be sanctioned for providing gas to keep the plant going. OFAC discovered the sharp limits to what Spiegelberger caustically described as the "what does this button do" approach to economic coercion. Soon afterward, OFAC wound down the sanctions on the condition that Deripaska give up formal control of the company.

After Trump was finally dragged out of office, the Biden administration seemed better placed to avoid mistakes like Rusal. It would talk to its allies in advance. But officials in the new administration had paradoxically taken heart from Trump's errors. Before Trump, they had feared that the overuse of U.S. power would completely alienate allies, radicalize adversaries, and push businesses to work around the choke points. The Trump years suggested that their cautions were largely misplaced. Perhaps mistakes wouldn't undermine U.S. power.

Trump had been both brutal and incompetent. His officials had pushed an extreme view of U.S. power, harshly punishing key allies and threatening to sanction their officials. They adopted tactics that no other administration had ever dared. Not only had they dismantled Huawei and threatened European governments with dire consequences, but they caused international uproar by designating International Criminal Court officials for investigating alleged war crimes by U.S. soldiers in Afghanistan. The designations didn't just affect the officials themselves: Trump's secretary of state, Mike Pompeo, threatened sanctions against businesses or individuals who supported them in any way.

But after four years of this behavior, the world financial system hadn't stopped using the U.S. dollar. U.S. technology and intellectual property still played a critical role in global supply chains. For all their complaints, U.S. allies hadn't cut their ties. China had punished Canada over the Huawei affair, holding a former diplomat and a North Korean tourism and investment consultant hostage in jail cells, but it had never dared punish the United States directly. Incoming officials surmised that U.S. power was far greater than anyone had realized. The new administration would forgo Trump's vicious stupidity, but it wouldn't fret much about overreach.

That was one reason why the Biden administration was willing to employ an enormous array of sanctions and technology restrictions against Russia in 2022. Unlike the previous administration, it took pains to consult with its allies. All the measures were debated, some over weeks and months.

Still, the knock-on consequences were hard to calculate. When the United States and Europe tried to isolate Putin, they destabilized global oil markets, leading to soaring prices. Drivers had to pay much more to refill their tanks. Businesses faced the threat of bankruptcy thanks to spiking electricity prices, while citizens worried that they couldn't pay their home heating bills. The higher the price of oil, the more likely it was that Trump would be elected in the United States, as well as pro-Russian populists in Europe. Russia would find it easier to withstand pressure, too, as its oil exports brought home even more dollars.

Both the United States and Europe wanted to cut off Moscow's access to hard currency, but they didn't want to sink their own economies. They began to experiment with alternative forms of punishment. What if they imposed a global cap on the price of Russian oil, threatening to sanction businesses that were willing to pay more as well as the ships willing to transport the oil? That might hurt Russia while keeping energy prices down.

The price cap was not particularly elegant but it seemed like it might work. Other countries, like China and India, did not like U.S. power, but they would have little incentive to cheat, since they did like cheaper oil. What the United States didn't anticipate was how badly its awkward and undemocratic ally, Saudi Arabia, would take it. The United States insisted that the price cap would only be used to hurt Russia, but Saudi Arabia feared that this new economic weapon might one day be deployed against it or other oil-producing states. According to Indonesia's finance minister, that was why Saudi Arabia and OPEC decided to decrease oil production, to fire a warning shot. She said that Saudi officials had told her that the price cap set a precedent and no one knew which country would be next. As supply fell, and prices started rising at gas stations, policy makers seemed caught off guard. Again, a chain of unanticipated actions and counteractions had spiraled outward with unexpected consequences.

No one had any good sense of how the sanctions might affect the administration's biggest foreign policy problem, the U.S.-China relationship. Both Trump and Biden had wanted the United States to start disentangling its economy from China's. This was a difficult and sensitive process since China was America's most important trade partner, accounting for $450.4 billion in imports and $164.9 billion in exports in 2020. The Biden administration wasn't as crude as Trump, who had claimed that cutting off China would "save $500 billion," or his trade adviser, Peter Navarro, who warned that America would "sink into the abyss" if it didn't decouple. Still, it feared that China was creating new choke points to use against the U.S.–China dominated production of photovoltaics and other clean energy technologies. China effectively controlled the processing of rare earths that were needed to manufacture complex electronics. But officials were almost more worried by what they couldn't see. There was no equivalent of SWIFT for supply chains, no straightforward way to map the whole. There might be myriads of weak points and vulnerabilities that China could exploit, and no obvious means of discovering them.

Perhaps offense could substitute for defense. As Matt Duss, Bernie Sanders's foreign policy adviser, told us, American politics became a "competition of who's tougher on China," where politicians fought over "who can come up with an ever more baroque setup of sanctions to slap on this or that official." Duss believed that some sanctions were appropriate—for example, against Chinese officials involved in the Uyghur genocide. But he also blamed a "sanctions industrial complex" that had grown up after 9/11, for creating "a self-licking ice cream cone" in which increasingly harsh sanctions always seemed to clear the way for more increasingly harsh sanctions.

This feedback loop kept on generating new ways to weaken China: ramped-up technology export bans, a crackdown on Chinese investments, stringent disclosure requirements for Chinese firms that wanted to sell their shares in the United States. The Biden administration did abandon the Trump administration's China Initiative, which had targeted scientists (often of Chinese ancestry) collaborating with Chinese institutions, charging them with lying to get U.S. government grants. But it, like the Trump administration, increasingly saw economic warfare as the first best response to China's inexorable rise. Biden's national security adviser, Jake Sullivan, warned that a technological "'relative' advantage" was no longer enough. There were areas, such as climate change, where the United States had to work with its rival, but America and the world would be better off with "as large of a lead as possible" and implicitly a weaker China.

Chinese policy makers were, if anything, even more inclined to believe the worst of their adversary than the United States. They hated having to depend on the United States. As Julian Gewirtz explained before he became a China director on Biden's National Security Council, Xi Jinping had already launched an initiative aimed at reducing

China's technological dependence in 2014. The Trump administration saw this as evidence of China's economic aggression and plan to "dominate" key sectors in the global economy. When Trump began his economic attacks on China, Xi announced a new economic doctrine for China, "dual circulation," which would build up China's domestic economy while securing its supply chains. Xi's regime clearly had ambitions to reunite China, to reshape its surrounding region, and perhaps to become a world-dominating power. An anonymous but well-connected Chinese academic told James Crabtree that the dual circulation program was a "Plan B," for "when international supply chains are shut off," as part of "preparations for a possible war across the Taiwan Straits."

These strategies were thrown into disarray by America and Europe's response to Russia, which "shocked" Chinese officials. Before the invasion, they had "never believed Washington would go so far as to weaponize the entire world's financial system" against a major country. Russia accounted for 2 percent of global trade—surely cutting its banks out of SWIFT would be too risky. But the United States and Europe didn't only weaponize SWIFT. They blocked access to Russia's currency reserves.

On April 22, 2022, the Chinese government's Finance Ministry and Central Bank convened an emergency meeting of dozens of local and international banks to ask how China might respond if it, too, were cut off. Chinese officials talked about moving their foreign currency holdings into euros and yen, but U.S. allies might be no more reliable in a crisis than the United States itself. As the *Financial Times'* source described the exchange, "No one on site could think of a good solution to the problem. China's banking system isn't prepared for a freeze of its dollar assets or exclusion from the SWIFT messaging system." A former adviser to China's central bank lamented that "if the US stops playing by the rules, what can China do to guarantee the safety of its foreign assets? We do not have an answer yet."

China's financial vulnerabilities made it more likely to comply with U.S. measures against Russia. Blinken threatened that "China will bear responsibility for any actions it takes to support Russia's aggression, and we will not hesitate to impose costs," while the U.S. secretary of commerce, Gina Raimondo, announced that "we could essentially shut SMIC [China's biggest domestic semiconductor manufacturer] down because we [can] prevent them from using our equipment and our software." Even worse, the U.S. secretary of the Treasury, Janet Yellen, warned that no one should "doubt our ability and resolve to do the same" to China if it invaded Taiwan.

It wasn't surprising that Xi started talking about building an alternative world economy that would be less vulnerable to U.S. pressure. At a virtual meeting with Brazil, Russia, India, and South Africa (the so-called BRICS countries), he urged his fellow leaders to "oppose unilateral sanctions and abuse of sanctions, and reject the small circles built around hegemonism by forming one big family belonging to a community with a shared future for humanity."

But there wasn't any easy way for China to start building a global alternative. No one who wasn't Chinese wanted to use CIPS unless they had to. It relied on the yuan, which wasn't fully convertible on international markets, because China needed to control money flows in and out of the country. CIPS handled roughly thirteen thousand transactions a day, almost exclusively in mainland China and Hong Kong, while SWIFT processed over forty million across the world.

Nor did it make sense for other countries to shift their financial assets to a Chinese-dominated system that was partly disconnected from the rest of the world and beholden to official whims. The United States was sometimes unpredictable, but it at least had the rule of law. There wasn't any law strong enough to stop the Chinese government from grabbing hold of whatever it felt it needed. The government had no compunction about isolating its key financial centers, Hong Kong and Shanghai, from the world in pursuit of its zero-COVID policy. As the monetary economist Barry Eichengreen said, "[I]t is no coincidence that every leading reserve-currency issuer in history has had a republican or democratic form of government, with checks on executive power." Without such checks, government couldn't be trusted.

That didn't stop the United States from worrying that Beijing was building a global economy with Chinese characteristics. Blinken warned in 2022 that "Beijing, despite its rhetoric, is pursuing asymmetric decoupling, seeking to make China less dependent on the world and the world more dependent on China." The irony was, of course, that his words described America's policy nearly as well as they did China's. The United States, too, wanted to become less dependent on the world, either bringing production back home or "friendshoring" it, to use Janet Yellen's term, so that the dangerous choke points in supply chains were on U.S. territory or the territories of allies. As the United States struggled to hold China down and strangle its access to technology, it still wanted to make the world more dependent on it.

And the United States was tempted to make ever greater use of choke points to strangle China. A single Dutch company, ASML, made the extreme ultraviolet lithography machines that were needed to produce the latest generation of semiconductors. The Trump administration had already worked with the Dutch government to stop ASML from exporting its most advanced machines to China. In mid-2022, the Biden administration pressed ASML to stop exporting older machines, too.

The Dutch government was willing to talk, but ASML made it clear that it didn't want to cooperate. In a call with investors, its CEO warned that the world "cannot ignore the fact" that Chinese chip manufacturers feed world markets. If the United States blocked China from making less advanced chips, it might disrupt the world economy.

But if it didn't, China might figure out how to make more advanced semiconductors with less advanced equipment. SMIC had apparently started doing this on a small scale. So should the U.S. government work through allies and the power of persuasion? Or should it accede to the demands of Senator Marco Rubio and the Republican leader on the House Foreign Affairs Committee, Mike McCaul, and threaten dire punishments for companies like ASML if they sold to SMIC? The former risked being ineffective. The latter risked angering allies and disrupting global markets.

Eventually, the Biden administration decided to use the tools that the Trump administration had developed, weaponizing intellectual property through export controls and the foreign direct product rule on a grander scale than Trump had ever dared. This time, the target wasn't a single firm like Huawei. It was China as a whole. The United States imposed the most far-reaching export controls on a single country since the end of the Cold War, blocking China from acquiring technologies that would allow it to produce high-end semiconductors. This was, as Wolf described it, "a fundamental shift in the use of export controls."

As the needs and ambitions of the United States grew, so, too, did the risk of consequences spiraling out of control. The more U.S. officials tried to pin China's economy down, the more resistance they encountered from allies and businesses. European leaders had lost their faith in the gospel of global markets. Germany's chancellor Scholz mournfully accepted that the notion that "close economic ties and mutual dependence would foster stability and security" had "now been destroyed." But the United States hadn't asked Europe to make real sacrifices yet. As Constanze Stelzenmüller at the Brookings Institution said, Germany had "outsourced . . . its export-led growth to China, and its energy needs to Russia." Big European companies, in Germany and elsewhere, depended on the Chinese market and would fight hard to keep it. Volkswagen's chief executive, Herbert Diess, admitted, "China probably doesn't need VW . . . but VW needs China a lot."

Even at home, firms kept their options open while proclaiming their support for the United States. Pat Gelsinger was still arguing that the United States needed to give chip manufacturers tens of billions of dollars to move semiconductor production back from Asia. While he was a "free marketer" and a "globalist," he wanted "manufacturing on American shore," for the "long-term success of the nation." But he didn't talk about how Intel wanted to build up its presence in China, too. Biden administration officials had to push back hard when Intel tried to revive a $10 billion fab in Chengdu, China.

As the United States considered new and harsher coercive options against China, it risked coming to resemble its adversary, driving other countries, businesses, and individuals away. That would mean the decline of America's empire rather than the necessary rise of China's, as dark spaces grew within the world economy where anything could be bought or sold.

Trump's reimposition of sanctions against Iran in 2018 turned out to have been an even bigger mistake than it seemed at the time. Iran had set up an "unprecedented governmental money-laundering operation" with proxies, cutouts, and cash payments, working through banks in China, Hong Kong, Singapore, Turkey, and the UAE. This was less efficient and more costly than open financial relations, but it still generated $80 billion in annual trade. A senior Iranian official boasted that "the majority of our exports of gasoline, steel, petrochemicals—all are under hidden subsidiary activities." If the United States tried to squeeze China too hard, many banks and businesses would be tempted to abandon the bright, centrally lit thoroughfares of the underground empire, and seek out dark twisty passages where no one could see what they were doing.

That would not allow China to dominate the world economy, but

China might be better able to defend itself by going dark. As China realized the dangers of its relationship with the United States, it tried ever harder to build networks outside U.S. oversight and control. The United States treated these bids for independence as bids for empire, widening the spiral further. They had excellent reason to be worried—a more self-sufficient China would be more likely to invade Taiwan. But if the spiral fed upon itself, it might end in a hard decoupling between the largest two economies on the planet, with real consequences for the everyday lives of billions.

A new history book suggested that economic isolation might trigger something much more dangerous. *The Economic Weapon* was Nicholas Mulder's first book. It revisited the history of sanctions and economic blockades between World War I and World War II. Mulder's history explained how the League of Nations, a precursor to today's United Nations, used collective sanctions against aggressive governments. Paradoxically, the League's efforts to build peace helped precipitate World War II. Fear of sanctions helped spur Nazi Germany to embark on conquest so that it could secure the raw materials that the Third Reich feared it would be denied; fear of sanctions also encouraged Japan to create a "yen bloc" including Korea and parts of China. Their fear of economic blockade led them to try to secure themselves by other means, helping to precipitate global war and the deaths of millions.

Mulder worried that economic warfare risked destabilizing the world again. The preferred tools of the U.S. government were "no longer scalpel-like instruments that exploit globalization." Rather than an alternative to war, these weapons had become an essential part of a peacetime arsenal, threatening a "tempest that will change the nature of globalization itself in major ways," and perhaps "quickly spiral out of control."

Like the World War II Axis powers, China is nationalistic,

militaristic, and ruthlessly nondemocratic. It has reason to be paranoid: the world economic order is being retooled to try to hold it down. As the United States and its allies keep loading restrictions onto China, how will it respond? Will it acquiesce, hoping that it will one day be powerful enough to break out of the trap that America had built for it? Will it retaliate through economic means, exploiting choke points and doing everything it can to destabilize the economic empire from beneath? Or might it turn, as Nazi Germany turned, to military aggression, securing its interests through force and territorial gain?

Not only does the United States not have good answers to these questions; it doesn't really have the means to find them. The Pentagon has spent decades thinking about military coercion and the complex dance of military force, counterforce, and deterrence. The responsibility for economic coercion is scattered instead across different parts of the U.S. government: Treasury, Justice, Commerce, and other smaller outfits. None of these agencies was designed to think about economic and national security in any broader strategic way. That was why they pressed buttons to see what would happen. Nor is there a well-organized body of academic research on coercion and counter-coercion that they could have mined for insights. People who studied economic coercion mostly asked when sanctions worked and when they failed. They didn't investigate how coercion might change the world.

Perhaps things could still work out. The masters of the underground empire may steer between the risks of failure and the dangers of succeeding all too well. But it is hard to discern a navigable course. As the CBDC mess demonstrates, the United States and China can't help but see each other's actions as bids for global control. Each thinks it is fundamentally vulnerable to the other, and one's fear builds on the other's as they struggle for control of their economic and political destinies. Neither has a clear understanding of their adversary's motivations or of the new and complex world that they both have to inhabit.

The danger that everything will spin out of control keeps growing, as ever greater financial weapons are developed and deployed. But no one seems to know what to do about it.

———————

The original Sputnik moment, in 1957, spurred a political crisis in America. Worry about Sputnik quickly grew into alarm that the United States was on the wrong side of the "missile gap" because the Soviet Union seemed to have far more intercontinental ballistic missiles (ICBMs). The Soviet premier, Nikita Khrushchev, claimed that his military was turning out ICBMs "like sausages," and the Eisenhower administration believed that the Soviet Union had enough ICBMs to eliminate U.S. nuclear armed forces in a "single massive attack." The missile gap was the central issue in John F. Kennedy's presidential campaign and helps explain why the United States spent vast amounts of money on silicon semiconductors for its missile guidance systems. Today's Silicon Valley is an accidental by-product of 1960s Cold War terrors.

But the missile gap was a myth. When the records were opened up after the Cold War, it turned out that the Soviet Union had only ever deployed four first-generation ICBMs. America's massive arms buildup was based on a fundamental mistake about what the Soviet Union could do. The same story happened again and again during the Cold War. The United States feared that the Soviet Union was gaining some advantage and poured money into catching up, while the Soviet Union was itself struggling desperately to catch up with the United States. The United States thought that the Soviet Union was ready and willing to carry out a devastating first strike with nuclear weapons. The Soviet Union believed that the United States was ready and willing to do the same. Each side's fears fed the other's, leading to an arms race and occasional critical mistakes that could easily have escalated into global nuclear catastrophe.

We're at a pivotal moment, when a similarly dangerous feedback loop is starting to build up again. Now again, a dynamic of mutual fear is taking hold between two great powers, the United States and China, which threatens to pull Europe, businesses, and ordinary people into an ever-widening vortex.

How can we avoid this? Since it is the United States that created the underground empire, it is the United States that must take the first steps. First, it needs to understand the problem that it faces, recognizing that with great powers come great responsibilities. Then, it needs to make sure that others understand the problem, too, especially including its adversaries.

The Cold War offers some important lessons. Mutually escalating fears nearly led to global nuclear war during the Cuban Missile Crisis. Afterward, leaders on both sides were terrified about how near they had come to toppling into Armageddon. An economist turned nuclear strategist, Thomas Schelling, wrote a paper suggesting one straightforward way to dampen down future crises: a hotline that would allow the U.S. president and Soviet premier to communicate directly. Amazingly, one hadn't existed before.

But Schelling and his colleagues also provided something much bigger—a coherent body of ideas that allowed policy makers to think systematically about the dangers of the world they found themselves in and how to mitigate them. Schelling drew paradoxical-seeming insights from mathematical game theory and his own experiences as a parent. Weakness could be strength: your promises and threats would be more believable if you had no power to change your mind. Effective defenses against nuclear attacks might be a terrible idea. If you started building them, your adversary might worry that your next move would be a first strike and decide to attack before it was too late. Such initially bizarre-seeming ideas later won Schelling the Nobel Prize in Economic Sciences. Game theory allowed the United States to think about the Soviet Union strategically—not as a mindless aggressor but as another powerful actor with its own interests that America had to live with.

The United States needs a framework like Schelling's today. It didn't have to think strategically about its economic weapons so long as nobody was really paying attention to them. But now that others have woken up to the underground empire, they are responding, each looking to protect its own interests. Without strategic planning, their responses, and possible counterresponses to these responses, could escalate rapidly in unexpected directions. The problems we confront today are far more complicated than the ones Schelling confronted in the 1960s. He famously compared nuclear confrontation to a game of chess, in which aggressive moves had a random chance of blowing up both players. The stakes may be lower in today's strategic games, but the players are both blindfolded and are playing on a board whose shape they do not know.

As professors of international politics, we have begun to map the chessboard. And it clearly looks different than in the Cold War. As John Lewis Gaddis, the preeminent historian of the Cold War, noted, the surprise of the Cold War was that the two major players never directly went to war with each other. The Long Peace, as he dubbed it, resulted in no small part because of "independence, not interdependence." The United States and the Soviet Union had few economic ties with each other and as a result avoided a host of frictions. Our research on weaponized interdependence—governments' use of global networks as a tool of geopolitics—has shaped how policy makers think about the world exactly because it forces them to think about great power interactions in a world of dense economic ties. Those ties among and between firms have become a source of enormous power. We are ourselves a small part of the story that we tell in this book.

Others are compiling their own maps, some reinforcing, some complementing, some contradicting, some ignoring our own understanding of an irreducibly complex landscape. Properly understanding these problems will require a huge new scientific endeavor, both inside and outside government, to map the business networks that bind the world together, building data on relationships that are hopelessly obscure today, probing for potential vulnerabilities, and assessing how best they could be mitigated. Schelling and his colleagues worked together with military strategists and nuclear scientists. Today's problems require large-scale cooperation among people who understand international relations, financial networks, supply chains, information science, history, and materials science—a Manhattan Project aimed not at blowing things up but at figuring out how they are made.

That already is hard, but it's only the first step. The next is to figure out strategies that preserve the possibility of action—for example, to deter China from attacking Taiwan—but that minimize the risk of actions and retaliations spiraling out of control. That would require the United States to construct a new architecture of institutions, within itself and with its allies. In October 2021, Japan created a ministry of economic security, and in May 2022 its Diet (parliament) passed a law to create a comprehensive economic security strategy. Remarkably, the United States has no similar institution or strategies. People who we spoke to have explained how this absence makes it hard for the United States to think collectively about economic security or to respond to economic security threats. The United States needs to create a new agency with oversight of American economic security measures and build the expertise necessary to create a strategic doctrine that can provide common purpose.

The United States and its partners have already forged new forums to coordinate policy with its allies, including the U.S.-EU Trade and Technology Council (TTC) and the Quad partnership with India, Japan, and Australia. Once it has developed a better strategic understanding, it needs to take the much more uncomfortable step of starting to talk with adversaries, too. The real moment at which the Cold War became more stable was when American and Soviet officials, generals, and scientists started to interact in earnest, sharing and applying the ideas that Schelling and his colleagues had developed. They didn't have an instruction sheet for nuclear chess but had to learn the rules of the game as they went along. That required "the passage of time" and a lot of good luck. Every mistake—the Bay of Pigs, the Cuban Missile Crisis, the Korean War—risked extinction. As they began to understand each other better, they became better able to predict which moves would provoke the other and which would grudgingly be viewed as acceptable. They also began to negotiate the arms control treaties that minimized the risk of escalation into nuclear war from the 1970s on.

America, China, and other powers need a forum where they can frankly discuss the risks of weaponizing the world economy and build the necessary guardrails to mitigate them. Existing economic institutions, such as the World Trade Organization, will not work unless they are radically reformed to reflect the world that is emerging. They reflect the free trade assumptions of a world that has disappeared. But even adversaries may identify informal shared rules that allow them to live together as they start to fill in the blank spaces on the maps, in a world where they will never be able to disconnect fully from each other.

The lessons of the Cold War provide a practical but pessimistic vision of managing great risks through a return to great power politics. Might something better still be possible? After all, Sputnik didn't just lead to nuclear confrontation. It opened up the possibilities of space, of communications satellites that could connect the world, and of new frontiers to boldly explore in future centuries.

Today it might be possible to redirect the spiral inward rather than out, making our own world better instead of seeking to discover new ones. The science fiction writer Kim Stanley Robinson warned in 2015 that dreams of outer space were no substitute for solving our planet's ecological problems. A few years later, he won world fame and the praise of readers like Barack Obama for his science fiction novel *The Ministry for the Future*, which described how a tiny UN organization created a coalition to solve climate change. As Robinson willingly admitted, his thought experiment had holes. His goal was to get people thinking and doing rather than to provide a comprehensive blueprint for them to implement. In particular, the book struggled with the question of how the powerful interests that preferred the status quo could be defeated.

As Europe began to feel its way toward a commonwealth of wind and light, it started mapping a possible route to a new world economy. That economy would not be a utopia, any more than Europe itself, with its bureaucracy, unacknowledged colonial legacies, and sundry rationalized cruelties is a utopia. But it might solve at least some of the world's besetting problems, helping avert the dangers of climate change, and freeing countries from bullying by fossil fuel authoritarians.

We are finishing writing this book in an unlikely future where America has somehow passed legislation that allows it, at last, to put its shoulder behind the enormous task of pushing toward a post-carbon economy. If it doesn't falter, the machineries of its underground empire could help to propel that vision further, providing an imperfect but effective solution to many of the problems that Robinson raises.

Before he took office in 2021, as the U.S. National Security Council's senior director for economics and competitiveness, Peter Harrell described how Trump had pushed the envelope of American economic policy making, using his authority to reshape trade relations in unprecedented ways. Harrell recognized the problems with what Trump had done, but he also saw the possibilities. Global climate change was "arguably the single greatest national security challenge the United States faces."

Harrell described how the tools that Trump had used against economic competition could be turned against the global carbon economy. The United States could impose tariffs on carbon-intensive imports. It could restrict U.S. companies from investing in high-emissions projects, such as extracting oil from tar sands, and designate foreign companies under sanctions laws or restrict their access to U.S. technology. All of the weapons of the underground empire could be deployed to defend a new conception of U.S. national security, combating the dangers of climate change.

These ideas have already allowed the United States to help Europe press toward a post-carbon future. When the EU started to impose its tariffs on high carbon imports, the Biden administration didn't announce countermeasures, as past administrations would have done. Instead, it negotiated a deal to impose a common green tariff on steel and aluminum imports, both of which are currently produced in carbon-intensive ways. That temporarily disadvantaged countries like China, which used more carbon to produce steel than EU and U.S. producers. But it also provided an incentive for China and other countries to develop technologies that would allow lower-intensity production.

The United States has not yet embraced Harrell's more radical suggestions, but they might provide the basis for a different kind of imperium, one that would demonstrably serve the global as well as national interest. That could create a new and very different set of feedback loops, in which national power reinforced global legitimacy and global legitimacy reinforced national power. China would benefit indirectly. It will suffer more from severe climate change than many countries—its economy depends on low-lying coastal cities and its interior is already at heavy risk from drought.

Such measures could be the seed of a different vision of power and global politics. The United States could use similar measures to counter tax evasion and corruption, which it recognizes as a major security threat. On June 3, 2021, the Biden administration announced a national security memorandum directing all U.S. government agencies to identify how they can "modernize, coordinate, and further resource efforts to better fight corruption, tackle illicit finance, hold corrupt actors accountable." The same week that the administration declared corruption a national security priority, OFAC initiated the "largest action targeting corruption" in its history. By the fall of 2021, the administration had released its Strategy on Countering Corruption, describing corruption as a "core" national security interest.

For two decades, America deployed the weapons of its underground empire against adversaries and enemies. Sometimes, especially in the early years, other countries and people benefited, too. Few complained when the United States targeted terrorist organizations like Al-Qaeda and states like North Korea. As the empire's ambitions expanded, it inspired resentment and pushback and began to risk undermining itself.

Now, perhaps, the United States could deploy its empire to build a commonwealth, in which power and legitimacy reinforce each other. Like all such efforts, it would be highly imperfect. It would be most active where U.S. self-interest and global self-interest overlapped. Some urgent problems would be carved out and left unaddressed. Economic coercion would be most effective in pushing other countries to make necessary choices that they already know they have to make than ones they starkly oppose.

But helping build such a commonwealth, with all its flaws, compromises, contradictions, and blind spots, is a far better path than that of confrontation breeding confrontation. Such a project wouldn't substitute for the less ambitious strategies, alliance building, and measured use of power that we have described already. We still need to check the vicious chain reactions of a world in which antagonistic powers are lashed together to their enormous distress. What it would do is to offer the hope that working toward collective goals can generate its own virtuous feedbacks, building security and remaking economies to counter the threat of oppression or collective disaster.

There is no visible exit from the underground empire. Every tunnel that seems to lead out ends up turning back in on itself. Business leaders hoped to free themselves from the chains of government but discovered that they had only forged new manacles for themselves and others. Politicians once dreamed that global markets would guarantee their security. They have had a cold and bitter awakening as markets became battlefields. Dreams of undermining empire from the outside in provoked the empire to dig its own countermines from the center out.

The roots of imperium go far too deep to ever fully be torn out. Yet even if we cannot escape the darkness underneath, we can strive to bend the growth of empire upward, toward the sun and air.

NOTES

Introduction: All Roads Lead to Rome

1 **Palladian facades:** Cecelia Lahiff, "*Aemulatio* and *Sprezzatura*: Palladio and the Legacy of Vitruvius," *Art Journal* no. 1 (2018): 12–22.

2 **like the mycelium:** Eben Bayer, "The Mycelium Revolution Is upon Us," *Scientific American*, July 1, 2019, retrieved on November 11, 2022, from https://blogs.scientificamerican.com/observations/the-mycelium-revolution-is-upon-us/.

3 **in the footsteps of their merchants:** See, for example, John Gallagher and Ronald Robinson, "The Imperialism of Free Trade," *Economic History Review* 6, no. 1 (1953): 1–15.

3 **imagine them as roads:** Like all metaphors, this leaves some important things out. As we explain later, the Internet, for example, is now made up of mirrors as much as international thoroughfares. That doesn't affect the main logic of our argument, although it does affect the detail of how it works in practice.

3 **a highway with millions of lanes:** Strictly speaking, fiber-optic cables do not have as many individual strands as that, but they have enough total capacity to carry millions of seemingly simultaneous exchanges.

4 **an "Information Superhighway":** "Remarks by Al Gore," Royce Hall, UCLA, Los Angeles, California, January 11, 1994, retrieved November 11, 2022, from

https://clintonwhitehouse1.archives.gov/White_House/EOP/OVP/other/superhig
.html.

6   a "CIA Project": Ewen MacAskill, "Putin Calls Internet a 'CIA Project' Renew-
     ing Fears of Web Breakup," *Guardian*, April 24, 2014.

7   an old world divided by a Wall: Thomas Friedman, "DOScapital," *Foreign Policy*
     116 (1999): 110–16.

7   like nailing Jell-O to the wall: William Clinton, "Remarks on Permanent Normal
     Trade Relations with China," March 8, 2000, retrieved on July 22, 2022, from https:
     //www.c-span.org/video/?c4893404/user-clip-clinton-firewall-jello.

7   "intimidate everybody": James Carville, quoted, "The World Economy," *Econo-
     mist*, October 7, 1995.

7   attacking your own economy: Thomas Friedman, *The World Is Flat: A Brief History
     of the Twenty-First Century* (New York: Farrar, Straus and Giroux, 2005).

8   As in previous historical moments: See Simone Müller and Heidi Tworek, "'The
     Telegraph and the Bank': On the Interdependence of Global Communications and
     Capitalism, 1866–1914," *Journal of Global History* 10, no. 2 (2015): 259–83. Müller
     and Tworek (p. 263) describe how the submarine cables that carried telegraphs
     were laid down according to theories of "natural monopoly," only later being used
     for "military, imperial, or strategic control."

8   social scientists often talk about path dependence: Paul Pierson, "Increasing
     Returns, Path Dependence, and the Study of Politics," *American Political Science
     Review* 94, no. 2 (2000): 251–67.

9   According to an NSA estimate: Charlie Savage, *Power Wars: Inside Obama's Post
     9–11 Presidency* (New York: Little, Brown, 2015), 177.

10   every single phone call in an entire country: Barton Gellman and Ashkan Sol-
     tani, "NSA Surveillance Program Reaches 'into the Past' to Retrieve, Replay
     Phone Calls," *Washington Post*, March 18, 2014.

11   options for gathering data from the world: Juan Zarate, *Treasury's War: The
     Unleashing of a New Era of Financial Warfare* (New York: PublicAffairs, 2013).

12   the Internet itself was at risk: Rob Price, "Eric Schmidt Thinks a Ruling by
     Europe's Top Court Threatens One of the Greatest Achievements of Humanity,"
     Business Insider, October 15, 2015, retrieved on December 21, 2021, from https://
     www.businessinsider.com/eric-schmidt-ecj-safe-harbor-ruling-threatens-one-of
     -the-great-achievements-of-humanity-2015-10.

12   if the United States overused its powers: Jack Lew, "Remarks of Secretary Lew on
     the Evolution of Sanctions and Lessons for the Future," delivered at the Carnegie
     Endowment for International Peace, Washington, DC, May 30, 2016.

12   few people outside Colson Whitehead novels: Colson Whitehead's wonder-
     ful novel, *The Intuitionist* (New York: Knopf Doubleday, 1999), depicts warring
     factions of elevator inspectors as a means of disentangling the racial politics of

America's internal empire. Francis Spufford's similarly excellent *Red Plenty* (London: Faber and Faber, 2010) uses a novelist's tools to grasp the economic infrastructure of the Soviet economy and the ideas that animated it.

13 **a toddler with new toys:** Daniel Drezner, *The Toddler in Chief: What Donald Trump Teaches Us about the Modern Presidency* (Chicago: University of Chicago Press, 2020).

13 **As a cynical European official put it:** "America's War on Huawei Nears Its Endgame," *Economist*, July 18, 2020, retrieved on July 20, 2022, from https://www.economist.com/briefing/2020/07/16/americas-war-on-huawei-nears-its-endgame.

14 **"cooperation becomes dependence":** Roger Cohen, "Macron Tells Biden That Cooperation with US Cannot Be Dependence," *New York Times*, January 29, 2021, retrieved on July 20, 2022, from https://www.nytimes.com/2021/01/29/world/europe/macron-biden.html.

14 **months of disruption:** Vasco M. Carvalho, Makoto Nirei, Yukiko U. Saito, and Alireza Tahbaz-Salehi, "Supply Chain Disruptions: Evidence from the Great East Japan Earthquake," *Quarterly Journal of Economics* 136, no. 2 (2021), 1255–1321.

15 **it revealed similar vulnerabilities:** Jill Kilpatrick and Lee Barter, *COVID-19: Managing Supply Chain Risk and Disruption*, Deloitte Development LCC, 2020, 14.

Chapter 1: Walter Wriston's World

17 **His book:** Walter B. Wriston, *The Twilight of Sovereignty: How the Information Revolution Is Transforming Our World* (New York: Charles Scribner, 1992).

17 **"decentralize power":** Wriston, *The Twilight of Sovereignty*, 4.

17 **"once vital strategic 'choke points'":** Wriston, *The Twilight of Sovereignty*, 8.

18 **the irresistible challenge:** Walter Wriston, *Information, Electronics and Gold*, speech written for the International Monetary Conference, London, June 11, 1979.

18 **to help found the Mont Pèlerin Society:** For discussion of the origin and disparate aims of the Society, see Angus Burgin, *The Great Persuasion: Reinventing Free Markets since the Depression* (Cambridge, MA: Harvard University Press, 2015). On the invitation to Wriston's father, see Bruce Caldwell, *Mont Pèlerin 1947* (Palo Alto, CA: Hoover Institution Press, 2020), 9. Wriston's father, who later joined the Society, shared his son's fascination with technology and interdependence, marveling in a 1924 speech about how "the cable and the wireless have been shrinking the effective size of the world beyond the dreams of our fathers." The quote comes from Phillip L. Zweig, *Wriston: Walter Wriston, Citibank, and the Rise and Fall of American Financial Supremacy* (Digital Edition, PLZ Publishers, 2019), 17.

18 **Walter was a globalist:** Zweig, *Walter Wriston*. For historical discussion of

globalism and neoliberalism, see Quinn Slobodian, *Globalists: The End of Empire and the Birth of Neoliberalism* (Cambridge, MA: Harvard University Press, 2018).

18 **"the most influential banker"**: Roy C. Smith, *The Global Bankers: A Top Investment Banker Explores the New World of International Deal-Making and Finance* (New York: Truman Talley, 1989), 33–34.

18 **"all others copy shamelessly"**: Smith, *The Global Bankers*, 34.

18 **"the perspective of a participant"**: Wriston, *The Twilight of Sovereignty*, xiii.

19 **a distinct piratical flair**: Zweig, *Walter Wriston*, 797 and passim.

19 **the high seas of global markets**: Wriston, *Information, Electronics and Gold*.

19 **had risked causing apoplexy**: Marc Levinson tells this story in his book, *The Box: How the Shipping Container Made the World Smaller and the World Economy Bigger* (Princeton, NJ: Princeton University Press, 2006). Also see Zweig, *Walter Wriston*.

19 **As he explained**: Wriston, *Information, Electronics and Gold*.

19 **Instead it might master them**: Wriston, *Information, Electronics and Gold*. See also Wriston, *The Twilight of Sovereignty*, 66: "Not only are governments losing control over money, but this newly free money in its own way is asserting its control over them, disciplining irresponsible policies."

19 **the free movement of information**: Wriston, *Information, Electronics and Gold*.

19 **As Wriston explained later**: Wriston, *The Twilight of Sovereignty*, 81, 85.

20 **"centralization . . . is a fascist state"**: Zweig, *Walter Wriston*, 242.

20 **"international banking is a system"**: Wriston, *Information, Electronics and Gold*.

21 **pneumatic tube networks**: Susan V. Scott and Markos Zachariadis, *The Society for Worldwide Interbank Financial Telecommunication (SWIFT): Cooperative Governance for Network Innovation, Standards, and Community* (London: Routledge, 2014), 12.

21 **cases of Scotch whisky**: Zweig, *Walter Wriston*, 112.

22 **"branch of the information business"**: Walter B. Wriston, *Risk and Other Four-Letter Words* (New York: Harper & Row, 1986), 135.

22 **like J. P. Morgan and Warburg**: Ron Chernow, *The House of Morgan: An American Banking Dynasty and the Rise of Modern Finance* (New York: Atlantic Monthly Press, 1990).

23 **the political economist Eric Helleiner**: See the classic account in Eric Helleiner, *States and the Re-emergence of Global Finance* (Ithaca, NY: Cornell University Press, 1994).

23 **U.S. officials**: Gary Burn, *The Re-emergence of Global Finance* (London: Palgrave, 2006), chap. 6.

23 **the Soviet Union**: Wriston, *The Twilight of Sovereignty*, 63–64.

23 **As Wriston explained**: Wriston, *The Twilight of Sovereignty*, 69.

24 **"system to a halt"**: Zweig, *Walter Wriston*, 579.

25 **"de facto payments mechanism of the world"**: Walter B. Wriston, "De Facto

Payments Mechanism" in *If You Ask Me: A Global Banker Reflects on Our Times*, Walter B. Wriston Papers, Tufts University, 1980, retrieved on September 17, 2021, from https://dl.tufts.edu/teiviewer/parent/vq27zz94c/chapter/c1s36.

25   **shared code books:** Scott and Zachariadis, *The Society for Worldwide Interbank Financial Telecommunication*, 12.

25   **branches in over ninety countries:** Mark S. Mizruchi and Gerald F. Davis, "The Globalization of American Banking, 1962–1981" in *The Sociology of the Economy*, ed. Frank Dobbin (New York: Russell Sage Foundation, 2004).

26   **"nexus of the world's payments system":** Zweig, *Walter Wriston*, 477.

26   **"We advise you to use MARTI":** Scott and Zachariadis, *The Society for Worldwide Interbank Financial Telecommunication*, 18.

26   **"you make yourself captive":** Scott and Zachariadis, *The Society for Worldwide Interbank Financial Telecommunication*, 18.

27   **SWIFT had 270 member banks:** Scott and Zachariadis, *The Society for Worldwide Interbank Financial Telecommunication*, 18.

27   **"people's resistance to MARTI":** Zweig, *Walter Wriston*, 382.

27   **Robert Moore of Chemical Bank:** Scott and Zachariadis, *The Society for Worldwide Interbank Financial Telecommunication*, 109.

27   **Citibank's Yawar Shah:** Yawar Shah's LinkedIn page, retrieved on September 16, 2021, from https://www.linkedin.com/in/yawar-shah-42514b16.

27   **ten billion messages annually:** SWIFT, *Highlights 2021, Messaging Traffic and Operational Performance* (Brussels, Belgium: SWIFT, 2021).

27   **"no real alternative":** Scott and Zachariadis, *The Society for Worldwide Interbank Financial Telecommunication*, 127.

28   **North Korean hackers exploited weaknesses:** PYMENTS, "Anatomy of a Bank Heist, SWIFT-ly Done by Phishers," Pyments.com, September 17, 2018, retrieved on September 17, 2021, from https://www.pymnts.com/news/security-and-risk/2018/bangladesh-bank-heist-swift-phishing-scam-fraud-doj/.

28   **Walter Wriston enthused:** Thomas A. Bass, "The Future of Money," *WIRED*, October 1, 1996, retrieved on September 7, 2021, from https://www.wired.com/1996/10/wriston/.

29   **Wriston had intimate and painful experience:** This paragraph draws on Wriston, *The Twilight of Sovereignty*, 42–43.

29   **"utterly dependent on the new world communications network":** Wriston, *The Twilight of Sovereignty*, 47.

30   **"interprets censorship as damage":** The phrase is attributed to John Gilmore in Philip Elmer-DeWitt, "First Nation in Cyberspace," *Time*, December 6, 1993.

30   **"bullseye of America's Internet":** Andrew Blum, "The Bullseye of America's Internet," Gizmodo, May 29, 2012, retrieved on July 19, 2022, from https://gizmodo.com/the-bullseye-of-america-s-internet-5913934.

31   "command and control networks": *Paul Baran and the Origins of the Internet* (Santa
      Monica, CA: RAND Corporation, undated), retrieved on July 20, 2021, from
      https://www.rand.org/about/history/baran.html; and Paul Baran, *On Distributed
      Communications I. Introduction to Distributed Communications Networks*, Memoran-
      dum RM-3420-PR (Santa Monica, CA: RAND Corporation, 1964).

31   one kind of crossroad: "Internet Exchange Points (IXPs)," *Internet Society*,
      undated, retrieved on December 1, 2022, from https://www.internetsociety.org
      /issues/ixps/.

32   developed the basic "protocols": Ben Tarnoff, "How the Internet Was Invented,"
      Guardian, July 15, 2016.

32   A new microeconomy: See Paul E. Ceruzzi's history of the area in *Internet Alley:
      High Technology in Tysons Corner, 1945–2005* (Cambridge, MA: MIT Press, 2008).

32   a long spike: Ceruzzi, *Internet Alley.*

32   computer "mutant": Kara Swisher, "Anticipating the Internet," *Washington Post*,
      May 6, 1996.

32   forty-eight-ounce porterhouses: Nathan Gregory, *Securing the Network: F. Scott
      Yeager and the Rise of the Commercial Internet* (Palo Alto, CA: privately published by
      Reprivata Corporation, 2016), 135.

33   "UUNET would become the default route": Gregory, *Securing the Network*, 137.

33   over 90 percent of all Internet traffic: Gregory, *Securing the Network*, 150.

33   members of MAE-East: James Bamford, *The Shadow Factory: The Ultra-Secret
      NSA from 9/11 to the Eavesdropping on America* (New York: Doubleday, 2008), 187.

33   smaller companies were turned away: Gregory, *Securing the Network*, 161.

33    $93.25 a share: Om Malik, *Broadbandits: Inside the $750 Billion Telecom Heist*
      (New York: John Wiley, 2003), 11.

33   their own old-boys club: As Jay Adelson described it, "[I]t was a who you know
      game." See the interview at: "Jay Meets Other Equinox Co-founder Al Avery
      (Part 3 of Jay Adelson Visiting PAIX)," September 18, 2013, YouTube video, 1:39,
      https://www.youtube.com/watch?v=QtVMdFlsck0.

34   its seventy-second consecutive quarter of growth: Abigail Opiah, "Equinix
      Projects 10–11% Increase in 2021 Annual Revenue Growth," Capacity Media,
      February 11, 2021.

34   build a "neutral exchange": Authors' interview with Jay Adelson, July 8, 2021.

34   "most dense [interconnection point] in the world": Authors' interview with
      Jay Adelson. See also Penny Jones, "Equinix—It Was Always a Big Idea," Data
      Center Dynamics, July 23, 2013, retrieved on July 22, 2022, from https://www
      .datacenterdynamics.com/en/news/equinix-it-was-always-a-big-idea/.

34   a hand grasping a bunch of old-school analog phone cords: Authors' interview
      with Jay Adelson.

35   the largest colocation provider on the planet: Yevgeniy Sverdlik, "2021:

These Are the World's Largest Data Center Colocation Providers," Data Center Knowledge, January 15, 2021, retrieved on July 19, 2022, from https://www .datacenterknowledge.com/archives/2017/01/20/here-are-the-10-largest-data -center-providers-in-the-world.

35   **Ashburn is its largest facility:** Chris Kimm, "Inside Equinix Data Centers: A View of the Top 5 North American Metros," *Equinix* (blog), September 19, 2019, retrieved on July 19, 2022, from https://blog.equinix.com/blog/2019/09/19/inside -equinix-data-centers-a-view-of-the-top-5-north-american-metros/.

35   **"a dominating force":** Jones, "Equinix."

35   **"engine of profitability":** Brad Stone, *Amazon Unbound: Jeff Bezos and the Invention of a Global Empire* (New York: Simon & Schuster, 2021), 96.

36   **By poring through municipal property records:** Ingrid Burrington, "Why Amazon's Data Centers Are Hidden in Spy Country," *Atlantic*, January 8, 2016.

36   **"the inconvenience of transferring it back out":** Brad Stone, *Amazon Unbound*, 99.

36   **websites across the globe . . . crashed:** Jay Greene, "Amazon's Cloud-Computing Outage on Wednesday Was Triggered by Effort to Boost System's Capacity," *Washington Post*, November 28, 2020; "Summary of the Amazon Kinesis Event in the Northern Virginia Region," *Amazon* (corporate blog), November 25, 2020, retrieved on July 19, 2022, from https://aws.amazon.com/message/11201/.

36   **"kill off about 70 percent of the Internet":** Katie Shepherd, "He Brought a Sawed-Off Rifle to the Capitol on Jan. 6. Then He Plotted to Bomb Amazon Data Centers," *Washington Post*, June 10, 2021.

37   **"fuck up the Amazon servers":** Katie Shepherd, "He Brought a Sawed-Off Rifle to the Capitol on Jan. 6."

37   **C-4 plastic explosives:** Brian Barrett, "A Far-Right Extremist Allegedly Plotted to Blow Up Amazon Data Centers," *WIRED*, April 9, 2021, retrieved on July 19, 2022, from https://www.wired.com/story/far-right-extremist-allegedly-plotted-blow -up-amazon-data-centers/.

37   **seventy nondescript low-slung warehouses:** Ally Schweitzer, "The Pandemic Is Driving a Data Center Boom in Northern Virginia," *DCist*, March 25, 2021, retrieved on July 19, 2022, from https://dcist.com/story/21/03/25/the-pandemic-is -driving-a-data-center-boom-in-northern-virginia/.

37   **an estimated 4.5 gigawatts:** "Clicking Clean Virginia: The Dirty Energy Powering Data Center Alley," Greenpeace, February 13, 2019, retrieved on July 19, 2022, from https://www.greenpeace.org/usa/reports/click-clean-virginia/.

37   **up to 70 percent:** Joel St. Germain, "Why Is Ashburn the Data Center Capital of the World?" Datacenters.com, August 29, 2019, retrieved on July 19, 2022, from https://www.datacenters.com/news/why-is-ashburn-the-data-center-capital-of -the-world.

37   **nearly twice the capacity:** St. Germain, "Why Is Ashburn."

37 **lure Jeff Bezos:** Chris Hudgins and Katie Arcieri, "Amazon Hiring for Cloud Services, Alexa Products at HQ2 in Arlington, VA," S&P Global Market Intelligence, September 4, 2019, retrieved on July 19, 2022, from https://www.spglobal .com/marketintelligence/en/news-insights/latest-news-headlines/amazon-hiring -for-cloud-services-alexa-products-at-hq2-in-arlington-va-53798578.

37 **laying new roads on top of old ones:** Sometimes this was literally true. In Manhattan, optical fibers were run along the old system of pneumatic tubes. Personal communication from Tom Standage, https://twitter.com/tomstandage/status/148499 0326183972864.

37 **"a very small number of bottlenecks":** Neal Stephenson, "Mother Earth Mother Board," *WIRED*, December 1, 1996, retrieved on July 6, 2022, from https://www .wired.com/1996/12/ffglass/.

38 **"fundamental change in the world's work":** Wriston, *The Twilight of Sovereignty*, 78.

38 **"the dominant factor of production":** Wriston, *The Twilight of Sovereignty*, 78.

38 **Adam Smith's wealth of nations:** Adam Smith, *An Inquiry into the Nature and Causes of the Wealth of Nations with an Introductory Essay and Notes by J. Shield Nicholson* (London: T. Nelson and Sons, 1887).

39 **an outgrowth of U.S. military spending:** Margaret O'Mara, *The Code: Silicon Valley and the Remaking of America* (New York: Penguin Books, 2019).

39 **Fremont, California, and the East Bay:** O'Mara, *The Code*, 264.

39 **Singapore and Ireland:** Everett M. Rogers and Judith Larsen, *Silicon Valley Fever* (New York: Basic Books, 1984), 122.

39 **As O'Mara explained to us:** Personal communication from Margaret O'Mara, April 15, 2022.

39 **Its first Singapore plant:** *1968–1978: The First Decade*, Singapore Semiconductor Industry Association, retrieved on July 6, 2022, from https://ssia.org.sg/wp -content/uploads/2018/12/Semiconductor50_Timeline_R5_flatten_forWeb.pdf.

39 **source components from a single supplier:** Leander Kahney, *Tim Cook: The Genius Who Took Apple to the Next Level* (New York: Portfolio Books, 2019), 60.

40 **an estimated 1.3 million workers:** Kahney, *Tim Cook*, 76.

41 **it wasn't going to happen:** Charles Duhigg and Keith Bradsher, "How the U.S. Lost Out on iPhone Work," *New York Times*, January 21, 2012.

41 **a lifetime of around five years:** Daniel Nenni and Paul McLellan, *Fabless: The Transformation of the Semiconductor Industry* (n.p.: SemiWiki.com, 2014), 18.

42 **Gordon Campbell, a well-known entrepreneur:** Nenni and McLellan, *Fabless*.

42 **a $50 million investment:** *Morris Chang's Last Speech*, April 2021, translated by Kevin Xu, retrieved on July 22, 2022, from https://web.archive.org/web /20211016142636/https://interconnected.blog/morris-changs-last-speech/.

42 **a market opportunity:** Nenni and McLennan, *Fabless*.

42 **With $100 million in support:** Chad Bown, "How the United States Marched

the Semiconductor Industry into Its Trade War with China," *East Asian Economic Review* 24, no. 4 (2020): 349–88.

42   **relationships with its customers:** Hau Lee, Seungjin Whang, and Shiri Sneorson, *Taiwan Semiconductor Manufacturing Company: The Semiconductor Services Company.* Case GS-40, Stanford Business School, 2006.

43   **a beautiful and extraordinarily complex global ecology:** Nathan Associates, *Beyond Borders: The Global Semiconductor Value Chain. How an Interconnected Industry Promotes Innovation and Growth*, Semiconductor Industry Association, 2016, retrieved on September 21, 2021, from https://www.semiconductors.org/wp-content/uploads /2018/06/SIA-Beyond-Borders-Report-FINAL-June-7.pdf.

43   **"a globally interdependent industry":** Nathan Associates, *Beyond Borders.*

43   **advanced logic chip:** John VerWey, "From TSMC to Tungsten: Semiconductor Supply Chain Risks," Semi-Literate, May 3, 2021, retrieved on August 29, 2022, from https://semiliterate.substack.com/p/from-tsmc-to-tungsten-semiconductor.

45   **a skeptical riposte:** Eric Helleiner, "Electronic Money: A Challenge to the Sovereign State?" *Journal of International Affairs* 51, no. 2 (1998): 387–409.

45   **"increasingly concentrated":** Helleiner, "Electronic Money," 395.

45   **"'choke points'":** Helleiner, "Electronic Money," 394.

45   **power of governments:** Helleiner, "Electronic Money," 397.

Chapter 2: The STORMBREW Map

46   **"STORMBREW at a Glance":** National Security Agency, "Special Source Operations: Corporate Partner Access," retrieved on November 7, 2022, from https: //www.aclu.org/sites/default/files/field_document/Special%20Source%20Operations%20(Corporate%20Partners).pdf.

47   **a papal bull:** "AD 1493: The Pope Asserts Rights to Colonize, Convert, and Enslave," U.S. National Library of Medicine timeline, retrieved on July 28, 2021, from https://www.nlm.nih.gov/nativevoices/timeline/171.html.

47   **terra nullius:** China Miéville, *Between Equal Rights: A Marxist Theory of International Law* (London: Brill, 2005).

47   **Other rulers drew up their own maps:** On the relationship between the pope's division of the world and John Dee's maps for Queen Elizabeth, see Christopher Whitby, "John Dee's Actions with Spirits, 22 December 1581 to 23 May 1583" (PhD diss., University of Birmingham, 1981), vol. 1, 388–89.

47   **exquisite maps:** William H. Sherman, "Putting the British Seas on the Map: John Dee's Imperial Cartography," *Cartographica* 35, nos. 3–4 (1998): 1–10.

47   **"iust Arthurien clayme":** Glyn Parry, "John Dee and the Elizabethan British Empire in Its European Context," *Historical Journal* 49, no. 3 (2006): 643–75.

47   **Created by the Truman administration:** "The Origins of NSA," Center for Cryptologic History, National Security Agency, retrieved on November 29, 2021, from https://www.nsa.gov/portals/75/documents/about/cryptologic-heritage/historical-figures-publications/publications/NSACSS/origins_of_nsa.pdf?ver=2019-08-09-091926-677.

48   **which has been identified as Verizon/MCI:** Julia Angwin, Charlie Savage, Jeff Larson, Henrik Moltke, Laura Poitras, and James Risen, "AT&T Helped U.S. Spy on Internet on a Vast Scale," *New York Times*, August 15, 2015.

48   **Such as PRISM:** "NSA Slides Explain the PRISM Data-Collection Program," *Washington Post*, July 10, 2013.

50   **testimony to the House:** Michael V. Hayden, "Statement for the Record by Lt Gen Michael V. Hayden, USAF, Director before the House Permanent Select Committee on Intelligence," speech, April 12, 2000, retrieved on November 7, 2022, from https://www.nsa.gov/Press-Room/Speeches-Testimony/Article-View/Article/1620510/statement-for-the-record-by-lt-gen-michael-v-hayden-usaf-director-before-the-ho/.

50   **the Rev. Martin Luther King Jr.:** Matthew M. Aid and William Burr, "'Disreputable If Not Outright Illegal': The National Security Agency Versus Martin Luther King, Muhammad Ali, Art Buchwald, Frank Church, et al.," National Security Archives, George Washington University, September 25, 2013.

50   **if Osama bin Laden:** Vernon Loeb, "Test of Strength," *Washington Post*, July 29, 2001.

50   **Hayden wanted to defend his embattled agency:** *Statement for the Record of NSA Director Lt Gen Michael V. Hayden, USAF, House Permanent Select Committee on Intelligence*, 12 April 2000, retrieved on July 28, 2021, from https://fas.org/irp/congress/2000_hr/hayden.html (checked July 28, 2021).

50   **the NSA was targeting the homeland:** Michael V. Hayden, *Playing to the Edge: American Intelligence in the Age of Terror* (New York: Penguin, 2016), 4.

50   **He shrank into his seat:** Loeb, "Test of Strength."

51   **programs like ECHELON:** Duncan Campbell, "My Life Unmasking British Eavesdroppers," *Intercept*, August 3, 2015. For a broader history, see Patrick Radden Keefe, *Chatter: Dispatches from the Secret World of Global Eavesdropping* (New York: Random House, 2005).

51   **submarine cables:** Phil Edwards, "A Map of All the Underwater Cables That Connect the Internet," *Vox*, November 8, 2015.

51   **a far harder time:** Franco Piodi and Iolanda Mombelli, *The Echelon Affair: The EP and the Global Interception System*, Historical Archives Unit, European Parliamentary Research Service, November 2014.

51   **apparently failed dismally:** Whitfield Diffie and Susan Landau, *Privacy on the Line: The Politics of Wiretapping and Encryption* (Cambridge, MA: MIT Press,

1998). The word "apparently" is used deliberately. It turned out later that the NSA used its influence over cryptographic standards to create at least one standard that it could easily compromise. See Nicole Perlroth, Jeff Larson, and Scott Shane, "N.S.A. Able to Foil Basic Safeguards of Privacy on Web," *New York Times*, September 5, 2013.

51 **pushed out the boundaries:** *NSA's Key Role in Major Developments in Computer Science*, National Security Agency, July 19, 2017, retrieved on August 29, 2022, from https://www.nsa.gov/portals/75/documents/news-features/declassified-documents/nsa-early-computer-history/6586785-nsa-key-role-in-major-developments-in-computer-science.pdf.

51 **thousands of patents:** Shane Harris, "The NSA's Patents, in One Searchable Database," *Foreign Policy*, July 30, 2014.

51 **"the *whole* system":** Hayden, *Playing to the Edge*, 1.

51 **The crash lasted for days:** Jamie McIntyre and Pam Benson, "U.S. Intelligence Computer Crashes for Nearly 3 Days," CNN, January 29, 2000.

51 **"We can't actually do that":** Hayden, *Playing to the Edge*, 12.

51 **the agency had sixty-eight different email systems:** Loeb, "Test of Strength."

52 **Politicians had cut 30 percent from its budget:** Loeb, "Test of Strength."

52 **When Hayden returned to this imaginary example:** "Statement for the Record by Lieutenant General Michael V. Hayden, USAF Director, National Security Agency/Chief, Central Security Service, before the Joint Inquiry of the Senate Select Committee on Intelligence and the House Permanent Select Committee on Intelligence," October 17, 2002; "Remarks by General Michael V. Hayden: What American Intelligence and Especially the NSA Have Been Doing to Defend the Nation," National Press Club, January 23, 2006.

52 **employing unencrypted email:** Bruce W. Don, David R. Frelinger, Scott Gerwehr, Eric Landree, and Brian A. Jackson, *Network Technologies for Networked Terrorists: Assessing the Value of Information and Communication Technologies to Modern Terrorist Organizations* (Santa Monica, CA: RAND, 2007).

52 **funded the hijackers:** John Roth, Douglas Greenburg, and Serena Wille, "Monograph on Terrorist Financing: Staff Report to the Commission," National Commission on Terrorist Attacks Upon the United States, Washington, DC, August 24, 2004, retrieved on November 29, 2021, from https://govinfo.library.unt.edu/911/staff_statements/911_TerrFin_Monograph.pdf.

52 **"enemy in the global war on terrorism":** Hayden, "Remarks by General Michael V. Hayden."

52 **As Hayden saw it:** Hayden, *Playing to the Edge*, 405.

53 **to redraw the line:** "Michael V. Hayden, who led the NSA on 9/11 and later took over the CIA, was fond of saying that in carrying out intelligence activities, 'I had a duty to play aggressively—right up to the line.' . . . The catch was that the Bush

legal team's secret memos defined what those legal limits were—and weren't." Charlie Savage, *Power Wars: Inside Obama's Post-9/11 Presidency* (New York: Little, Brown, 2017), 45–46.

53 **"Mogadishu":** Hayden, *Playing to the Edge*, 132.

53 **As far back as the 1980s:** Savage, *Power Wars*, 173–75.

53 **Writers, including Savage:** Savage, *Power Wars*; Laura K. Donohue, *The Future of Foreign Intelligence: Privacy and Surveillance in a Digital Age* (New York: Oxford University Press, 2016); and Jennifer Stisa Granick, *American Spies: Modern Surveillance, Why You Should Care, and What to Do about It* (New York: Cambridge University Press, 2017).

54 **John Yoo provided:** Granick, *American Spies*.

54 **"Stellar Wind" program:** Granick, *American Spies*.

54 **Hayden liked to compare:** Hayden, *Playing to the Edge*, 132.

54 **"exploitation of entire populations":** Hayden, *Playing to the Edge*, 132.

54 **the "remarkable transition":** Hayden, *Playing to the Edge*, 141–42.

54 **If "you were not protected by the US Constitution":** Hayden, *Playing to the Edge*, 146.

55 **Mark Klein, a skilled technician:** Our account draws on Mark Klein, *Wiring Up the Big Brother Machine . . . and Fighting It* (Charleston, SC: Booksurge, 2009), and our interview with Mark Klein, conducted on August 5, 2021.

56 **another former AT&T employee:** Ryan Gallagher and Henrik Moltke, "The Wiretap Rooms: The NSA's Hidden Spy Hubs in Eight U.S. Cities," *Intercept*, June 25, 2018.

56 **"froze" in his seat:** Klein, *Wiring Up the Big Brother Machine*, 42.

56 **The NSA's Fairview program:** Gallagher and Moltke, "The Wiretap Rooms."

56 **"extreme willingness":** Quoted in an NSA slideshow, "SSO Corporate Portfolio Overview," retrieved on August 29, 2022, from https://www.eff.org/files/2015/08/15/20150815-nyt-att-fairview-stormbrew.pdf.

57 **was paid to telecommunications firms:** Craig Timberg and Barton Gellman, "NSA Paying U.S. Companies for Access to Communications Networks," *Washington Post*, August 29, 2013.

57 **"30 minutes of warning":** Craig Timberg and Ellen Nakashima, "Agreements with Private Companies Protect U.S. Access to Cables' Data for Surveillance," *Washington Post*, July 6, 2013.

57 **a secret NSA presentation:** National Security Agency, *PRISM/US-984-XN Overview*, retrieved on November 29, 2021, from https://nsa.gov1.info/dni/prism.html.

58 **"quietly encourage[d] the telecommunications industry":** Eric Lichtblau and James Risen, "Spy Agency Mined Vast Data Trove, Officials Report," *New York Times*, December 24, 2005.

58   **Yahoo! refused:** Craig Timberg, "U.S. Threatened Massive Fine to Force Yahoo to Release Data," *Washington Post*, September 11, 2014.

59   **As Hayden described it years later:** Michael Hirsh and National Journal, "Silicon Valley Doesn't Just Help the Surveillance State—It Built It," *Atlantic*, June 10, 2013.

59   **"we still do not know all of that even today":** Brad Smith, interviewed by Cameron Kerry, "The Future of Global Technology, Privacy, and Regulation," Brookings Institution, Washington, DC, June 24, 2014, retrieved on November 29, 2021, from https://news.microsoft.com/download/exec/smith/2014/06 -24brookingsinstitution.pdf.

59   **"a blank space on the map":** Keefe, *Chatter*, 238.

60   **presidential policy directive:** Henry Farrell and Abraham Newman, *Of Privacy and Power: The Transatlantic Struggle over Freedom and Security* (Princeton, NJ: Princeton University Press, 2019).

60   **"Obama's favorite non-combatant command":** David E. Sanger, "Global Crises Put Obama's Strategy of Caution to the Test," *New York Times*, March 16, 2014.

61   **As one senior Treasury official described it:** David Aufhauser, "Testimony: Counterterror Initiatives in the Terror Finance Program," *Hearings before the Committee on Banking, Housing, and Urban Affairs, United States Senate, September 25, October 22, 2003, and April 29 and September 29, 2004*, retrieved on October 1, 2021, from https://www.govinfo.gov/content/pkg/CHRG-108shrg20396/html /CHRG-108shrg20396.htm.

61   **"few resources to collecting the strategic financial intelligence":** Roth, Greenburg, and Wille, "Monograph on Terrorist Financing," 5.

61   **"not a priority":** Roth, Greenburg, and Wille, "Monograph on Terrorist Financing," 4.

61   **violently allergic:** John B. Taylor, *Global Financial Warriors: The Untold Story of International Finance in the Post-9/11 World* (New York: W. W. Norton, 2008), xxv.

61   **"could crumble [*sic*] U.S. credibility":** Juan Carlos Zarate, *Treasury's War: The Unleashing of a New Era of Financial Warfare* (New York: PublicAffairs, 2013), 60.

61   **As the news came in:** Quotes here and in next paragraph from David Aufhauser, "Testimony: An Assessment of the Tools Needed to Fight the Financing of Terrorism," *Hearing before the Committee on the Judiciary, United States Senate, November 20, 2002*, serial no. J-107–112.

62   **the problem of terrorism:** Aufhauser, "Testimony: An Assessment of the Tools Needed to Fight the Financing of Terrorism."

63   **"nerve center of the global banking industry":** Eric Lichtblau, *Bush's Law: The Remaking of American Justice* (New York: Pantheon, 2008), 253.

63   **a "Rosetta Stone":** Lichtblau, *Bush's Law*, 253.

63   **tried to get access to SWIFT's data:** Zarate, *Treasury's War*, 50.

63   **it would simply move it overseas:** Lichtblau, *Bush's Law*, 242.

63   **"think the unthinkable"**: Scott and Zachariadis, *The Society for Worldwide Inter-bank Financial Telecommunication*, 128.

63   **"We don't do subpoena"**: Scott and Zachariadis, *The Society for Worldwide Inter-bank Financial Telecommunication*, 128.

64   **"James Bond–level security"**: Katy Burne and Robin Sidel, "Hackers Ran Through Holes in Swift's Network," *Wall Street Journal*, April 30, 2017.

64   **the NSA seems also to have hacked into SWIFT's system independently:** "NSA Spies on International Payments," *Der Spiegel*, September 15, 2013, retrieved on September 29, 2021, from https://www.spiegel.de/international/world/spiegel -exclusive-nsa-spies-on-international-bank-transactions-a-922276.html; Clare Baldwin, "Hackers Release Files Indicating NSA Monitored Global Bank Trans-fers," Reuters, April 14, 2017, retrieved on September 29, 2021, from https://www .reuters.com/article/us-usa-cyber-swift/hackers-release-files-indicating-nsa -monitored-global-bank-transfers-idUSKBN17G1HC.

64   **"What took you so long?"**: Zarate, *Treasury's War*, 52. Eric Lichtblau reports Schrank using the same words in *Bush's Law*, though they differ over where the meeting took place (Washington, DC, or Brussels).

65   **"unique and powerful"**: Eric Lichtblau and James Risen, "Bank Data Is Sifted in Secret to Block Terror," *New York Times*, June 23, 2006.

65   **"never-before-seen financial links"**: Zarate, *Treasury's War*, 50.

65   **ending the meeting:** Zarate, *Treasury's War*, 58.

65   **nearly as impatient:** Farrell and Newman, *Of Privacy and Power*.

65   **program was finally revealed:** Lichtblau and Risen, "Bank Data Is Sifted in Secret to Block Terror."

65   **Europe and the United States struck a deal:** We provide a detailed account of the negotiation of this deal in *Of Privacy and Power*.

66   **"the new era of financial warfare"**: Zarate, *Treasury's War*, xiii.

66   **"every financial influence"**: George W. Bush, "Address to a Joint Session of Con-gress and the American People," White House, September 20, 2001, available at https://georgewbush-whitehouse.archives.gov/news/releases/2001/09/20010920 -8.html.

66   **"knew little about disrupting the flow of funds"**: Taylor, *Global Financial War-riors*, 6.

67   **"cut off these evil people's money"**: George W. Bush, "Remarks to Federal Emer-gency Management Agency Employees Online by Gerhard Peters and John T. Woolley," American Presidency Project, October 1, 2001, available at https://www .presidency.ucsb.edu/documents/remarks-federal-emergency-management-agency -employees.

68   **the "battle for turf"**: Taylor, *Global Financial Warriors*.

69   **"dollar unilateralism"**: Suzanne Katzenstein, "Dollar Unilateralism: The New Frontline of National Security," *Indiana Law Journal* 90 (2015): 292–351.

69 **"mapping the regime's"**: David L. Asher, "Pressuring Kim Jong-Il: The North Korean Illicit Activities Initiative, 2001–2006," in David Asher, Patrick M. Cronin, and Victor Comras, eds., *Pressure: Coercive Economic Statecraft and U.S. National Security* (Washington, DC: Center for a New American Security, 2011), 34.

69 **"financial battle map"**: Zarate, *Treasury's War*, 219.

69 **"neutron bomb"**: Joanna Caytas, "Weaponizing Finance: U.S. and European Options, Tools, and Policies," *Columbia Journal of European Law* 23, no. 2 (2017): 441–75.

69 **froze $25 million in assets**: Asher, "Pressuring Kim Jong-II," 44.

69 **"smash in the mouth"**: Zarate, *Treasury's War*, 245.

70 **"the sort of impact that it did"**: Authors' interview with Victor Cha, November 2, 2021.

70 **it had received the message:** Asher, "Pressuring Kim Jong-Il."

70 **"striking one financial node"**: Anna Yukhananov, "After Success on Iran, US Treasury's Sanctions Team Faces New Challenges," Reuters, April 14, 2014.

70 **"finding chokepoints"**: Zarate, *Treasury's War*, 102.

71 **began to prosecute foreign banks:** Cornelia Woll, "Economic Lawfare: The Geopolitics of Corporate Justice," GRIPE: Global Research in International Political Economy, Webinar in IPE, March 3, 2021, retrieved on December 1, 2022 from https://s18798.pcdn.co/gripe/wp-content/uploads/sites/18249/2021/02/Woll-GRIPE-Corporate-Prosecutions.pdf.

71 **"hunting whales"**: Bryan Early and Kevin Preble, "Going Fishing Versus Hunting Whales: Explaining Changes in How the US Enforces Economic Sanctions," *Security Studies* 29, no. 2 (2020): 231–67.

71 **BNP Paribas pleaded guilty:** Department of Justice, "BNP Paribas Agrees to Plead Guilty and to Pay $8.9 Billion for Illegally Processing Financial Transactions for Countries Subject to U.S. Economic Sanctions," press release, June 20, 2014, https://www.justice.gov/opa/pr/bnp-paribas-agrees-plead-guilty-and-pay-89-billion-illegally-processing-financial.

71 **"not worth the risk"**: *Testimony of Stuart Levey, Under Secretary for Terrorism and Financial Intelligence before the Senate Committee on Banking, Housing and Urban Affairs, March 21, 2007*, retrieved on December 2, 2022, from https://web.archive.org/web/20140605060731/https://www.treasury.gov/press-center/press-releases/Pages/hp325.aspx.

71 **important side benefits:** Pierre-Hugues Verdier, *Global Banks on Trial: U.S. Prosecutions and the Remaking of International Finance* (New York: Oxford University Press, 2020).

72 **an OFAC compliance office:** Verdier, *Global Banks*, 137.

72 **trade sanctions:** Anu Bradford and Omri Ben-Shahar, "Efficient Enforcement in International Law," *Chicago Journal of International Law* 12 (2012), 390.

73 **combined to change the game:** Peter Feaver and Eric Lorber, *Coercive Diplomacy and the New Financial Levers: Evaluating the Intended and Unintended Consequences of Financial Sanctions* (London: Legatum Institute, 2010).

73 **He was traveling in Bahrain:** Robin Wright, "Stuart Levey's War," *New York Times*, October 31, 2008.

73 **"major businesses simply couldn't function":** Jay Solomon, *The Iran Wars: Spy Games, Bank Battles and the Secret Deals That Reshaped the Middle East* (New York: Random House, 2016), 145.

73 **blocking Iranian banks' backdoor access:** Katzenstein, "Dollar Unilateralism."

73 **U-turn transactions:** Katzenstein, "Dollar Unilateralism," 316.

74 **"significant" transactions:** Iran Freedom and Counterproliferation, U.S. Code Ch. 95, Title 22 Foreign Relations and Intercourse (2013).

74 **"a split-second's worth of business":** *Committee on Banking, Housing and Urban Affairs, United States Senate, Hearing on the Nomination of Adam J. Szubin to Be Under Secretary for Terrorism and Financial Crimes, Department of the Treasury, September 15, 2015*, retrieved on October 15, 2021, from https://www.congress.gov/114/chrg/shrg97884/CHRG-114shrg97884.htm.

74 **they went directly to the banks:** Rachel L. Loeffler, "Bank Shots: How the Financial System Can Isolate Rogues," *Foreign Affairs* 88, no. 2 (March/April 2009): 101–10.

74 **In Bagley's description:** *U.S. Vulnerabilities to Money Laundering, Drugs, and Terrorist Financing: HSBC Case History, Majority and Minority Staff Report. Permanent Subcommittee on Investigations. United States Senate. Released in Conjunction with the Permanent Subcommittee on Investigations, July 17, 2012, Hearing, 165*, retrieved on October 10, 2021, from https://www.hsgac.senate.gov/imo/media/doc/PSI%20REPORT-HSBC%20CASE%20HISTORY%20(9.6).pdf.

74 **"almost purposefully confusing":** Sean M. Thornton, "Iran, Non-U.S. Banks and Secondary Sanctions: Understanding the Trends," Skadden, Arps, Slate, Meagher and Flom LLP, retrieved on October 10, 2021, from https://www.jdsupra.com/post/contentViewerEmbed.aspx?fid=1bb53e84-6c76-429d-ac09-4129c821ba8c.

75 **The group targeted SWIFT:** United Against Nuclear Iran, *SWIFT Campaign* (Washington, DC: UANI, 2012).

75 **nineteen Iranian banks . . . had access:** *Annual Review 2010: Common Challenges, Unique Solutions*, SWIFT, Brussels, 2010.

75 **UANI wrote to SWIFT:** Letter re: SWIFT and Iran, UANI, January 30, 2012, retrieved on August 29, 2022, from https://www.unitedagainstnucleariran.com/sites/default/files/IBR%20Correspondence/UANI_Letter_to_SWIFT_013012.pdf.

75 **forcing SWIFT to kick out Iranian banks:** Sascha Lohmann, "The Convergence of Transatlantic Sanction Policy against Iran," *Cambridge Review of International Affairs* 29, no. 3 (2016): 930–51.

75   **prohibiting SWIFT:** "US Presses EU to Close SWIFT Network to Iran," Agence France Presse, February 16, 2012; Samuel Rubenfeld, "SWIFT to Comply with EU Ban on Blacklisted Entities," *Wall Street Journal*, March 15, 2018.

75   **"an extraordinary and unprecedented step":** Reuters staff, "Payments System SWIFT to Cut Off Iranian Banks," Reuters, March 15, 2012.

75   **Its exports dipped:** Jay Solomon, *The Iran Wars*, 201, 206.

75   **a key bargaining point:** Henry Farrell and Abraham Newman, "Weaponized Interdependence: How Global Economic Networks Shape State Coercion," *International Security* 44 (2019): 42–79.

76   **"[t]he deal will be made or broken":** Aaron Arnold, "The True Cost of Financial Sanctions," *Survival* 58 (2016), 85.

76   **no one wanted to listen:** Laurence Norman, "U.S., EU Urge European Banks, Businesses to Invest in Iran," *Wall Street Journal*, May 19, 2016.

76   **"pushing non-U.S. banks":** Stuart Levey, "Kerry's Peculiar Message about Iran for European Banks," *Wall Street Journal*, May 12, 2016.

77   **"kind of sanctions doomsday machine":** Christopher Hill, *Outpost: A Diplomat at Work* (New York: Simon & Schuster, 2015), 248. See Hill more generally on the Six Party Talks.

77   **"lose their effectiveness":** Loeffler, "Bank Shots," 110.

77   **awesome financial power:** Jack Lew, "Remarks of Secretary Lew on the Evolution of Sanctions and Lessons for the Future," delivered at the Carnegie Endowment for International Peace, Washington, DC, May 30, 2016.

77   **"plumbing is being . . . tested":** David A. Wemer, "Buy-In from Allies Critical for Effective Sanctions, Says Former U.S. Treasury Secretary Lew," *Atlantic Council*, February 19, 2019, retrieved on December 1, 2022, from https://www .atlanticcouncil.org/blogs/new-atlanticist/buy-in-from-allies-critical-for-effective -sanctions-says-former-us-treasury-secretary-lew/.

Chapter 3: War without Gunsmoke

79   **When Meng Wanzhou finally returned:** (video) "Huawei CFO Meng Wanzhou Welcomed by Employees in Shenzhen Headquarters After Extradition Drama," *Standard* (Hong Kong), October 25, 2021, retrieved on October 29, 2021, from https://www.thestandard.com.hk/breaking-news/section/3/181960/(Video)-Hua wei-CFO-Meng-Wanzhou-welcomed-by-employees-in-Shenzhen-headquarters-a fter-extradition-drama.

79   **"Meng Wanzhou is back at work":** Iris Deng, "Huawei CFO Meng Wanzhou Returns to Hero's Welcome at Company Headquarters After 21-Day Quarantine," *South China Morning Post*, October 25, 2021.

79   **"suffered for three years":** James Griffiths, "Meng Wanzhou Lands in China with Fanfare After Release from Canadian Custody," *Globe and Mail*, September 25, 2021.

79   **"Ode to the Motherland":** Griffiths, "Meng Wanzhou Lands in China with Fanfare."

79   **"If faith has a color":** Xu Zihe and Yang Ruoyu, "If Faith Has a Color, It Must Be China Red," *Global Times*, September 2021.

80   **its lonely stand:** Yang Shaolong, *The Huawei Way* (New York: McGraw-Hill Education, 2017), 24.

80   **the world's biggest smartphone brand:** Sherisse Pham, "Samsung Slump Makes Huawei the World's Biggest Smartphone Brand for the First Time, Report Says," CNN, July 30, 2020.

81   **"like a small ant":** (video) "Huawei CEO Says His Daughter Should Be Proud She Became a 'Bargaining Chip' in the Trade War," CNN Business, December 1, 2019, retrieved on October 29, 2021, from https://www.cnn.com/2019/12/01/tech/huawei-ceo-ren-zhengfei-daughter/index.html.

81   **"war without gunsmoke":** Rush Doshi, *The Long Game: China's Grand Strategy to Displace American Order* (New York: Oxford University Press, 2021), 52 and 74.

82   **first take control of the countryside:** Yang, *The Huawei Way*, 29.

82   **"a bloody path for itself":** Yang, *The Huawei Way*, 29.

82   **"military attitude to business":** Yang, *The Huawei Way*, 15.

82   **"Guidelines and Strategies for War":** Tian Tao, David De Cremer, and Wu Chunbo, *Huawei: Leadership, Culture and Connectivity* (Thousand Oaks, CA: SAGE, 2017), 197.

83   **studying at the Chongqing Institute of Civil Engineering and Architecture:** Yang, *The Huawei Way*, 11.

83   **the Shenzhen Special Economic Zone:** Ezra F. Vogel, *Deng Xiaoping and the Transformation of China* (Cambridge, MA: Belknap Press, 2011), 219.

83   **he had been a delegate:** Tian Tao with Wu Chunbo, *The Huawei Story* (Thousand Oaks, CA: SAGE, 2015).

84   **"encircling the cities":** Yang, *The Huawei Way*, 29.

84   **"sequence of very targeted war plans":** Yang, *The Huawei Way*, 29.

84   **a pack of wolves:** Tian, De Cremer, and Chunbo, *Huawei*, 40.

85   **Ren, like many of the technology entrepreneurs who came after him:** Yang, *The Huawei Way*. On Alibaba founder Jack Ma's fascination, see *The Alibaba Story—Crocodile in the Yangtze* (2012 documentary film directed by Porter Erisman).

85   **Mao and . . . Lou Gerstner:** Dan Steinbock, *The Case for Huawei in America* (The Difference Group, 2012), 23.

85   **"Song of Huawei":** Zhi-Xue Zhang and Jianjun Zhang, eds., *Understanding Chinese Firms from Multiple Perspectives* (New York: Springer Verlag, 2014), 42.

85   **"switching equipment technology was related to national security":** Eric

Harwit, "Building China's Telecommunications Network: Industrial Policy and the Role of Chinese State-Owned, Foreign and Private Domestic Enterprises," *China Quarterly* 190 (2007): 311–32. Quote on p. 327.

86 **"something must have happened to help":** Kathrin Hille, "Ren Zhengfei: Huawei's General Musters for a Fight," *Financial Times*, December 14, 2018.

86 **neglected by the big international telecommunications companies:** Steinbock, *The Case for Huawei.*

86 **"placed limits":** Julian Gewirtz, "The Chinese Reassessment of Interdependence," *China Leadership Monitor*, June 1, 2020.

86 **to steal valuable technologies:** Susan Sell, "Intellectual Property and Public Policy in Historical Perspective: Contestation and Settlement," *Loyola of Los Angeles Law Review* 38 (2004), retrieved on December 1, 2022, from https://digitalcommons .lmu.edu/llr/vol38/iss1/6/.

87 **cutting-edge chips:** John VerWey, "Chinese Semiconductor Industrial Policy: Past and Present," *Journal of International Commerce and Economics*, July 2019.

87 **dubious entrepreneurs:** Hua Tse Gan, "Semiconductor Fraud in China Highlights Lack of Accountability," *Nikkei Asia*, February 12, 2021.

87 **"original technologically":** Alexandra Harney, "Huawei: The Challenger from China," *Financial Times*, January 10, 2005.

88 **"play by the rules":** Don Clark, "Cisco CEO Wary of Huawei," *Wall Street Journal*, April 6, 2012.

88 **the Chinese military:** U.S. Senate Committee on Homeland Security and Governmental Affairs, *Congressional Leaders Cite Telecommunications Concerns with Firms That Have Ties with Chinese Government*, October 19, 2010.

88 **threats to U.S. national security:** *Investigative Report on the U.S. National Security Issues Posed by Chinese Telecommunications Companies Huawei and ZTE. A Report by Chairman Mike Rogers and Ranking Member C.A. Dutch Ruppersberger of the Permanent Select Committee on Intelligence*, U.S. House of Representatives, 112th Cong., October 8, 2012.

88 **"one former telecommunications executive":** undated conversation on background.

89 **global market:** Dell'Oro Group, "Total Telecom Equipment Market Share," Reuters, https://graphics.reuters.com/HUAWEI-USA-CAMPAIGN/0100924N31D /index.html.

89 **"Huawei strongly supports the Communist party":** Kathrin Hille, "How Huawei Lost Its PR Battle in the West," *Financial Times*, February 20, 2019.

89 **Huawei marketing material:** Eva Dou, "Documents Link Huawei to China's Surveillance Programs," *Washington Post*, December 14, 2021.

90 **"political persons of interest":** Eva Dou, "Documents Link Huawei to China's Surveillance Programs."

90 **easier for authoritarian countries:** Stacie Hoffmann, Dominique Lazanski, and Emily Taylor, "Standardising the Splinternet: How China's Technical Standards Could Fragment the Internet," *Journal of Cyber Policy* 5 (2020): 239–64.

90 **"trying to encircle China":** Authors' interview with Kevin Wolf, September 3, 2022.

91 **everything to do with national security:** Authors' interview with Kevin Wolf. A Biden administration official who we talked to provided indirect support for Wolf's claim, highlighting the limits of policy regulations that focused on national security, with no real consideration of economic security.

91 **persuaded his colleagues:** David Bond, George Parker, Sebastian Payne, and Nic Fildes, "US Cyber Chief Warns UK against Giving Huawei 'Loaded Gun,'" *Financial Times*, April 24, 2019.

91 **fired:** "Defence Secretary Gavin Williamson Sacked over Huawei Leak," BBC, May 1, 2019, https://www.bbc.com/news/uk-politics-48126974 (checked December 11, 2021).

91 **"loaded gun":** Bond, Parker, Payne, and Fildes, "US Cyber Chief Warns UK against Giving Huawei 'Loaded Gun.'"

91 **"China to control the Internet":** Guy Faulconbridge, Kylie MacLellan, and Andrew MacAskill, "No Time to Go 'Wobbly': Pompeo Scolds Britain over China and Huawei," Reuters, May 8, 2019.

92 **One of their stories:** Steve Stecklow, Farnaz Fassihi, and Loretta Chao, "Chinese Tech Giant Aids Iran," *Wall Street Journal*, October 27, 2011.

92 **a detailed report:** Steve Stecklow, *Chinese Firm Helps Iran Spy on Citizens*, Reuters Special Report, March 22, 2012, retrieved on September 18, 2022, from http://graphics.thomsonreuters.com/12/03/IranChina.pdf.

92 **Skycom:** Steve Stecklow, "Exclusive: Huawei Partner Offered Embargoed HP Gear to Iran," Reuters, December 30, 2012.

92 **Meng Wanzhou had been the secretary:** Steve Stecklow, "Exclusive: Huawei CFO Linked to Firm That Offered HP Gear to Iran," Reuters, January 31, 2013.

93 **"Top Secret":** ZTE (undated), "Proposal for Import and Export Control Risk Avoidance—YL as an Example," available at https://www.bis.doc.gov/index.php/documents/about-bis/newsroom/1436-proposal-for-english/file.

93 **"treasure trove":** Karen Freifeld, "Exclusive: U.S. Probe of China's Huawei Includes Bank Fraud Accusations: Sources," Reuters, December 6, 2018.

93 **the "Top Secret" document:** Karen Freifeld, "INSIGHT: Long Before Trump's Trade War with China, Huawei's Activities Were Secretly Tracked," Reuters, March 6, 2019.

94 **leadership's intentions:** Bureau of Industry and Security, U.S. Department of Commerce, "Proposed Charging Letter," https://www.bis.doc.gov/index.php/documents/about-bis/newsroom/1658-zte-final-pcl/file.

94 **a second secret ZTE document:** "ZTE Corporation Document Submitted for Ratification (Review) Form," ZTE, August 25, 2011, available at https://www .bis.doc.gov/index.php/documents/about-bis/newsroom/1438-report-regarding -english/file.

94 **As he acknowledged:** USC US-China Institute, "Steve Stecklow Talks about Reporting on Huaiwei [sic]," retrieved on September 22, 2022, from https://www .youtube.com/watch?v=GfpLY10YtPo.

94 **chief financial officer:** *Huawei Annual Report Details Directors, Supervisory Board for the First Time,* Open Source Center, October 5, 2011.

95 **"not adhering to the rules":** Li Tao, "Huawei CFO Sabrina Meng Wanzhou Comments about Compliance in Internal Meeting Before Her Arrest in Canada," *South China Morning Post,* December 6, 2018.

95 **over $12 million:** Michael Bristow, "Meng Wanzhou: The Huawei Exec Trapped in a Gilded Cage," BBC, January 24, 2019.

95 **met by a contingent:** Gordon Corera, "Meng Wanzhou: Questions over Huawei Executive's Arrest as Legal Battle Continues," BBC, October 31, 2020.

95 **secret information:** David E. Sanger and Nicole Perlroth, "N.S.A. Breached Chinese Servers Seen as Security Threat," *New York Times,* March 22, 2014.

96 **to launder $881 million:** "HSBC Holdings Plc. and HSBC Bank USA N.A. Admit to Anti-Money Laundering and Sanctions Violations, Forfeit $1.256 Billion in Deferred Prosecution Agreement," Department of Justice, December 11, 2012.

96 **$1.9 billion in fines:** Aruna Viswanatha and Brett Wolf, "HSBC to Pay $1.9 Billion U.S. Fine in Money-Laundering Case," Reuters, December 11, 2012.

96 **an independent monitor:** Karen Freifeld and Steve Stecklow, "Exclusive: HSBC Probe Helped Lead to U.S. Charges against Huawei CFO," Reuters, February 26, 2019.

96 **"Discredit, Deny, Deflect and Delay":** Greg Farrell, "Sealed HSBC Report Shows U.S. Managers Battling Cleanup Squad," Bloomberg, July 7, 2015.

96 **considering criminal charges:** Greg Farrell and Keri Geiger, "U.S. Considers HSBC Charge That Could Upend 2012 Settlement," Bloomberg, September 11, 2016.

96 **collapse of HSBC:** George Osborne, Britain's chancellor of the Exchequer, had warned earlier that a criminal conviction might prevent HSBC from being able to clear U.S. dollars, risking "destabilizing the bank globally, with very serious implications for financial and economic stability, particularly in Europe and Asia." Quoted in Verdier, *Global Banks on Trial,* 132.

96 **providing information on its dealings:** Freifeld and Stecklow, "Exclusive: HSBC Probe Helped Lead to U.S. Charges against Huawei CFO."

97 **she had arguably misled:** U.S. Department of Justice, "Huawei CFO Wanzhou Meng Admits to Misleading Global Financial Institution," Office of Public

Affairs press release, September 24, 2021, retrieved on November 13, 2022 from https://www.justice.gov/opa/pr/huawei-cfo-wanzhou-meng-admits-misleading -global-financial-institution.

97   **"more than $100 million worth of Skycom-related transactions":** "Chinese Telecommunications Conglomerate Huawei and Huawei CFO Wanzhou Meng Charged with Financial Fraud," Department of Justice, January 28, 2019.

97   **shackled to an electronic bracelet:** "Huawei Executive Meng Wanzhou Released on Bail in Canada," BBC, December 12, 2018.

97   **high-end shopping trips:** Natalie Obiko Pearson, "Huawei CFO Meng Wanzhou's Life on Bail: Private Dining, Shopping Sprees and More," *Financial Post*, January 12, 2021.

98   **a "trap" for Huawei:** Shen Weiduo and Chen Qingqing, "Update: HSBC Could Face Dead End for Conspiring with US against Huawei," *Global Times*, July 24, 2020. See also Reuters Staff, "HSBC Denies Chinese Media Reports That It 'Framed' Huawei," Reuters, July 25, 2020.

99   **an "apoplectic" phone call:** Sebastian Payne and Katrina Manson, "Donald Trump 'Apoplectic' in Call with Boris Johnson over Huawei," *Financial Times*, February 6, 2020.

99   **"jeopardize our ability to share Intelligence":** Richard Grenell (@Richard Grenell), Twitter, February 16, 2020, 2:03 p.m., retrieved on December 1, 2022, from https://web.archive.org/web/20200320194951/https://twitter.com /RichardGrenell/status/1229164331738312706.

99   **"black hole":** John Bolton, *The Room Where It Happened* (New York: Simon & Schuster, 2020), 263 and 277.

99   **Trump kept on hinting:** Sherisse Pham and Abby Philip, "Trump Suggests Using Huawei as a Bargaining Chip in US-China Trade Deal," *CNN Business*, May 24, 2019, retrieved on December 1, 2022, from https://www.cnn.com/2019/05/24 /tech/donald-trump-huawei-ban.

99   **"the Ivanka Trump of China":** Bolton, *The Room Where It Happened*, 276.

100   **Entity List:** *Entity List*, Bureau of Industry and Security, U.S. Department of Commerce, 2020, retrieved on November 11, 2022, from https://www.bis.doc.gov /index.php/policy-guidance/lists-of-parties-of-concern/entity-list.

100   **"to buy grain from Nebraska or whatever":** Authors' interview with Kevin Wolf.

100   **"prevent American technology from being used":** U.S. Department of Commerce, "Department of Commerce Announces the Addition of Huawei Technologies Co. Ltd. To the Entity List," press release, May 15, 2019.

100   **"a fucking great statement":** Bolton, *The Room Where It Happened*, 279.

100   **"agreed to allow Chinese company Huawei":** Donald Trump, June 29, Twitter .com. Reported in Colin Lecher, "Trump Says He'll Ease Huawei Restrictions, But No One's Sure How," *Verge*, July 3, 2019.

100   **"loose comment"**: Bolton, *The Room Where It Happened*, 280.

101   **"effectively disrupt our adversary"**: Ben Sasse, "Sasse Statement on Executive Order and Huawei," Office of Senator Ben Sasse, May 15, 2019, https://www.sasse .senate.gov/public/index.cfm/2019/5/sasse-statement-on-executive-order-and -huawei (checked November 22, 2021).

101   **As Wolf described it:** Interview with Kevin Wolf.

101   **what we called "weaponized interdependence":** Farrell and Newman, "Weaponized Interdependence."

101   ***Chip War*:** Chris Miller, *Chip War: The Fight for the World's Most Critical Technology* (New York: PublicAffairs, 2022).

102   **"I almost fell out of my chair":** Personal communication from Chris Miller, October 7, 2022. Miller emphasized that "playbook" was his own term, rather than a term used by his interviewee.

102   **"beautiful thing":** Chris Miller, *Chip War*, 317.

102   **more than 25 percent:** Ian F. Ferguson and Paul K. Kerr, "The U.S. Export Control System and the Export Control Reform Initiative," *Congressional Research Service*, January 28, 2020.

102   **"trillions with a 'T'":** Interview with Kevin Wolf.

103   **a special cargo plane:** Phate Zhang, "Huawei Reportedly Chartered a Plane to Bring Back All the Kirin Chips," *CnTechPost*, September 12, 2020.

103   **market share:** "Global Smartphone Market Share," Counterpoint, retrieved on November 29, 2021, from https://www.counterpointresearch.com/global -smartphone-share/.

103   **"lobbying Taiwan":** Kathrin Hille, "U.S. Urges Taiwan to Curb Chip Exports to China," *Financial Times*, November 3, 2019.

103   **a generation ahead:** "Silicon Foundries Surge to New Revenue Records, but Texas Cold Snap Sent Samsung Backwards; TSMC Is Well on Truly on Top with 55 Percent Market Share," *Register*, June 1, 2021.

103   **a near monopoly:** "From TSMC to Tungsten: Semiconductor Supply Chain Risks," Semi-Literate, May 2, 2021, https://semiliterate.substack.com/p/from -tsmc-to-tungsten-semiconductor.

104   **second-largest customer after Apple:** Iain Morris, "Huawei Chips Crisis Shortens Odds on China-US Conflict," Light Reading, March 25, 2021.

104   **"it will be harder for us to be confident":** Ian Levy, "A Different Future for Telecoms in the UK," NCSC blogpost, July 14, 2020, retrieved on October 2, 2022, from https://www.ncsc.gov.uk/blog-post/a-different-future-for-telecoms -in-the-uk.

104   **reached an agreement:** *Huawei CFO Wanzhou Meng Admits to Misleading Global Financial Institution*, U.S. Department of Justice, September 24, 2021.

104   **"untrue statements":** United States of America v. Wanzhou Meng, Deferred

Prosecution Agreement, Cr. No. 18–457 (S-3) (AMD). United States District Court, Eastern Division of New York, 2021, retrieved on December 15, 2021, from https://www.justice.gov/opa/press-release/file/1436211/download.

104   **"more theoretical breakthroughs"**: Ren Zhengfei, *Conversation with Scientists, Experts, and Interns at the Academia Sinica Innovation Pioneer Symposium*, retrieved on October 2, 2022, from https://xinsheng.huawei.com/cn/index.php?app=forum&mod=Detail&act=index&id=6228877.

104   **new research program:** Dave Yin, "China's Plan to Leapfrog Foreign Chipmakers: Wave Goodbye to Silicon," *Protocol*, November 8, 2021.

105   **"we may forever lag behind"**: Yin, "China's Plan to Leapfrog Foreign Chipmakers."

105   **emerging markets:** Takashi Kawakami and Yusuke Hinata, "Huawei Focuses on Emerging Markets as Outlook in West Remains Dim," *Nikkei Asia*, August 19, 2021.

105   **"choose the lesser evil"**: Alexander Gabulev, "Huawei's Courtship of Moscow Leaves West in the Cold," *Financial Times*, June 21, 2020.

105   **setback:** Matt Walker, "Ericsson, Nokia Benefit Most from First-Half 2021 Telco Network Spend," *FierceTelecom*, September 9, 2021.

106   **"core technologies are controlled by others"**: Elizabeth Chen, "Semiconductor Scandal a Concerning Backdrop to Xi's Pursuit of 'Core Technologies,'" Jamestown Foundation, March 26, 2021.

106   **"to start over again"**: Meng Jing and Zen Soo, "Tech Cold War: How Trump's Assault on Huawei Is Forcing the World to Contemplate a Digital Iron Curtain," *South China Morning Post*, May 26, 2019.

106   **"choke points"**: "Ministry of Industry and Information Technology: Closely Focus on Technological Self-Reliance and Strive to Solve the Problem of 'Chokepoint'", China News Service, March 1, 2021, https://www.chinanews.com/cj/2021/03-01/9421391.shtml.

106   **Unreliable Entity List:** Adrianna Zhang, "China Releases Details on Its Own Unreliable Entity List," Voice of America, September 2020.

106   **A secretive committee:** "Secretive Chinese Committee Draws Up List to Replace U.S. Tech," Bloomberg, November 16, 2021.

106   **a three-year plan:** Xinmei Shen, "US-China Tech War: Beijing Draws Up Three-Year Plan to Revamp State Technology System," *South China Morning Post*, November 25, 2021.

106   **a core goal:** *Outline of the People's Republic of China 14th Five-Year Plan for National Economic and Social Development and Long-Range Objectives for 2035*, Xinhua News Agency (translation by CSET, Georgetown University), available at https://cset.georgetown.edu/wp-content/uploads/t0284_14th_Five_Year_Plan_EN.pdf (checked December 15, 2021).

106 **totaling $118 billion:** James Lewis, "Learning the Superior Techniques of the Barbarians: China's Pursuit of Semiconductor Independence," Center for Strategic and International Studies, January 2019.

106 **"asking to build rockets":** Cheng Ting-Fang and Lauly Li, "US-China Tech War: Beijing's Secret Chipmaking Champions," *Nikkei Asia*, May 5, 2021.

106 **"a matter of survival":** "Xi Jinping Picks Top Lieutenant to Lead China's Chip Battle against U.S.," Bloomberg, June 17, 2021.

107 **spying and subversion:** This paragraph draws on Yeling Tan, Mark P. Dallas, Henry Farrell, and Abraham Newman, "Driven to Self-Reliance: Coercion and the US-China Innovation Ecosystem," unpublished paper.

107 **"safeguard the security":** "Be Alert to 'Prism Gate' and Advance the Localization of Core Technology," Government Procurement Information, July 5, 2013, on file with author.

107 **couldn't get a bank account:** Carrie Lam, from her interview at https://www .facebook.com/hkibcnews/videos/484173425894280/?ref=sharing.

107 **"flattered" by China's attention:** Michael Martina, "US Religious-Rights Official Gayle Manchin 'Flattered' by China's Sanctions in Dispute over Uyghurs," Reuters, March 29, 2021.

108 **new "financial war":** Orange Wang, "China-US Rivalry on Brink of Becoming a 'Financial War,' Former Minister Says," *South China Morning Post*, November 9, 2019.

108 **prepare for the "nuclear option":** Samuel Shen, Winni Zhou, and Kevin Yao, "In China, Fears of Financial Iron Curtain as U.S. Tensions Rise," Reuters, August 13, 2020.

108 **they started using yuan:** "Russia Gives China's Yuan a Boost as Firms Cope with Sanctions," Bloomberg, September 14, 2022.

108 **its own international payment system:** Michelle Chen, "China's International Yuan Payment System Pursues World Finance," Reuters, October 8, 2015.

108 **$12.68 trillion:** Emily Jin, "Under the Radar: Alternative Payment Systems and the National Security Impacts of Their Growth," Testimony before the House Financial Services Subcommittee on National Security, International Development, and Monetary Policy, September 20, 2022, retrieved on December 1, 2022, from https://financialservices.house.gov/uploadedfiles/hhrg-117-ba10-wstate-jine -20220920.pdf.

108 **"a good punch to the enemy":** "Chinese Banks Urged to Switch Away from SWIFT as U.S. Sanctions Loom," Reuters, July 29, 2020.

109 **Norwegian salmon:** Bjørnar Sverdrup-Thygeson, "The Flexible Cost of Insulting China: Trade Politics and the 'Dalai Lama Effect,'" *Asian Perspective* 39, no. 1 (2015): 101–23. See also Xianwen Chen and Roberto Javier Garcia, "Economic Sanctions and Trade Diplomacy: Sanction-Busting Strategies, Market Distortion

and Efficacy of China's Restrictions on Norwegian Salmon Imports," *China Information* 30, no. 1 (2016).

109 **indicted five Chinese military officials:** Robert Blackwill and Jennifer Harris, *War by Other Means: Geoeconomics and Statecraft* (Cambridge, MA: Belknap Press, 2016), 136.

109 **When Australia called for an investigation:** Paulina Duran and Kirsty Needham, "Australia and China Spat Over Coronavirus Inquiry Deepens," *Reuters*, May 18, 2020.

109 **quietly started importing it again:** Primrose Riordan and Neil Hume, "China Unloads Australian Coal Despite Import Ban amid Power Shortage," *Financial Times*, October 4, 2021.

109 **hosting the Dalai Lama:** Outlook Web Bureau, "Meeting Dalai Lama Major Offence, China Warns World Leaders," *Outlook*, October 21, 2017.

109 **U.K. barristers stayed quiet:** Primrose Riordan, Tabby Kinder, and Jane Croft, "UK Lawyers Feel Ripples of Chinese Sanctions on Essex Court Chambers," *Financial Times*, April 4, 2021.

109 **roughly $400 million:** Ross Dellenger, "NBA Responds to U.S. Senator's Letter about League's Relationship with China," *Sports Illustrated*, July 21, 2020.

110 **"If the U.S. crackdown is like bombardment":** Cheng Ting-Fang and Shunsuke Tabeta, "China's Chip Industry Fights to Survive U.S. Tech Crackdown" *Nikkei Asia*, November 30, 2022.

Chapter 4: Waking into Winter

112 **a protégé:** Christina Goßner and Philipp Grüll, "Merkel and von der Leyen: Two Long-Time Companions Guiding Europe," *Euractiv*, July 3, 2020, retrieved on March 11, 2022, from https://www.euractiv.com/section/future-eu/news/merkel-and-von-der-leyen-two-long-time-companininos-guiding-europe/.

112 **a new beginning:** *Speech by President von der Leyen at the European Parliament Plenary on the Russian Aggression against Ukraine*, retrieved on March 11, 2022, from https://ec.europa.eu/commission/presscorner/detail/en/speech_22_1483.

113 **The ECSC:** "The Founding of the European Communities," *CVCE.EU*, retrieved on December 2, 2022, from https://www.cvce.eu/en/education/unit-content/-/unit/d5906df5-4f83-4603-85f7-0cabc24b9fe1/7550d654-18b4-4e04-86d1-9bd3a8dddf5a.

113 **"ever closer union":** "Treaty of Rome (EEC)," European Union, 2017, retrieved on November 14, 2022 from https://eur-lex.europa.eu/legal-content/EN/TXT/?uri=LEGISSUM:xy0023.

114 **stable energy supplies:** Helen Thompson, *Disorder: Hard Times in the 21st Century* (Oxford: Oxford University Press, 2022).

114   **"economic warfare"**: Antony J. Blinken, *Ally Versus Ally: America, Europe and the Siberian Pipeline Crisis* (New York: Praeger, 1987).

114   **"reconsider military commitments"**: Bruce Jentleson, *Pipeline Politics: The Complex Political Economy of East-West Energy Trade* (Ithaca, NY: Cornell University Press, 1986), 199. On the Cold War politics of gas, see also Michael Mastanduno, *Economic Containment: CoCom and the Politics of East-West Trade* (Ithaca, NY: Cornell University Press, 1992).

114   **They were furious**: Blinken, *Ally Versus Ally*, 105.

115   **Cold War *Ostpolitik***: Angela Stent, *From Embargo to Ostpolitik: The Political Economy of West German-Soviet Relations* (New York: Cambridge University Press, 1981).

115   **notoriously eager**: Erika Solomon, "Gerhard Schröder Draws German Ire by Keeping Faith with Russia," *Financial Times*, March 28, 2022.

115   **"make money"**: Katrin Bennhold, "The Former Chancellor Who Became Putin's Man in Germany," *New York Times*, April 23, 2022.

116   **obscure changes to phytosanitary regulations**: One of the authors was once a stagiaire (a glorified intern) in the European Commission's unit for keeping track of legislation. The unexpected departure of half the unit's personnel meant that he had to suddenly learn a lot more about the intricacies of EU regulation than he ever expected or desired.

116   **a halfhearted afterthought**: Wolfgang Wagner, "Why The EU's Common Foreign and Security Policy Will Remain Intergovernmental: A Rationalist Institutional Choice Analysis of European Crisis Management Policy," *Journal of European Public Policy* 10, no. 4 (2003): 576–95.

117   **"basic issue"**: Authors' interview with Max Schrems, January 21, 2016.

117   **lacked the resources**: "Berlin to Create Task Force to Enact Russia Sanctions—Report," Deutsche Welle, March 12, 2022.

117   **"persistent and dogged"**: Catherine Mayer, "Meet the Woman Who Helped Negotiate the Iran Nuclear Deal," *Time*, November 25, 2013.

117   **"decisive role"**: Peter Spiegel, "EU Foreign Policy Chief Lady Ashton Comes of Age in Iran Talks," *Financial Times*, November 26, 2013.

118   **"sunset clauses"**: Robert Einhorn, "'Fix' the Iran Deal, but Don't Move the Goalposts," Brookings, January 18, 2018.

118   **global relevance**: Tarja Cronberg, "No EU, No Iran Deal: The EU's Choice Between Multilateralism and the Transatlantic Link," *Nonproliferation Review* 24, nos. 3–4 (2018): 243–59.

118   **weren't terribly worried**: Authors' interview with Peter Wittig.

118   **had sparred**: Brakkton Booker, "Trump, Cruz Headline Tea Party Rally against Iran Nuclear Deal," NPR, September 9, 2015.

118   **"worst," "terrible," "bad"**: "Trump on the Iran Deal: 'Worst, Horrible, Laughable,'" *BBC News*, April 26, 2018.

118 **personal pique:** Jake Sullivan, "Trump's Only Iran Strategy Is to Punish Iran," *Atlantic*, May 19, 2018.

118 **"the art of the deal":** Donald Trump and Tony Schwartz, *The Art of the Deal* (New York: Random House, 2016).

119 **"disastrous flaws":** Robert Einhorn, "'Fix' the Iran Deal, But Don't Move the Goalposts."

119 **"pride of authorship":** Authors' interview with Brian Hook, February 12, 2021.

119 **Macron visited Washington:** Julian Borger and David Smith, "Macron Pitches New Iran Deal to Sweeten Existing Agreement for Trump," *Guardian*, April 24, 2018.

119 **"Just weeks later":** Reuters Staff, "Factbox: How Trump Is Reimposing Iran Sanctions after Ditching Deal," Reuters, May 8, 2018.

119 **"Pandora's box":** William Dobson, "Macron Doesn't Believe He Changed Trump's Mind on the Iran Deal," NPR, April 25, 2018.

119 **to pull out:** "French Energy Giant Total Officially Pulls Out of Iran," Deutsche Welle, August 21, 2018.

120 **"there [was] no solution":** Quoted in Eric Maurice, "EU Has No 'Magic Bullet' against US Iran Sanctions," *EUobserver*, May 16, 2018.

120 **put it bluntly:** Reuters Staff, "Maersk Latest Company to Shun Iran as EU Scrambles to Save Nuclear Deal," Reuters, May 17, 2018.

120 **"signaling value":** Robin Emmott, "EU Considers Iran Central Bank Transfers to Beat US Sanctions," Reuters, May 18, 2018.

120 **getting Iran kicked out:** Matthew Lee, "US Lawmakers Urge Iran Expulsion from SWIFT Banking Network," Associated Press, October 18, 2018; Richard Goldberg and Jacob Nagel, "Here's How Trump Can Bring Iran Back to the Table," Foundation for the Defense of Democracies, August 28, 2018.

120 **"publicly gloating":** Adam Kredo, "Trump Admin Will Allow Iran Key Financial Lifeline in Major Concession," *Washington Free Beacon*, October 24, 2018.

120 **Bolton badmouthed Mnuchin:** John Bolton, *The Room Where It Happened* (New York: Simon & Schuster, 2020).

121 **thin legal fiction:** Hilary Hurd, "U.S. Reimposes the Second Round of Iran Sanctions," *Lawfare* (blog), November 9, 2018, retrieved on April 2, 2022, from https://www.lawfareblog.com/us-reimposes-second-round-iran-sanctions.

121 **might sanction:** "U.S. Warns Europe That Its Iran Workaround Could Face Sanctions," Bloomberg, May 29, 2019, retrieved on April 2, 2022, from https://www.bloomberg.com/news/articles/2019-05-29/u-s-warns-europe-that-its-iran-workaround-could-face-sanctions.

121 **its first transaction:** "INSTEX Successfully Concluded First Transaction," German Federal Foreign Office, March 31, 2020.

121 **"unusual workarounds":** Authors' interview with financial industry expert.

121 **"the weight of the US":** Lili Bayer, "EU Shield Looks Flimsy against Trump's Iran Sanctions," *Politico*, July 17, 2018.

121 **the EU's impotence:** Authors' interview with German industry official.

122 **"they're a foe":** Cat Contiguglia, "Trump: EU Is One of United States' Biggest Foes," *Politico*, July 15, 2018.

122 **he didn't "care about the Europeans":** Adam Forrest, "Trump Says 'I Don't Care about the Europeans' After Questions on Iran Crisis," *Independent*, June 24, 2019.

122 **Trump said privately:** Julian E. Barnes and Helene Cooper, "Trump Discussed Pulling U.S. from NATO, Aides Say Amid New Concerns over Russia," *New York Times*, January 14, 2019.

123 **"toxic quibble":** Franziska Brantner, "We Need to Pull Our Own Weight," European Council on Foreign Relations, December 10, 2020.

123 **This catchphrase:** *Shared Vision, Common Action: A Stronger Europe: A Global Strategy for the European Union's Foreign and Security Policy*, European External Action Service, June 2016.

123 **"does not like . . . the term 'strategic autonomy'":** Authors' interview with former German defense department official.

123 **provocative catchphrase:** Authors' interview with French foreign policy official.

124 **"European sovereignty":** Emmanuel Macron, *Speech at the Sorbonne*, September 26, 2017, retrieved on May 6, 2022, from https://international.blogs.ouest-france.fr/archive/2017/09/29/macron-sorbonne-verbatim-europe-18583.html.

124 **"a vassal that obeys":** Patrick Wintour, "U.S. Faces European Backlash against Iran Sanctions," *Guardian*, May 11, 2018.

124 **wrote an essay:** Heiko Maas, "Wir Lassen Nicht Zu, Dass die USA über Unsere Köpfe Hinweg Handeln," *Handelsblatt*, August 21, 2018.

124 **"expression of opinion":** Matthew Karnitschig, "Merkel Quashes Foreign Minister's (Anti) American Dream," *Politico Europe*, August 22, 2018.

124 **sharply disagreed:** Jo Harper, "Maas Wants End to US Dominance," *Deutsche Welle*, August 27, 2018.

124 **"total reliance":** Susan B. Glasser, "How Trump Made War on Angela Merkel and Europe," *New Yorker*, December 24 and 31, 2018.

125 **U.S. financial coercion:** Ellie Geranmayeh and Manuel Lafont Rapnouil, "Meeting the Challenge of Secondary Sanctions," European Council on Foreign Relations, June 25, 2019.

125 **"on the table":** Authors' interview with former senior German official.

126 **greater organism:** Wolfgang Munchau, "Europe's Four Freedoms Are Its Very Essence," *Financial Times*, November 12, 2017.

126 **"the graveyard of German ministers":** Ben Judah, "The Rise of Mrs. Europe," *Critic*, October 2020.

126 **It was Macron who suggested:** Judah, "The Rise of Mrs. Europe."

126   **a "geopolitical Commission":** European Commission, "The von Der Leyen Commission: for a Union That Strives for More," press release, September 10, 2019.

126   **as Pierre Haroche . . . explained:** Pierre Haroche, "A 'Geopolitical Commission': Supranationalism Meets Global Power Competition," *Journal of Common Market Studies*, forthcoming.

127   **a widely reported speech:** *Speech by Commissioner Phil Hogan at Launch of Public Consultation for EU Trade Policy Review*, June 16, 2020.

127   **trade philosophy name generator:** "The All-New Trade Secrets Policy Philosophy Name-Generator," retrieved on September 25, 2022, from https://d1e00ek4ebabms .cloudfront.net/production/uploaded-files/name%20generator%20policy%202 -f8a5db5f-518a-4f96-b4f4-62ffea8cd44f.pdf.

127   **existential vulnerabilities:** Henry Farrell and Abraham Newman, "The New Age of Protectionism: Coronavirus 'Vaccine Wars' Could Herald a Broader Retreat from the Free Market," *Foreign Affairs*, April 5, 2021.

128   **"the vulnerability we had":** Authors' interview with senior Commission official.

128   **Trump had sabotaged:** Chad Bown and Soumaya Keynes, "Why Did Trump End the WTO's Appellate Body? Tariffs," Peterson Institute for International Economics, March 4, 2020.

128   **"vulnerabilities, not trade links":** Sabine Weyland interview with Henry Mance, "The EU Found Out We Are Dependent on Russia. We Can't Afford That," *Financial Times*, September 11, 2022.

128   **"We cannot watch on as others weaponize trade":** Sabine Weyland, "Anti-Coercion Instrument: How the EU Can Counter Sanctions, Boycotts and Economic Blackmailing," video, European Council on Foreign Relations, June 29, 2021, retrieved on October 1, 2022, from https://www.youtube.com/watch?v =mzLTKkml51k.

128   **"we will not have to use it":** Weyland, "Anti-Coercion Instrument."

128   **"deter a conflict":** Authors' interview with Commission official.

129   **"reverse dependencies":** Weyland, "Anti-Coercion Instrument," 14:39.

129   **to find weaknesses:** Authors' interview with Commission official.

130   **"I'm going to freeze your you-know-whats off":** Jim Yardley and Jo Becker, "How Putin Forged a Pipeline Deal That Derailed," *New York Times*, December 30, 2014.

130   **"totally controlled by Russia":** Quoted in Glasser, "How Trump Made War on Angela Merkel and Europe."

130   **In its early years:** Amanda Sloat, "Germany's New Centrists? The Evolution, Political Prospects, and Foreign Policy of Germany's Green Party," Brookings, October 2020.

131   **Gazprom formed a consortium:** This paragraph relies on Hannes Adomeit, *Sanctions as a Bone of Contention in the EU-Germany-US-Russia Quadrilateral*, Center for European Studies, Carleton University, December 2017.

131   **"better relationship with Russia"**: Adomeit, *Sanctions as a Bone of Contention*.

131   **"commercial project"**: Adomeit, *Sanctions as a Bone of Contention*, 4.

132   **"had ever agreed on anything"**: Guy Chazan, "Angela Merkel Stands Firm on Nord Stream 2 Despite Navalny Poisoning," *Financial Times*, September 22, 2020.

132   **a more enthusiastic audience**: Brett Forrest, "U.S., Russia Race to Outflank Each Other on Russian Pipeline," *Wall Street Journal*, November 29, 2020.

132   **by nearly 70 percent**: Jude Clemente, "Where Does US Natural Gas Production Go from Here?" *Forbes*, May 14, 2021.

132   **fawning admiration**: Katie Sheperd, "Sen. Ted Cruz Insulted a 'Woke, Emasculated' U.S. Army Ad. Angry Veterans Fired Back," *Washington Post*, May 21, 2021.

132   **"freedom gas"**: "Sen. Cruz Leads Congressional Push to Halt Putin's Nord Stream 2 Pipeline with Clarified and Expanded Sanctions," Office of Ted Cruz, June 15, 2020.

132   **munitions had been dumped**: "Permit for Nord Stream 2 Natural Gas Pipelines," Danish Energy Agency, October 30, 2019, available at https://ens.dk/sites/ens.dk/files/OlieGas/permit_nord_stream_2.pdf.

133   **"vessels that engage in pipe-laying"**: National Defense Authorization Act, US Congress, December 20, 2019.

133   **"potentially fatal legal and economic sanctions"**: Ted Cruz and Ron Johnson, "Sens. Cruz, Johnson Put Company Installing Putin's Pipeline on Formal Legal Notice," December 18, 2019.

133   **"crushing legal and economic sanctions"**: Letter from Ted Cruz, Tom Cotton, and Ron Johnson to Harm Sievers and Fridjof Ostenberg, August 5, 2020, retrieved on September 24, 2022, from https://www.cruz.senate.gov/imo/media/doc/Letters/2020.08.05%20Final%20Mukran%20Port%20Letter.pdf.

133   **stevedores**: Agathe Demarais, *Backfire: How Sanctions Reshape the World against U.S. Interests* (New York: Columbia University Press, 2022).

133   **"We do not approve"**: Guy Chazan, "Angela Merkel Hits Out at US Sanctions on Nord Stream 2 Pipeline," *Financial Times*, December 18, 2019.

133   **an "economic declaration of war"**: Erika Solomon and Katrina Manson, "US Senators' Letter on Nord Stream 2 Sparks Outrage in Germany," *Financial Times*, August 19, 2020.

133   **"European energy policy is decided in Europe"**: Chazan, "Angela Merkel Hits Out."

133   **"a strategy of burned bridges"**: Quoted in Patrick Wintour, "Nord Stream 2: How Putin's Pipeline Paralysed the West," *Guardian*, December 23, 2021.

134   **it didn't make sense**: Franziska Brantner, *Nordstream 2: Klimakiller und Spaltpilz für Europa*, February 8, 2021, retrieved on July 11, 2022, from https://www.youtube.com/watch?v=2I5K5HT1xjc&t=120s.

134 **"it was quite tragic"**: Authors' interview with Franziska Brantner, April 30, 2022.

134 **a German promise of $175 million:** Nikolaus Kurmayer, "Ukraine Gets Compensation in Exchange for US-Germany Deal on Nord Stream 2," *Euractiv*, July 22, 2021.

134 **final regulatory approval was delayed:** Timothy Jones, "Nord Stream 2 Unlikely to Start Operations before Summer—Regulator," Deutsche Welle, January 30, 2022.

134 **"geopolitical mistake":** "Nord Stream 2: German Minister Warns Russia over Ukraine," Deutsche Welle, December 18, 2022.

135 **spelled out the implied message:** Andrey Gurkov, "Can Europe Escape Gazprom's Energy Stranglehold?" Deutsche Welle, July 11, 2021.

135 **persistently declined to say:** Leela Jacinto, "Ex-German Chancellor Schröder's Russia Ties Cast a Shadow over Scholz's Trip to Moscow," France 24, February 15, 2022.

135 **his defense minister suggested:** Sabine Siebold, "Don't Drag Nord Stream 2 into Conflict over Ukraine, German Defmin Says," Reuters, January 13, 2022.

135 **an energy exemption:** Alberto Nardelli and Arne Delfs, "Germany Sought Energy Exemption in Russia Finance Sanctions," Bloomberg, January 25, 2022.

135 **"We will bring an end to it":** Missy Ryan, Rick Noack, Robyn Dixon, and Rachel Pannett, "Biden Vows to Stop Nord Stream 2 Pipeline to Europe If Russia Invades Ukraine," *Washington Post*, February 7, 2022.

135 **Robert Habeck reiterated:** "Nord Stream 2 Approval Depends on Geopolitical Developments, Habeck Says," Deutsche Welle, February 11, 2002.

135 **putting the project into deep freeze:** Philip Oltermann, "Germany Halts Nord Stream 2 Approval over Russian Recognition of Ukraine 'Republics,'" *Guardian*, February 22, 2022.

136 **a post-carbon economy:** Mark Leonard, Jean Pisani-Ferry, Jeremy Shapiro, Simone Tagliapietra, and Guntram Wolff, "The EU Can't Separate Climate Policy from Foreign Policy," *Foreign Affairs*, February 9, 2021.

136 **delusional screeds:** Vladimir Putin, "On the Historical Unity of Russians and Ukrainians," *Kremlin.ru*, retrieved on December 2, 2022, from http://en.kremlin.ru/events/president/news/66181.

137 **"high-impact economic measures":** Humeyra Pamuk, "Blinken Warns of 'High-Impact' Economic Steps If Russia Invades Ukraine," Reuters, December 1, 2021.

137 **cutting Russia out of SWIFT:** Martin Grieve and Moritz Koch, "Swift-Sanktionen vom Tisch: EU und USA rücken vom Ausschluss Russlands aus globalem Finanzsystem Ab," *Handelsblatt*, January 17, 2022.

137 **"not the highest common denominator":** Sam Fleming, Henry Foy, and James Shotter, "Ukraine: EU Wrestles with How to Inflict Sanctions 'Pain' on Russia," *Financial Times*, February 7, 2022.

138 **"secure calls or video conferences"**: Valentina Pop, Sam Fleming, and James Politi, "Weaponisation of Finance: How the West Unleashed 'Shock and Awe' on Russia," *Financial Times*, April 6, 2022.

138 **repeatedly waiting**: Michael D. Shear, Zolan Kanno-Youngs, and Katie Rogers, "10 Consequential Days: How Biden Navigated War, Covid and the Supreme Court," *New York Times*, February 27, 2022.

138 **willingness to "sacrifice"**: Pop, Fleming, and Politi, "Weaponisation of Finance."

138 **the British soccer club Chelsea**: Rory Smith and Tariq Panja, "Chelsea Is for Sale, Its Russian Owner Says," *New York Times*, March 2, 2022. See also Rachel Treisman, "The U.K. Sanctions Roman Abramovich, Halting His Plan to Sell Chelsea Football Club," NPR, March 10, 2022.

138 **its crew tried to flee**: Tassilo Hummel, Alasdair Pal, and Steve Holland, "Yacht Seized as U.S. Ramps Up Oligarch Sanctions So Putin 'Feels the Squeeze,'" Reuters, March 4, 2022.

139 **yacht that allegedly belonged to Putin**: Crispian Balmer and Emilio Parodi, "Italy Impounds Luxury Yacht Linked to Russian President," Reuters, May 6, 2022.

139 **implemented in just seventy-two hours**: Pop, Fleming, and Politi, "Weaponisation of Finance."

139 **$600 billion in reserves**: Nicholas Gordon, "Banks Are Stopping Putin from Tapping at $630 Billion War Chest Russia Stockpiled before Invading Ukraine," *Fortune*, March 3, 2022.

139 **hashed out the details**: Pop, Fleming, and Politi, "Weaponisation of Finance."

139 **"a geopolitical actor"**: See video, State of the Union, European University Institute, May 7–9, 2022, retrieved on September 26, 2022, from https://stateoftheunion.eui.eu/videos-on-demand/.

139 **"regulatory superpower to an actor"**: Alex Stubb, "Geopolitical Order and Change of Security Architecture in Europe Conversation," video, State of the Union, European University Institute, May 6, 2022, retrieved on September 26, 2022, from https://stateoftheunion.eui.eu/videos-on-demand/.

140 **"deterrence and solidarity"**: James Politi, "Former Nato Chief Calls for Mutual Pledge on Economic Coercion," *Financial Times*, June 10, 2022.

141 **euphemistically described the problem**: Sam Fleming and Andy Bounds, "Brussels Pushes for Tougher Sanctions Enforcement via EU-Wide Body," *Financial Times*, July 7, 2022.

141 **"competing major powers"**: Olaf Scholz, "Die EU Muss zu Einem Geopolitischen Akteur Warden," *Frankfurter Allgemeine*, July 17, 2022.

141 **Russia shut down the Nord Stream 1**: Larry Elliott, "Nord Stream 1: Russia Switches Off Gas Pipeline Citing Maintenance," *Guardian*, August 31, 2022.

141 **remarked pointedly**: Matthias Matthijs, "A German Word for How Others See Germany's Gas Crisis: Schadenfreude," *Washington Post*, July 26, 2022.

141   **"catastrophic" consequences:** David Sheppard and Polina Ivanova, "Putin Warns of 'Catastrophic' Energy Crisis If West Boosts Sanctions," *Financial Times*, July 8, 2022.

142   **Lavrov congratulated him:** Marton Dunai and Polina Ivanova, "Hungary Sends Foreign Minister to Moscow to Ask Russia for More Gas," *Financial Times*, July 22, 2022.

142   **"massive scaling up":** *REPowerEU: A Plan to Rapidly Reduce Dependence on Russian Fossil Fuels and Fast Forward the Green Transition*, European Commission, May 18, 2022.

142   **high carbon intensity products:** Kate Abnett, "EU Countries Support Plan for World-First Carbon Border Tariff," Reuters, March 16, 2022.

142   **wanted the authority:** "Commission Unveils New Approach to Trade Agreements to Promote Green and Just Growth," European Commission, June 22, 2022, retrieved on September 25, 2022, from https://ec.europa.eu/commission /presscorner/detail/en/ip_22_3921.

142   **Edoardo Saravalle proposed:** Edoardo Saravalle, "Why World Leaders Should Impose Green Sanctions," *Financial Times*, August 2, 2019.

142   **"He delayed the shutdown of nuclear power plants":** Marina Kormbaki, Serafin Reiber, Jonas Schaible, and Gerald Traufetter, "Germany's Green Party Confronts Its Last Taboo," *Der Spiegel*, June 9, 2022.

143   **"interdependence also involves risks":** Annalena Baerbock, "Comments at the Business Forum of the 20th Conference of the Heads of German Missions," September 9, 2022.

143   **blunt in explaining:** Margethe Vestager, "Remarks of EVP Vestager at the Annual Conference of the EU Heads of Delegation," October 11, 2022, retrieved on October 23, 2022, from https://ec.europa.eu/commission/presscorner/detail/en /SPEECH_22_6115.

Chapter 5: Hook's Captain

145   **Demetri Sevastopulo discovered:** Our account of this story is taken from Demetri Sevastopulo, "US Offers Cash to Tanker Captains in Bid to Seize Iranian Ships," *Financial Times*, September 4, 2019.

145   **"mapping out . . . the pressure points":** Authors' interview with Brian Hook.

146   **assassinate dissidents abroad:** "EU Sanctions Iran over Assassination Plots," Agence France-Presse, September 1, 2019.

147   **businesses struggle to respond:** Steven Weber, *Bloc by Bloc: How to Build a Global Enterprise for the New Regional Order* (Cambridge, MA: Harvard University Press, 2019).

147 **a single phrase:** Aaron Tilley and Ryan Tracey, "How Microsoft Became Washington's Favorite Tech Giant," *Wall Street Journal*, April 2, 2022.

147 **antitrust enforcers had decided:** U.S. Department of Justice, "Justice Department Files Antitrust Suit against Microsoft for Unlawfully Monopolizing Computer Software Markets," press release, May 18, 1998, retrieved on November 18, 2022, from https://www.justice.gov/archive/atr/public/press_releases/1998/1764.htm

147 **"people in the federal government":** Brad Smith and Carol Anne Brown, *Tools and Weapons: The Promise and Peril of the Digital Age* (New York: Penguin, 2019), ix.

147 **making peace with a hostile power:** Michael Kinsley, "How Microsoft Learned ABCs of D.C.," *Politico*, April 5, 2011.

148 **it succeeded:** Cat Zakrewski, "Microsoft Is Bigger than Google, Amazon and Facebook. But Now Lawmakers Treat It Like an Ally in Antitrust Battles," *Washington Post*, January 22, 2022.

149 **a talk in Hamburg:** Caspar Bowden, *The Cloud Conspiracy*, speech given at Chaos Computer Club Congress, Hamburg, December 27, 2014, retrieved on May 26, 2022, from https://www.youtube.com/watch?v=d7TyBK-gMgk.

149 **Bowden had been a privacy activist:** Interviews with friends of Caspar Bowden.

149 **"going hard enough":** Interview with friend of Caspar Bowden.

150 **"nauseating cynicism":** Retrieved on September 24, 2022, from https://twitter.com/casparbowden/status/542588420611379201.

151 **drive a wedge:** Farrell and Newman, *Of Privacy and Power*.

152 **might break the global Internet:** Mark Bergen, "Eric Schmidt: Get Ready for 'a Lot' More Alphabet Companies," Vox.com, October 13, 2015.

152 **Brad Smith seemed less alarmed:** Brad Smith, "The Collapse of the US-EU Safe Harbor: Solving the New Privacy Rubik's Cube," *Microsoft on the Issues* (blog), October 25, 2015, retrieved on May 25, 2022, from https://blogs.microsoft.com/on-the-issues/2015/10/20/the-collapse-of-the-us-eu-safe-harbor-solving-the-new-privacy-rubiks-cube.

152 **"all hell broke loose":** Smith and Brown, *Tools and Weapons*, 136.

152 **that Microsoft give it information:** Microsoft, *US National Security Orders Report*, retrieved on November 18, 2022, from https://www.microsoft.com/en-us/corporate-responsibility/us-national-security-orders-report?activetab=pivot_1:primaryr2

152 **working with GCHQ:** Smith and Brown, *Tools and Weapons*, 13.

152 **"tech has gone global":** Smith and Brown, *Tools and Weapons*, 11.

153 **pretending that the chasm wasn't there:** Henry Farrell and Martha Finnemore, "The End of Hypocrisy," *Foreign Affairs*, November/December 2013.

153 **$22 billion in quarterly sales:** Microsoft, "Microsoft Cloud Strength Fuels Second Quarter Results," *Microsoft News Center* (blog), January 25, 2022, retrieved

on July 3, 2022, from https://news.microsoft.com/2022/01/25/microsoft-cloud
-strength-fuels-second-quarter-results-4/.

154   **They began to encrypt:** David E. Sanger and Nicole Perlroth, "Internet Giant
Erects Barriers to Spy Agencies," *New York Times*, June 6, 2014.

154   **a more lasting and lawful peace:** Brad Smith, "The Collapse of the US-EU Safe
Harbor."

154   **intelligence agencies grudgingly agreed:** Farrell and Newman, *Of Privacy and
Power.*

155   **Stuxnet was infecting machines:** Bruce Schneier, "The Story Behind the Stuxnet
Virus," *Forbes*, October 7, 2010.

155   **Obama had hesitated:** David Sanger, *The Perfect Weapon: War, Sabotage, and Fear
in the Cyber Age* (New York: Crown, 2018), 10.

155   **it was quietly willing to pay top dollar:** Nicole Perlroth, *This Is How They Tell Me
the World Ends: The Cyber Weapons Arms Race* (London: Bloomsbury Publishing,
2021).

155   **notorious SWIFT heist:** Jim O'Grady and Kenny Malone, "A SWIFT Getaway,"
NPR, February 9, 2022.

155   **forced TSMC to close down its plants:** Debby Wu, "iPhone Chipmaker Blames
WannaCry Variant for Plant Closures," Bloomberg, August 6, 2018.

155   **Smith told the RSA Conference:** Brad Smith, *Transcript of Keynote Address at
the RSA Conference 2017: "The Need for a Digital Geneva Convention,"* February 14,
2017.

156   **treasure trove of commercially sensitive information:** Michael Balsamo and
Eric Tucker, "North Korean Programmer Charged in Sony Hack, WannaCry
Attack," PBS News Hour, September 6, 2018.

156   **Russia "would retaliate":** Smith and Brown, *Tools and Weapons*, 83.

156   **"help the U.S. government spy":** Smith and Brown, *Tools and Weapons*, 115.

156   **banned government use of Windows:** Sean Gallagher, "Red Flag Windows: Microsoft Modifies Windows OS for Chinese Government," *Ars Technica*, March
21, 2017.

157   **"digital Switzerland":** Smith, *Keynote Address at the RSA Conference 2017.*

157   **"our own international agreements":** Smith and Brown, *Tools and Weapons*, 119.

158   **"as the ICRC did":** Brad Smith, *Keynote Address at the RSA Conference 2017.*

158   **regardless of the country from which we come:** Smith, *Keynote Address at the RSA
Conference 2017.*

158   **nonbinding "Paris Call for Trust and Security":** "Paris Call for Trust and Security in Cyberspace," November 12, 2018, retrieved on November 19, 2022, from
https://pariscall.international/en/.

158   **Biden administration signed on:** Ned Price, "The United States Supports the
Paris Call for Trust and Security in Cyberspace," press statement, U.S. Department

of State, November 10, 2021, retrieved on November 19, 2022, from https://www
.state.gov/the-united-states-supports-the-paris-call-for-trust-and-security-in
-cyberspace/.

158 **Cybersecurity Tech Accord:** "Cybersecurity Tech Accord," Tech Accord, n.d.,
retrieved on November 19, 2022, from https://cybertechaccord.org/accord/.

158 **Switzerland rethought their neutrality:** Michael Shield and Silke Koltrowitz,
"Neutral Swiss Join EU Sanctions against Russia in Break with Past," Reuters,
February 28, 2022.

158 **two carefully authored blog posts:** Brad Smith, "Digital Technology and the War
in Ukraine," *Microsoft on the Issues* (blog), February 28, 2022; Tom Burt, "The
Hybrid War in Ukraine," *Microsoft on the Issues* (blog), April 27, 2022.

158 **a remarkable keynote speech:** Except where stated otherwise, this and the other
details below are taken from the video of the 2022 Envision Conference, retrieved
on May 31, 2022, from https://www.microsoft.com/en-gb/events/envision-uk/.

159 **FoxBlade:** Microsoft, *Special Report: Ukraine. An Overview of Russia's Cyberattack
Activity in Ukraine,* April 27, 2022.

159 **twenty-four trillion daily signals:** Microsoft, *Special Report: Ukraine.*

159 **As the *New York Times* later described it:** David E. Sanger, Julian E. Barnes, and
Kate Conger, "As Tanks Rolled into Ukraine, So Did Malware. Then Microsoft
Entered the War," *New York Times,* February 28, 2022.

159 **compared Russia's cyberattacks:** Brad Smith, "Defending Ukraine: Early Lessons from the Cyber War," Microsoft, June 22, 2022.

160 **a "hybrid war":** Burt, "The Hybrid War."

160 **suspended sales:** "Microsoft Suspends Sales in Russia as Western Sanctions
Tighten," Reuters, March 4, 2022.

160 **a follow-up report:** Microsoft, *Defending Ukraine.*

160 **Smith boasted:** Brad Smith, speech at Envision Conference.

161 **a help wanted notice:** Chang Chien and Elizabeth Hsu, "TSMC Looking to Hire
Geopolitical Experts with PhDs," *Focus Taiwan,* February 16, 2022.

161 **an internal document:** "Morris Chang Speech, October 26, 2021," retrieved on
December 2, 2022, from https://semiwiki.com/forum/index.php?threads/morris
-chang-speech-oct-26-2021.14846/.

162 **"Switzerland of semiconductors":** Yang Jie, Stephanie Yang, and Asa Fitch, "The
World Relies on One Chip Maker in Taiwan, Leaving Everyone Vulnerable," *Wall
Street Journal,* June 19, 2021.

163 **Samsung, the one firm:** *Morris Chang's Last Speech,* April 2021, translated by Kevin
Xu, retrieved on July 22, 2022, from https://web.archive.org/web/20211016142636
/https://interconnected.blog/morris-changs-last-speech/.

163 **Intel struggled:** Michael Kan, "Intel's 7nm PC Chip to Arrive in 2023 Next to
TSMC-Made CPU," *PC Magazine,* March 24, 2021.

163   **began to compete with the iPhone:** Geoffrey Cain, "Samsung vs. Apple: Inside the Brutal War for Smartphone Dominance," *Forbes*, March 13, 2020.

163   **Apple-designed processors:** Apple, "Mac Computers with Apple Silicon," July 25, 2022, retrieved November 19, 2022, from https://support.apple.com/en-us /HT211814.

163   **consider dumping:** Ortenca Alliaj and Richard Waters, "Third Point Tells Intel to Consider Shedding Chip Manufacturing," *Financial Times*, December 29, 2020.

163   **"incredibly dependent":** Kathrin Hille, "TSMC: How a Taiwanese Chipmaker Became a Linchpin of the Global Economy," *Financial Times*, March 24, 2021.

164   **"a small industrial park":** Dan Wang, "How Technology Grows (A Restatement of Definite Optimism)," Danwang.co, July 24, 2018.

164   **15 to 20 percent:** Cheng-Ting Fang and Lauly Li, "TSMC Halts New Huawei Orders after US Tightens Restrictions," *Nikkei Asia*, May 18, 2020.

164   **"a sometime friend":** Raymond Zhong, "In U.S.-China Tech Feud, Taiwan Feels Heat from Both Sides," *New York Times*, October 1, 2020.

164   **TSMC's earnings didn't suffer:** Tim Culpan, "TSMC Shrugs Off Huawei Ban and Shows Who's King," *Washington Post*, July 17, 2020.

165   **a key "part":** Ming-Chin Monique Chu, *The East Asian Computer Chip War* (London: Routledge, 2013), 106.

165   **war was unlikely:** "TSMC Chairman Says Nobody Wants War over Taiwan as Chip Supplies Too Valuable," Reuters, July 15, 2021.

165   **"broken nest" strategy:** Jared McKinney and Peter Harris, "Broken Nest: Deterring China from Invading Taiwan," *Parameters* 51, no. 4 (2021): 23–36.

166   **how dangerous it was:** Eric Chang, "Intel Says US Chipmakers Should Be Priority over TSMC, Samsung," *Taiwan News*, December 2, 2021.

166   **restricted TSMC from supplying:** Reuters Staff, "TSMC Stops New Huawei Orders After U.S. Restrictions," Reuters, May 18, 2020.

166   **TSMC announced:** Cheng Ting-Fang, Lauly Li, and Yifan Yu, "TSMC to Build $12bn Cutting-Edge Chip Plant in US," *Nikkei Asia*, May 15, 2020.

166   **"deep American roots":** Pat Gelsinger, "More Than Manufacturing: Investments in Chip Production Must Support U.S. Priorities [sponsored story]," *Politico*, June 24, 2021.

166   **Gelsinger spent:** Asa Fitch and Bob Davies, "Intel CEO Pitches Pricey Chip Plants to Officials at Home and Abroad," *Wall Street Journal*, August 14, 2021.

166   **"where the oil reserves are":** See video at Ian King, "Intel CEO Urges Lawmakers to 'Not Waste This Crisis' in Chip Push," Bloomberg, January 19, 2022, retrieved on June 13, 2022, from https://www.bloomberg.com/news/articles/2022-01-19 /intel-urges-lawmakers-to-not-waste-this-crisis-with-chip-push.

166   **"implored us to do it":** Yu Nakamura, "Intel Slams US Subsidies for TSMC in Arizona's Clash of Chip Titans," *Nikkei Asia*, July 16, 2021.

166 **As Liu explained elsewhere:** Charlie Campbell, "Inside the Taiwan Firm That Makes the World's Tech Run," *Time*, October 1, 2021.

167 **The unfortunately named "Chipageddon":** Enrique Dans, "How We Got to 'Chipageddon,'" *Forbes*, February 25, 2021.

167 **a hundred-day review:** White House, "Executive Order on America's Supply Chains," February 24, 2021, retrieved on January 11, 2022, from https://www.whitehouse.gov/briefing-room/presidential-actions/2021/02/24/executive-order-on-americas-supply-chains/.

167 **"a shortage of computer chips":** Joseph Biden, "Remarks by President Biden at Signing of an Executive Order on Supply Chains," February 24, 2021, retrieved on January 11, 2022, from https://www.whitehouse.gov/briefing-room/speeches-remarks/2021/02/24/remarks-by-president-biden-at-signing-of-an-executive-order-on-supply-chains/.

167 **His executive order:** White House, "Executive Order on America's Supply Chains."

168 **invited comments from the semiconductor industry:** Bureau of Industry and Security, "Semiconductor Manufacturing and Advanced Packaging Supply Chain Notice Published 3/15/21. Comments Due 4/5/21," 86 FR 14308, March 15 2021.

168 **"data hub":** White House, *Building Resilient Supply Chains, Revitalizing American Manufacturing, and Fostering Broad-Based Growth*, June 2021, 17–18.

168 **"voluntarily share information":** White House, "Readout of Biden Administration Convening to Discuss and Address Semiconductor Supply Chain," retrieved on June 16, 2022, from https://www.whitehouse.gov/briefing-room/statements-releases/2021/09/23/readout-of-biden-administration-convening-to-discuss-and-address-semiconductor-supply-chain/.

168 **"if they don't comply":** Jenny Leonard, "White House Weighs Invoking Defense Law to Get Chip Data," Bloomberg, September 23, 2021.

168 **"unprecedented actions":** Reuters Staff, "Taiwan's TSMC Says Working to Overcome Global Chip Shortage," Reuters, September 24, 2021.

169 **"we definitely will not leak":** "Taiwan's TSMC, After US Request, Says It Won't Leak Sensitive Info," Reuters, October 7, 2021.

169 **a tranche of information:** Debby Wu, "World's Top Chipmakers Provide Data to US as Deadline Arrives," Bloomberg, November 7, 2021.

169 **a form of treachery:** Che Pan, "Chinese Media Continues Tirade against Taipei for Letting Chip Maker TSMC Comply with US Request for Semiconductor Supply Data," *South China Morning Post*, November 9, 2021.

169 **"seriously compromise":** "GT Voice: Chipmakers Risk Violating Chinese Laws over US' Hegemonic Data Request," *Global Times*, October 24, 2021.

169 **"help Washington impose sanctions":** Che Pan, "Chinese Critics Express

Dismay over Taiwan Chip Maker TSMC's Compliance with Washington's Semiconductor Data Request," *South China Morning Post*, November 8, 2021.

169 **If Xi just appreciated:** Thomas Friedman, "China's Bullying Is Becoming a Danger to the World and Itself," *New York Times*, October 19, 2021.

169 **commented briefly on globalization:** See response to audience after Morris Chang speech beginning approximately at 1:15, retrieved on June 20, 2022, from https://www.youtube.com/watch?v=Tiu0i6htq-U&t=74s.

170 **its home advantages:** Ting-Fang and Lauly Li, "From Somebody to Nobody: TSMC Faces Uphill Battle in U.S. Talent War," *Nikkei Asia*, May 27, 2022.

170 **"those good days are gone":** Jude Blanchett, Ryan Hass, and Morris Chang, Transcript, *Vying for Talent Podcast: Can Semiconductor Manufacturing Return to the US*, April 14, 2022.

170 **in London:** Vitalik Buterin, "The Not So Paranoid Case for Decentralization," *Ethereum London Meetup*, March 30, 2015, retrieved on June 23, 2022, from https://www.youtube.com/watch?v=tjxkdniYtkc.

170 **a chilly day:** Retrieved from https://www.timeanddate.com/weather/uk/london/historic?month=3&year=2015.

170 **it still hadn't launched:** See Laura Shin, *The Cryptopians: Idealism, Greed, Lies, and the Makings of the First Big Cryptography Craze* (New York: PublicAffairs, 2022), for an account of the personal conflicts and rivalries that complicated the launch.

171 **As Buterin described it to us:** Authors' interview with Vitalik Buterin, July 2, 2022.

172 **total notional value:** Ryan Browne, "Ethereum, the World's Second-Largest Cryptocurrency, Soars Above $4,000 for the First Time," CNBC, May 10, 2021.

172 **a billionaire for a while:** Scott Carpenter, "Ethereum Co-Founder Buterin Says He's No Longer a Billionaire," Bloomberg, May 20, 2022.

172 **happiest writing blogposts:** Vitalik Buterin, "My 40-Liter Travel Backpack Guide," June 20, 2022, retrieved on June 23, 2022, from https://vitalik.ca/general/2022/06/20/backpack.html.

173 **private currency:** Stefan Eich, "Old Utopias, New Tax Havens: The Politics of Bitcoin in Historical Perspective," in Philipp Hacker, Ioannis Lianos, Georgios Dimitropoulos, and Stefan Eich, eds., *Regulating Blockchain: Techno-Social and Legal Challenges* (New York: Oxford University Press, 2019).

173 **Libertarians proclaimed:** Most famously, John Perry Barlow, *A Declaration of the Independence of Cyberspace*, Davos, Switzerland, February 8, 1996.

173 **"anonymous transactions systems":** Eric Hughes, *A Cypherpunk's Manifesto*, March 9, 1993.

174 ***Cryptonomicon*:** Neal Stephenson, *Cryptonomicon* (New York: Avon, 1999).

174 **"required reading":** Peter Thiel (with Blake Masters), *Zero to One: Notes on Startups, or How to Build the Future* (New York: Penguin, 2014), 123.

174 **As Thiel later admitted:** Peter Thiel, "PayPal Co-Founder Peter Thiel—Bitcoin Keynote—Bitcoin 2022 Conference," retrieved on June 30, 2022, from https:// www.youtube.com/watch?v=ko6K82pXcPA&t=7s.

174 **"grand mission":** Peter Thiel, *Zero to One*, 17.

174 **"World Domination Index":** Jimmy Soni, *The Founders: The Story of PayPal and the Entrepreneurs Who Shaped Silicon Valley* (New York: Simon & Schuster, 2022), xiv.

174 **with a slide:** Peter Thiel, Bitcoin Keynote.

174 **reached a . . . settlement:** U.S. Department of the Treasury, *Settlement Agreement Between the U.S. Department of the Treasury's Office of Foreign Assets Control and PayPal, Inc.*, March 25, 2015.

174 **without demur:** John Adams, "These Payment Companies Are Cutting Off Russia," *American Banker*, March 7, 2022.

174 **slogan engraved on his cannons:** Neil Stephenson, *Snow Crash* (New York: Bantam, 1992).

175 **an ingenious mathematical trick:** For a detailed explanation, which does require some basic familiarity with cryptographic concepts, see Arvind Narayanan, Joseph Bonneau, Edward Felten, Andrew Miller, and Steven Goldfeder, *Bitcoin and Cryptocurrency Technologies: A Comprehensive Introduction* (Princeton, NJ: Princeton University Press, 2016).

176 **"decentralized computer":** Authors' interview with Vitalik Buterin.

176 **As Gavin Wood . . . explained:** Gavin Wood, *Allegality, Coinscrum and Proof of Work Media: Tools for the Future*, London, 2014, retrieved on June 29, 2022, from https://www.youtube.com/watch?v=Zh9BxYTSrGU.

176 **"forces of nature":** Wood, *Allegality*.

177 **Jentzsch began to fear:** These paragraphs summarize the much more detailed account in Shin, *The Cryptopians*.

177 **the self-declared Cryptoqueen:** BBC, "Cryptoqueen: How This Woman Scammed the World, Then Vanished," *BBC News*, November 24, 2019.

177 **"take the money and run":** María Luisa Paúl, "Former 'Cryptoqueen' Is Now One of 10 Most-Wanted Fugitives," *Washington Post*, July 1, 2022.

177 **dubbed Web3:** Arjun Kharpal, "What Is 'Web3'? Here's the Vision for the Future of the Internet from the Man Who Coined the Phrase," CNBC, April 19, 2022.

178 **conceptual artists:** Thomas McEvilley, "Art in the Dark," *Artforum*, June 1983, retrieved on July 1, 2022, from https://www.artforum.com/print/198306/art-in-the-dark-35485.

178 **Marlinspike warned:** Moxie Marlinspike, "My First Impressions of Web3," moxie.org, retrieved on July 1, 2022, from https://moxie.org/2022/01/07/web3-first-impressions.html.

178 **intermediary companies:** "Your NFT Journey Starts Here," OpenSea Learn, 2022, retrieved on November 20, 2022, from https://opensea.io/learn; "About

Coinbase," Coinbase, 2022, retrieved on November 20, 2022, from https://www
.coinbase.com/about; "About," Metamask, 2022, retrieved on November 20, 2022,
from https://metamask.io/about/.

178 **infrastructure providers like Alchemy and Infura:** @Amit0617, "Nodes and Clients," blogpost, ethereum.org, November 10, 2022, retrieved on November 20,
2022, from https://ethereum.org/en/developers/docs/nodes-and-clients/.

178 **Stablecoins like Dai and Tether:** "What Is a Stablecoin?" Coinbase, 2022,
retrieved on November 20, 2022, from https://www.coinbase.com/learn/crypto
-basics/what-is-a-stablecoin.

178 **As Buterin explained to us:** Interview with Vitalik Buterin.

178 **"most participants don't even know":** Marlinspike, "My First Impressions of Web3."

179 **professed surprise:** Retrieved on July 1, 2022, from https://twitter.com/nikil
/status/1290870587909443584.

179 **value triple:** "Alchemy Valuation Nearly Triples to $10.2 Billion in About Three
Months," Reuters, February 8, 2022.

179 **writer bemoaned:** Neel Chauhan, "Web3 Is Centralized (and Inefficient!),"
March 22, 2022, retrieved on December 2, 2022, from https://web.archive.org
/web/20220323031915/https://www.neelc.org/posts/web3-centralized/.

179 **use ShapeShift:** Shin, *The Crytopians*, 131.

179 **the *Wall Street Journal* accused it:** Justin Scheck and Shane Shiflett, "How Dirty
Money Disappears into the Black Hole of Cryptocurrency," *Wall Street Journal*,
September 28, 2018.

179 **helped Buterin:** Shin, *The Cryptopians*, 380.

179 **drawn a smiley face:** Bob Van Voris, "Crypto Expert Gets 63 Months in Prison
for Helping North Korea Evade U.S. Sanctions," Bloomberg, April 12, 2022.

179 **how "Facebook could succeed":** Robert Hackett, "Hanging in the Balance: Facebook and Libra," *Fortune*, December 19, 2019.

180 **Chinese competitors:** Lizhi Liu, "From Click to Boom: The Political Economy of
E-Commerce in China," unpublished book manuscript.

180 **"I hate everything":** Hackett, "Hanging in the Balance."

180 **"resolutely against Libra":** Taylor Telford, "Why Governments Around the World
Are Afraid of Libra, Facebook's Cryptocurrency," *Washington Post*, July 12, 2019.

180 **emphasized the risks:** Fabio Panetta, *The Two Sides of the (Stable)Coin*, speech at il
Salone di Pagamenti, Frankfurt am Main, November 4, 2020.

180 **"could facilitate money laundering":** Elizabeth Dwoskin and Damian Paletta,
"Facebook Privately Pitched Its Cryptocurrency Plan Last Month to Regulators.
They Were Left Even More Scared," *Washington Post*, July 16, 2019.

180 **"worked feverishly":** Hannah Murphy and Kiran Stacey, "Facebook Libra: The
Inside Story of How the Company's Cryptocurrency Dream Died," *Financial
Times*, March 10, 2022.

181 **Big crypto:** Allyson Versprille and Bill Allison, "Crypto Bosses Flex Political Muscle with 5,200% Surge in US Giving," Bloomberg, June 2, 2022.

181 **"how to" guide:** *How to Win the Future: An Agenda for the Third Generation of the Internet*, Andreessen Horowitz, October 2021, retrieved on November 20, 2022, from https://a16z.com/wp-content/uploads/2021/10/How-to-Win-the-Future-1.pdf.

181 **over four thousand DAOs:** Eric Lipton and Ephrat Livni, "Reality Intrudes on a Utopian Crypto Vision," *New York Times*, March 8, 2022.

181 **instituted proceedings against:** Securities and Exchange Commission, "SEC Seeks to Stop the Registration of Misleading Crypto Asset Offerings," press release, November 18, 2022, retrieved on December 2, 2022, from https://www.sec.gov/news/press-release/2022-208.

181 **"poker chips":** Gary Gensler, "The Path Forward: Cryptocurrency with Gary Gensler," *Washington Post*, September 21, 2021.

181 **if examined closely:** Lipton and Livni, "Reality Intrudes."

181 **much more centralized:** Alyssa Blackburn, Christoph Huber, Yossi Eliaz, Muhammad S. Shamim, David Weisz, Goutham Seshadri, Kevin Kim, Shengqi Hang, and Erez Lieberman Aiden, "Cooperation Among an Anonymous Group Protected Bitcoin During Failures of Decentralization," arXiv, retrieved on July 2, 2022, from https://arxiv.org/abs/2206.02871.

182 **Buterin told us:** Interview with Vitalik Buterin.

182 **He wrote a book:** Balaji Srinivasan, *The Network State: How to Start a New Country* (self-published, 2022).

182 **"Pax Bitcoinica":** Balaji S. Srinivasan, "Bitcoin Is Civilization," May 14, 2021, retrieved on July 17, 2022, from https://www.commonsense.news/p/is-bitcoin-anarchy-or-civilization.

183 **"a Chinese financial weapon":** Retrieved on July 18, 2022, from https://twitter.com/nixonfoundation/status/1379894036060864516.

183 **his headline speech:** Peter Thiel, Bitcoin Keynote.

183 **North Korean hackers:** U.S. Department of the Treasury, "U.S. Treasury Sanctions Notorious Virtual Currency Mixer Tornado Cash," retrieved on September 22, 2022, from https://home.treasury.gov/news/press-releases/jy0916.

183 **to donate money to Ukraine:** @VitalikButerin, retrieved on September 22, 2022, from https://twitter.com/VitalikButerin/status/1556925602233569280.

183 **"a crime":** "Ohio Resident Charged with Operating Darknet-Based Bitcoin 'Mixer,' Which Laundered over $300 Million," Department of Justice, Office of Public Affairs, February 13, 2020.

184 **blatantly suspect wallets:** Danny Nelson, "US Treasury Official Warns Crypto Industry to Proactively Sanction 'Problematic' Wallets," *CoinDesk*, May 19, 2022.

184 **selling tracking information:** Sam Biddle, "Cryptocurrency Titan Coinbase Providing 'Geotracking Data' to ICE," *Intercept*, June 29, 2022.

184 **"prosecute individuals":** *Testimony of John Kothanek before the Committee on Homeland Security*, Subcommittee on Intelligence and Counterterrorism, June 9, 2022.

184 **"to be unstoppable":** Quoted in Sam Reynolds, "Tornado Cash Co-Founder Says the Mixer Protocol Is Unstoppable," *CoinDesk*, January 25, 2022.

184 **"U.S. Treasury can't turn off Tornado Cash":** Jon Stokes, "Crypto Reaps the Whirlwind: Treasury Moves against Tornado Cash," Jonstokes.com, August 10, 2022.

184 **"technically impossible":** Muyao Shen, "Crypto Mixer Tornado Cash Says Sanctions Can't Apply to Smart Contracts," Bloomberg, March 10, 2022.

185 **colorfully jumbled metaphor:** Wood, *Allegality*.

185 **Italian plastic surgeon:** David Yaffe-Bellany, "The Coin That Could Wreck Crypto," *New York Times*, June 17, 2022.

185 **funded a lawsuit:** Rami Ayyub and Hannah Lang, Coinbase Backs Lawsuit against U.S. Treasury Over Tornado Cash Sanctions," Reuters, September 8, 2022.

185 **had been dusted:** U.S. Department of the Treasury, "Frequently Asked Questions: Cyber-related Sanctions 1078. Do OFAC Reporting Obligations Apply to 'Dusting' Transactions," updated November 8, 2022, retrieved November 20, 2022, from https://home.treasury.gov/policy-issues/financial-sanctions/faqs/.

185 **fired employees:** Alastair Marsh, "Crypto Rebels Trip over Each Other en Route to Financial Utopia," Bloomberg, October 5, 2019.

186 **community bank:** Vishal Chawla, "MakerDAO Approves $100 Million Stablecoin Loan Vault for 151-Year-Old US Bank," *Block*, July 7, 2022.

186 **long essay:** Rune Christensen, "The Path of Compliance and the Path of Decentralization: Why Maker Has No Choice but to Prepare to Free Float Dai," MakerDAO Forum, August 22, 2022, retrieved on September 25, 2022, from https://forum.makerdao.com/t/the-path-of-compliance-and-the-path-of-decentralization-why-maker-has-no-choice-but-to-prepare-to-free-float-dai/17466.

186 **cut off their connections:** Turner Wright, "Tornado Cash DAO Goes Down without Explanation Following Vote on Treasury Funds," *Cointelegraph*, August 12, 2022.

187 **"not a joke":** Scott Chipolina, "FT Cryptofinance: DeFi Is DeFi Until Washington Says It's Not," *Financial Times*, August 26, 2022.

Chapter 6: The Empire of Wind and Light

188 **Buterin happened to be in China:** Authors' interview with Vitalik Buterin.

188 **"one boss":** Frank Tang, "Facebook's Libra Forcing China to Step Up Plans for Its Own Cryptocurrency, Says Central Bank Official," *South China Morning Post*, July 8, 2019.

188 **Jinping demanded:** Robert Murray, "The U.S. Is Facing a 'Sputnik Moment' in the International Economy," Foreign Policy Research Institute, February 11, 2022.

189 **"dead end":** Authors' interview with Vitalik Buterin.

189 **"Sputnik moment":** Robert Murray, "The U.S. Is Facing a 'Sputnik Moment' in the International Economy."

189 **"urgency":** White House, "FACT SHEET: President Biden to Sign Executive Order on Ensuring Responsible Development of Digital Assets," March 9, 2022.

189 **"dollar's global status":** "Federal Reserve Vice Chair Testifies on Digital Currency," C-SPAN, May 26, 2022, https://www.c-span.org/video/?520618-1/federal-reserve-vice-chair-testifies-digital-currency.

189 **"something we really need to explore":** Helene Braun, "Powell Says Fed Plans Recommendation to Congress on CBDC," *CoinDesk*, June 23, 2022.

190 **despite government subsidies:** Theodore Benzmiller, "China's Progress Towards a Central Bank Digital Currency," Center for Strategic and International Studies, April 19, 2022.

190 **helped feed the widening gyre:** Ali Wyne, *America's Great-Power Opportunity: Revitalizing U.S. Foreign Policy to Meet the Challenges of Strategic Competition* (New York: Polity, 2022).

192 **encourage others to do the same:** Joseph Mayton, "Google Favors Encryption: HTTPS Sites to Get Search Ranking Boost," *Tech Times*, August 11, 2014.

192 **began to rearrange itself:** Hilary McGeachey, "The Changing Strategic Significance of Submarine Cables: Old Technology, New Concerns," *Australian Journal of International Affairs* 76 (2022): 161–77.

193 **"the dominant hub":** Quoted in McGeachey, "The Changing Strategic Significance of Submarine Cables."

193 **"Trump is the president":** Authors' interview with William Spiegelberger. Also see William R. Spiegelberger, "Anatomy of a Muddle: U.S. Sanctions against Rusal and Oleg Deripaska," Foreign Policy Research Institute, April 2019.

193 **reluctantly signed in 2017:** Emily Tamkin, "Trump Finally Signs Sanctions Bill, Then Adds Bizarre Statements," *Foreign Policy*, August 2, 2017.

193 **"supply bottleneck":** *Kurzposition: US-Russlandsanktionen*, WVMetalle, February 21, 2019, retrieved on December 2, 2022, from link at bit.ly/3uidgoe.

194 **"rerouted to China":** David O'Sullivan, Wolfgang Waldner, Gerard Araud, Emily Haber, Dan Mulhall, Armando Varrichio, Karin Olofsdotter, and Kim Darroch, "Letter to Charles Schumer," January 4, 2019, retrieved on October 1, 2022, from https://www.politico.eu/wp-content/uploads/2019/01/document1.pdf.

194 **"more difficult than it was":** Authors' interview with Dan Mulhall, March 31, 2022.

194 **"the gas supply would be cut off on Monday":** Authors' interview with Dan Mulhall.

194 **"what does this button do" approach:** Spiegelberger, "Anatomy of a Muddle," 10.

194 **designating International Criminal Court officials:** Human Rights Watch, *U.S. Sanctions on the International Criminal Court: Questions and Answers*, December 14, 2020.

194 **Trump's secretary of state, Mike Pompeo, threatened sanctions:** See video on State Department Account, September 2, 2020, https://twitter.com/statedept/status/1301157735652831232?s=12.

195 **China had punished Canada:** "As Canada Frees a Huawei Boss, China Lets Two Canadians Out of Jail," *Economist*, September 25, 2021.

196 **The price cap:** Florence Tan, David Lawder, and Timothy Gardner, "U.S. Says Russia Oil Price Cap Should Reflect Historical Prices, Curb Putin Profit," Reuters, September 9, 2022.

196 **According to Indonesia's finance minister:** Quoted in Iain Marlow and Shawn Donnan, "US Oil Price Cap May Backfire, Indonesia's Indrawati Says," Bloomberg, October 12, 2022.

196 **most important trade partner:** U.S. Trade Representative, "The People's Republic of China," undated, https://ustr.gov/countries-regions/china-mongolia-taiwan/peoples-republic-china (checked July 23, 2022).

196 **"save $500 billion":** "US Could Cut Ties with China over Coronavirus, 'Save $500 Billion': Trump," Deutsche Welle, May 15, 2020; Jason Lemon, "As Criticism of China Mounts, Trump Adviser Peter Navarro Continues to Urge Bringing Supply Chain Home," *Newsweek*, May 11, 2020.

197 **"an ever more baroque setup of sanctions":** Authors' interview with Matt Duss, February 13, 2021.

197 **"a self-licking ice cream cone":** Authors' interview with Matt Duss.

197 **stringent disclosure requirements:** Blair Wang, "CFIUS Ramps Up Oversight of China Deals in the U.S.," *Diplomat*, September 14, 2021; see also SEC, *Holding Foreign Companies Accountable Act*, undated, retrieved on July 24, 2022, from https://www.sec.gov/hfcaa.

197 **charging them with lying:** Michael German and Alex Liang, "End of Justice Department's 'China Initiative' Brings Little Relief to U.S. Academics," Brennan Center for Justice, March 22, 2022.

197 **"as large of a lead as possible":** Jake Sullivan, "Remarks at the Special Competitive Studies Project Global Emerging Technologies Summit," September 16, 2022.

197 **reducing China's technological dependence:** Gewirtz, "The Chinese Reassessment of Interdependence."

198 **China's economic aggression:** White House, *How China's Economic Aggression Threatens the Technologies and Intellectual Property of the United States and the World*, June 2018, retrieved on December 2, 2022, from https://www.hsdl.org/?view&did=812268

198 **"dual circulation":** James Crabtree, "China's Radical New Vision Of Globalization," *Noema*, December 10, 2020.

198 **"preparations for a possible war":** Crabtree, "China's Radical New Vision of Globalization."

198 **"weaponize the entire world's financial system":** Cissy Zhou, "China Scrambles for Cover from West's Financial Weapons," *Nikkei*, April 13, 2022.

198 **2 percent of global trade:** Zhou, "China Scrambles for Cover."

198 **moving their foreign currency holdings:** Iori Kaiwate and Yuta Saito, "China's Treasury Holdings Drop Below $1tn to 12-Year Low," *Nikkei Asia*, July 20, 2022.

198 **"China's banking system isn't prepared":** Sun Yu, "China Meets Banks to Discuss Protecting Assets from US Sanctions," *Financial Times*, April 30, 2022.

198 **"if the US stops playing by the rules":** Zhou, "China Scrambles for Cover."

199 **"we could essentially shut SMIC . . . down":** Ana Swanson, "Chinese Companies That Aid Russia Could Face U.S. Repercussions, Commerce Secretary Warns," *New York Times*, March 8, 2022.

199 **no one should "doubt our ability":** Christopher Condon, "Yellen Says U.S. Would Use Sanctions If China Invaded Taiwan," Bloomberg, April 6, 2022.

199 **"one big family":** CK Tan, "Xi Rallies BRICS against Sanctions 'Abuse,' Cold War Mentality," *Nikkei Asia*, June 23, 2022.

199 **thirteen thousand transactions a day:** Bloomberg News, "Why China's Payment System Can't Easily Save Russian Banks Cut Off from Swift," *Washington Post*, March 15, 2022.

200 **isolating its key financial centers:** Takeshi Kihara, "Hong Kong's 'Zero COVID' Policy Risks Status as Financial Hub," *Nikkei Asia*, January 23, 2022.

200 **"it is no coincidence":** Barry Eichengreen, "Ukraine War Accelerates the Stealth Erosion of Dollar Dominance," *Financial Times*, March 27, 2022.

200 **"asymmetric decoupling":** Antony J. Blinken, *The Administration's Approach to the People's Republic of China*, speech delivered at George Washington University, May 22, 2022.

200 **"friendshoring":** David Lawder and Andrea Shalal, "Yellen to China: Help Stop Russia's War in Ukraine or Lose Standing in the World," Reuters, April 13, 2022.

200 **stop exporting older machines:** Jillian Deutsch, Eric Martin, Ian King, and Debby Wu, "US Wants Dutch Supplier to Stop Selling Chipmaking Gear to China," Bloomberg, July 5, 2022.

200 **"cannot ignore the fact":** Cheng Ting-Fang and Lauly Li, "ASML Warns Chip Gear Ban against China Will Disrupt Supply Chain," *Nikkei Asia*, July 21, 2022.

201 **apparently started doing this:** Debby Wu and Jenny Leonard, "China's Top Chipmaker Achieves Breakthrough Despite US Curbs," Bloomberg, July 21, 2022.

201 **threaten dire punishments:** Office of Senator Rubio, "Rubio, McCaul Demand

Tougher Protections against Chinese Semiconductor Maker SMIC, Warn of Possible Beijing-Moscow Coordination," March 17, 2022.

201 **"a fundamental shift":** Ana Swanson, "Biden Administration Clamps Down on China's Access to Chip Technology," *New York Times*, October 7, 2022.

201 **Scholz mournfully accepted:** Scholz, "Die EU Muss."

201 **"export-led growth to China":** Constanze Stelzenmüller, "Putin's War and European Energy Security: A German Perspective on Decoupling from Russian Fossil Fuels," Testimony to the U.S. Commission on Security and Cooperation in Europe, Brookings Institution, June 7, 2022.

202 **"VW needs China a lot":** Joe Miller, "Volkswagen and China: The Risks of Relying on Authoritarian States," *Financial Times*, March 15, 2022.

202 **tens of billions of dollars:** David Ignatius, "Transcript: The Path Forward: American Competitiveness with Pat Gelsinger, CEO, Intel," *Washington Post*, July 12, 2022.

202 **had to push back hard:** Jenny Leonard and Ian King, "White House Spurns Intel Plan to Boost Chip Production in China," Bloomberg, November 12, 2021. For the $10 billion figure, see Yvonne Geng, "GlobalFoundries Abandons Chengdu Wafer Fab," *EE Times*, May 26, 2020.

202 **"governmental money-laundering operation":** Ian Talley, "Clandestine Finance System Helped Iran Withstand Sanctions Crush, Documents Show," *Wall Street Journal*, March 18, 2022.

202 **"under hidden subsidiary activities":** Talley, "Clandestine Finance System Helped Iran Withstand Sanctions Crush."

203 *The Economic Weapon*: Nicholas Mulder, *The Economic Weapon: The Rise of Sanctions as a Tool of Modern War* (New Haven, CT: Yale University Press, 2022).

203 **"scalpel-like instruments":** Nicholas Mulder, "By Invitation: Nicholas Mulder, Who Studies Sanctions, Declares a Watershed Moment in Global Economic History," *Economist*, March 4, 2022.

205 **"like sausages":** Edward J. Langer, "Cuban Missile Crisis—Khrushchev's Last Bluff," Military History Online.

205 **enough ICBMs:** Roy E. Licklider, "The Missile Gap Controversy," *Political Science Quarterly* 85, no. 4 (1970): 600–615.

205 **had only ever deployed:** Jonathan Renshon, "Assessing Capabilities in International Politics: Biased Overestimation and the Case of the Imaginary 'Missile Gap,'" *Journal of Strategic Studies* 32 (2009): 115–47.

205 **again and again:** Greg Thielmann, "Looking Back: The Missile Gap Myth and Its Progeny," *Arms Control Today* 41, no. 4 (2011): 44–48.

205 **willing to do the same:** Pavel Podvig, "The Window of Vulnerability That Wasn't: Soviet Military Vulnerability in the 1970s—a Research Note," *International Security* 33, no. 1 (2008): 118–38.

206 **hadn't existed before:** Steven E. Miller, *Nuclear Hotlines: Origins, Evolution, Applications*, Belfer Center for Science and International Affairs, Harvard Kennedy School, undated. See also Webster Stone, "Moscow's Still Holding," *New York Times*, September 18, 1988.

206 **experiences as a parent:** Richard Zeckhauser, "Distinguished Fellow: Reflections on Thomas Schelling," *Journal of Economic Perspectives* 3, no. 2 (Spring 1989): 153–64.

207 **won Schelling the Nobel Prize in Economic Sciences:** "Thomas C. Schelling, Biographical," NobelPrize.org, retrieved on November 21, 2022, from https://www.nobelprize.org/prizes/economic-sciences/2005/schelling/biographical/.

207 **a game of chess:** Thomas C. Schelling, *Arms and Influence* (New Haven, CT: Yale University Press, 2020).

207 **"independence, not interdependence":** John Lewis Gaddis, "The Long Peace: Elements of Stability in the Postwar International System," *International Security* 10, no. 4 (1986): 110.

207 **weaponized interdependence:** Henry Farrell and Abraham Newman, "Weaponized Interdependence"; Henry Farrell and Abraham Newman, "Weak Links in Finance and Supply Chains Are Easily Weaponized," *Nature* 605 (May 10, 2022): 219–22; Henry Farrell and Abraham Newman, "Chained to Globalization: Why It's Too Late to Decouple," *Foreign Affairs*, January–February 2020.

207 **how policy makers think:** "Remarks by EU High Commissioner Borrell at the European University Institute," May 5, 2022, https://www.youtube.com/watch?v=akftTQo_MVk&t=1s.

208 **a comprehensive economic security strategy:** Sheila A. Smith, "Japan Turns Its Attention to Economic Security," Council on Foreign Relations, May 16, 2022.

209 **that Schelling and his colleagues had developed:** Emanuel Adler, "The Emergence of Cooperation: National Epistemic Communities and the International Evolution of the Idea of Arms Control," *International Organization* 46, no. 1 (1992): 101–45.

209 **"the passage of time":** Gaddis, "The Long Peace."

209 **the arms control treaties:** "Treaties & Agreements," Arms Control Association, n.d., retrieved on November 21, 2022, from https://www.armscontrol.org/treaties.

210 **Kim Stanley Robinson warned:** Kim Stanley Robinson, *Aurora* (New York: Hachette, 2015).

210 ***The Ministry for the Future:*** Kim Stanley Robinson, *The Ministry for the Future* (New York: Hachette, 2020).

211 **"the single greatest national security challenge":** Peter Harrell, "How Biden Could Use Trump's Trade War Thumbscrews to Fight Climate Change," *Foreign Policy*, August 5, 2020.

211 **didn't announce countermeasures:** Bentley Allen and Todd Tucker, "The

E.U.-U.S. Steel Deal Could Transform the Fight against Climate Change," *Washington Post*, October 31, 2021.

212 **"to better fight corruption":** White House, "Background Press Call by Senior Administration Officials on the Fight against Corruption," June 3, 2021.

212 **"largest action targeting corruption":** U.S. Department of Treasury," Treasury Sanctions Influential Bulgarian Individuals and Their Expansive Networks for Engaging in Corruption," press release, June 2, 2021.

212 **a "core" national security interest:** White House, "United States Strategy on Countering Corruption," December 2021.

ACKNOWLEDGMENTS

This book had its beginning in our first meeting, twenty years ago, over beer on a sunny day in Bonn, Germany. We didn't know it then. We were two hungry young upstarts without permanent positions. Since we were both working on similar ideas, and would certainly be applying for similar jobs, things could have gone sour very quickly. Instead, we became friends and eventually started working and writing together. It wasn't just the kind of partnership where neither of us knows anymore who came up with which idea. It's the kind where that question doesn't even make sense.

That our journey has culminated in this book is thanks to the amazing guidance of our agent, Margo Beth Fleming. She forced us to abandon the instincts of decades pent up in the ivory tower, tearing down our idea for a book and rebuilding it on completely new foundations. Her guiding mantra was "Would someone spend the money in their wallet on this book, or would they buy a latte instead?" It's a humbling question but a good one. Without it, we wouldn't have written the book you're reading, which is completely different from the book we thought that we wanted to write. You'd be happily finishing your latte. We owe her, and we hope you'll find out that you owe her, too.

Tim Duggan and the team at Henry Holt saw the seed of something promising in our book proposal and took a chance on us. We've benefited from both Tim's specific advice and his trust in our ability to bring it home. He has ceaselessly pushed us to bring out our argument, focus on the narrative, and keep the reader engaged. If there are still some boring parts, it is our fault, not Tim's. We cannot thank him enough for believing in us and bringing the book into the world.

Underground Empire draws on ideas and arguments that we have been developing for nearly a decade. It would not have been possible without the many individuals who gave their time to be interviewed. Their insights and words tell the story. Some of them are named and thanked in the book. Others preferred to remain anonymous. We are so grateful to them all.

We're also grateful to the colleagues and friends who have helped us refine and craft the core claims. Mark Blyth and Dan Drezner were the first people to tell us that this had to become a book, written for a broad audience. As we figured out how we wanted to tell the story, we talked to novelists as well as nonfiction writers. Henry owes particular personal debts to John Crowley (for angels and mirrors), Stan Robinson (for how the hidden systems of the world might be used to transform it), and Francis Spufford (for showing how to use smaller personal stories to tell big impersonal ones). We also want to thank Thomas Banchoff, Tanja Börzel, danah boyd, Daniel Byman, Miles Evers, Martha Finnemore, Claire Fitzgibbon, Charles Glaser, Jack Goldsmith, Jonathan Hackenbroich, Marina Henke, Llewelyn Hughes, Bill Janeway, Erik Jones, Nikhil Kalyanpur, Charles King, Margaret Levi, Ed Luce, Kathleen McNamara, Jonas Nahm, Tadgh

O'Brien, Margaret O'Mara, Kurt Opsahl, Thomas Risse, Emer Rocke, Dani Rodrik, Jeremy Wallace, Glen Weyl, and John Zysman. A special thanks to Heather Kreidler, who provided invaluable fact checking on the manuscript. Their support, help in temporary crises, comments, correction of mistakes, and lively arguments have improved every page.

The book benefited from the continued engagement with our students at Johns Hopkins and Georgetown University. In particular, we thank Advait Arun, Naz Gocek, Jonas Heering, and Brooke Tanner, who served as tireless research assistants. Both Johns Hopkins and Georgetown played decisive roles in supporting our research, and we owe them a huge debt. Henry began his work on this project at George Washington University and finished it on a fellowship at Stanford's Center for Advanced Study in the Behavioral Sciences. Colleagues in both institutions provided unstinting friendship and support. Abe thanks the Georgetown Board of Regents, the Georgetown Initiative for U.S.-China Dialogue, the Open Society Foundation, and the William and Flora Hewlett Foundation, who supported various elements of the research financially. We also want to thank MIT Press and the editors of the journal *International Security*, who published our first article on these topics, "Weaponized Interdependence: How Global Economic Networks Shape State Coercion." The book is vastly different from the article, but it would never have come into being without it.

We are deeply grateful to the journalists, scholars, and writers whose work we have used to write this book. It is impossible to write a book on great global transformations without relying on the hard work and deep understanding of those who have investigated the specifics. We hope that our effort to understand the broader picture does not do too much violence to their work. Also, we recognize that ours is far from the only possible or useful map of this new world. Our book is mostly about the powerful. Another book deserves to be written, looking at the empire from the perspective of those with little power.

Our own journey into the understanding of empire started long ago and was made possible by the unending support of our families. To our parents, Paul and Louise, and Barb and Phil, who believed we could do anything. To our spouses, Nicole and Craig, for staying up late listening through our arguments and their endless patience with our days at the computer. Craig read countless drafts, and Nicole provided unstinting support. Their love has kept us going even when we felt like putting our heads under a pillow. And finally to our children, Jack, Kieran, Micah, and Sadie. Let's hope for wind and light.

INDEX

ABOUT THE AUTHORS

Henry Farrell is the SNF Agora Professor at Johns Hopkins SAIS, the 2019 winner of the Friedrich Schiedel Prize for Politics and Technology, former editor in chief of *The Monkey Cage* at the *Washington Post*, and cofounder of the popular academic blog *Crooked Timber*. A member of the Council on Foreign Relations, Farrell has written for publications such as the *New York Times*, the *Financial Times*, *Nature*, *Foreign Affairs*, *Foreign Policy*, the *Washington Monthly*, the *Boston Review*, *Aeon*, *New Scientist*, and the *Nation*.

Abraham Newman is a professor at the School of Foreign Service and Government Department at Georgetown University. Known for his research on the politics generated by globalization, he serves as a frequent commentator on international affairs, appearing on news programs ranging from Al Jazeera to Deutsche Welle and NPR. He is a 2022–2023 Berlin Prize winner and his work has been published in leading outlets like the *New York Times*, the *Washington Post*, *Nature*, *Science*, *Foreign Affairs*, *Foreign Policy*, *Harvard Business Review*, and *Politico*.